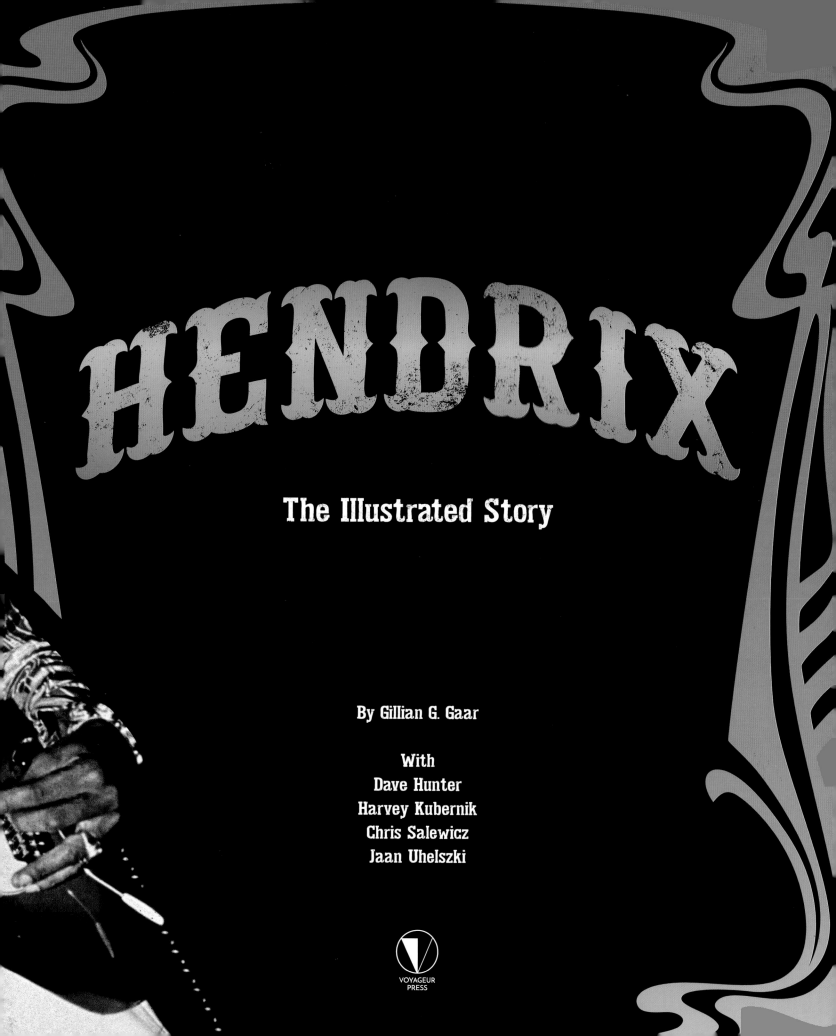

HENDRIX

The Illustrated Story

By Gillian G. Gaar

With
Dave Hunter
Harvey Kubernik
Chris Salewicz
Jaan Uhelszki

VOYAGEUR
PRESS

Brimming with creative inspiration, how-to projects, and useful information to enrich your everyday life, Quarto Knows is a favourite destination for those pursuing their interests and passions. Visit our site and dig deeper with our books into your area of interest: Quarto Creates, Quarto Cooks, Quarto Homes, Quarto Lives, Quarto Drives, Quarto Explores, Quarto Gifts, or Quarto Kids.

Inspiring | Educating | Creating | Entertaining

First published in 2017 by Voyageur Press, an imprint of The Quarto Group, 401 Second Avenue North, Suite 310, Minneapolis, MN 55401 USA. T (612) 344-8100 F (612) 344-8692 www.QuartoKnows.com

Voyageur Press titles are also available at discount for retail, wholesale, promotional, and bulk purchase. For details, contact the Special Sales Manager by email at specialsales@quarto.com or by mail at The Quarto Group, Attn: Special Sales Manager, 401 Second Avenue North, Suite 310, Minneapolis, MN 55401 USA.

10 9 8 7 6 5 4 3

ISBN: 978-0-7603-5223-6

Library of Congress Cataloging-in-Publication Data

Names: Gaar, Gillian G., 1959- | Hunter, Dave, 1962- | Kubernik, Harvey, 1951- | Salewicz, Chris. | Uhelszki, Jaan.
Title: Hendrix : the ultimate illustrated history / by Gillian G. Gaar, with Dave Hunter, Harvey Kubernik, Chris Salewicz, Jaan Uhelszki.
Description: Minneapolis, MN : Voyageur Press, 2017. | Includes bibliographical references and index.
Identifiers: LCCN 2017011921 | ISBN 9780760352236 (plc)
Subjects: LCSH: Hendrix, Jimi. | Rock musicians–United States–Biography. | Guitarists–United States–Biography.
Classification: LCC ML410.H476 G33 2017 | DDC 787.87166092 [B] –dc23
LC record available at https://lccn.loc.gov/2017011921

Acquiring Editor: Dennis Pernu
Project Manager: Madeleine Vasaly
Art Director: James Kegley
Cover Designer: Brad Norr
Layout: Kim Winscher

Page one: Falkoner Centret, Copenhagen, Denmark, January 10, 1969. *Jan Persson/Redferns/Getty Images*
Title pages: Jimi onstage, circa 1969. *Bridgeman Images*
Copyright page: Jimi circa 1967. *Pictorial Press Ltd./Alamy Stock Photo*
Contents: Mitchell, Hendrix, and Redding in West Germany, March 1967. *K & K Ulf Kruger OHG/Redferns/Getty Images*

Printed in China

INTRODUCTION

HEAR MY TRAIN A COMIN'

May 12, 1966: For Jimi Hendrix—though he was then known as "Jimmy"—the two-week engagement he'd signed on for at the Cheetah Club in Manhattan was nothing more than a welcome regular gig (for simplicity's sake this book will use the spelling "Jimi"). The journeyman guitarist had played hundreds of shows just like it as a backing musician since he'd been discharged from the army in 1962, and a residency was certainly much easier than a string of one nighters—at least he'd be able to sleep in his own bed every night. The club was located in Midtown, and Jimi would be

Locarno Ballroom, Bristol, England, February 9, 1967. *Trinity Mirror/Mirrorpix/Alamy Stock Photo*

9

playing with Curtis Knight & the Squires, an R & B act with which he'd previously recorded on a number of occasions. He even received his first-ever label credit on Knight's recently released "How Would You Feel"/"Welcome Home" single; underneath the producer's name on the label was the notation "Arr. by Jimmy Hendrix."

Jimi had built up an impressive résumé since leaving military service, backing some of the biggest names in R & B and rock 'n' roll: Little Richard, the Isley Brothers, and Ike and Tina Turner. He'd also notched up a few credits as a session musician (mostly uncredited). As yet, no one had fully grasped what kind of a musician Jimi was or what he could actually *do*. As he arrived for the first night at the Cheetah Club, strapped on his guitar, and took to the stage, he could hardly have imagined that during the run he'd meet someone who would change the course of his life—and rock history—forever.

Sitting in the sparse audience one night was Linda Keith, a British model, a girlfriend of the Rolling Stones' Keith Richards, and—most importantly—a big music fan. When Jimi met Linda after the gig, it provided him with his first step out of the realm of anonymity. Just one year later he'd be the hottest rising talent in rock, boasting a Top 10 album in the UK, drawing sellout crowds both there and in Europe, dazzling audiences with his superlative skills, and on the verge of returning to the United States to make one of the landmark performances of his career at the Monterey International Pop Festival.

It would all come to an end far too soon with Jimi's death on September 18, 1970, at the age of twenty-seven. But decade after decade, his legacy has continued to grow, his music inspiring generation after generation of musicians. He took the electric guitar in directions no other guitarist had even dreamed of going.

Part of Jimi's skill on his chosen instrument was due to his long fingers, giving him a dexterity other guitarists lacked. But he had more than just physical attributes working in his favor. From a young age, Jimi had a fascination with music and sound—and a strong determination to master the secrets of both. From the moment he got his first guitar (which initially only had one string), he set about figuring out just how many different sounds he could get out of the instrument. Though he exhibited a decided lack of discipline in other areas of his life, he never tired of picking up his guitar. Even when Jimi had a full schedule of concert dates, he'd frequently head out after a show, looking to sit in at a local club. On the last night of his life, he was expected to turn up at a London club to jam with Sly Stone.

Star-Club, Hamburg, Germany, March 1967. *Sueddeutsche Zeitung Photo/Alamy Stock Photo*

Do a search of "Best Guitarists of All Time" lists, and Jimi Hendrix is invariably on top. As David Fricke put it in his own "100 Greatest Guitarists" list for *Rolling Stone* in 2010, "In the end, I looked at it this way: Jimi Hendrix was Number One in every way; the other 99 were all Number Two." People don't just cite Hendrix's skill on the guitar. They talk about his imaginative approach to playing, his fusion of blues and rock to create something more powerful, his ability to push equipment to the limit in creating new sounds, and, most of all, how easy he made it all look.

David Fricke also wrote of his experiences seeing Jimi in live performance:

> I feel sad for people who have to judge Jimi Hendrix on the basis of recordings and film alone; because in the flesh he was so extraordinary. He had a kind of alchemist's ability; when he was on the stage, he changed. He physically changed. He became incredibly graceful and beautiful. . . . He did this thing where he would play a chord, and then he would sweep his left hand through the air in a curve, and it would almost take you away from the idea that there was a guitar player here and that the music was actually coming out of the end of his fingers.

Fricke added that while watching Jimi play at the Scotch of St. James club in London, he and Eric Clapton gripped each other's hands in their excitement: "What we were watching was so profoundly powerful." No one can have that kind of experience again, of course, but there's still much to discover in Jimi's music, not least because there's now so much out there. Jimi released three studio albums and one live album during his lifetime, but that number has since been dwarfed by posthumous releases. Now the listener can really get inside to learn how his music was created, tracing a song from demo to completion, or marvel at how he really stretched out when performing on stage.

Jimi's own story is fascinating as well. He started out in impoverished circumstances, largely raised by a single father, often going hungry and stuffing cardboard in his shoes when he got a hole in the sole. His early years in the music business weren't much easier as he scrabbled to find work and barely made enough to make ends meet. But when he finally stepped out front to head up his own band and make his own music, it didn't take him long to find a receptive audience. The years of preparation had stood him in good stead.

Jimi Hendrix's fondest wish was to succeed in music. He loved nothing more than talking about music, listening to music, recording music, and playing music. The music he left behind provides a rich legacy, one that can be—and will be—explored for new inspiration, time and again.

Star-Club, Hamburg, Germany, March 16, 1967. *Gunter Zint/K & K Ulf Kruger OHG/Redferns/Getty Images*

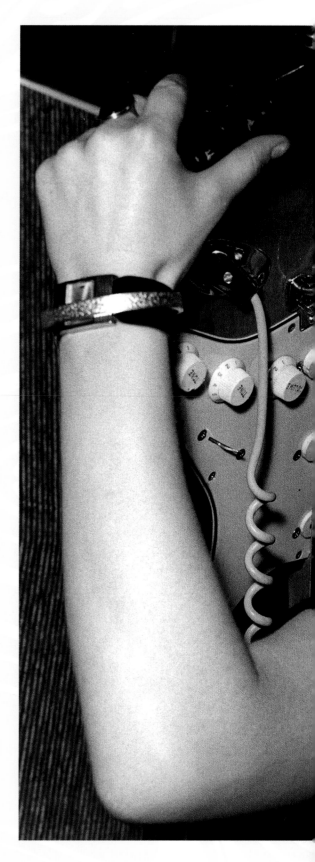

CHAPTER 1

SPANISH CASTLE MAGIC DAYS

When Johnny Allen Hendrix was born on November 27, 1942, in Seattle, Washington, his family was already in a state of flux. From the very beginning, the future guitar hero was adrift in a world of instability. It was something that would follow him throughout his short life.

His mother, the former Lucille Jeter, had met her husband, James Allen Ross Hendrix (Al), just the previous November at a friend's home prior to attending a Fats Waller concert held at Washington Hall (a venue where Jimi himself would later perform). Born in 1925, Lucille was sixteen years old and still at school. Al was six years older, born in 1919 in Vancouver, British Columbia, Canada, 142 miles north of Seattle. Both were of mixed race: there was African American, Native American, and Caucasian blood on both sides of the family.

Al Hendrix with his three-year-old son, James (then named Johnny), in 1945. *Apic/Getty Images*

Washington Hall, where Jimi's parents attended a Fats Waller concert on the night they met in November 1941. *Gillian G. Gaar*

Al wasn't very tall, only growing to a height of five feet six inches, but he was stocky and a good fighter and had briefly taken up boxing. He moved to Seattle in 1940 in search of more job opportunities and was working at an iron foundry when he met Lucille. The two began dating; both enjoyed going out and dancing. (Al had entered a number of dance contests when he was living in Canada.)

Their casual relationship quickly became serious, and in February 1942, Lucille learned she was pregnant. The same week, Al learned he was being drafted, only weeks after the United States entered World War II following the Japanese attack on the US base in Pearl Harbor, Hawaii, on December 7, 1941. Lucille's parents were unhappy about the situation, as she was still in school, but they reluctantly accepted Al's offer to marry her. A hasty marriage was arranged on March 31. Al's induction date was three days later.

Al was first sent to Fort Lewis, just outside of Tacoma, Washington, 26 miles south of Seattle. He was then sent to Fort Sill, Oklahoma, for basic training, transferred to Fort Benning, Georgia, and finally posted to Camp Rucker in Alabama. Back in Seattle, Lucille had dropped out of school to work as a waitress until she was forced to quit in the latter stages of her pregnancy. She moved in with a family friend, Dorothy Harding, before giving birth to her child at Harborview Medical Center. Al had asked for a furlough to return to Seattle to be with his wife, but it was denied; he was even locked up in the stockade to prevent him from going AWOL.

Al was still in the stockade when he received a telegram from Lucille's sister, Delores, telling him that his son had been born. But when he learned Lucille had named the baby Johnny, he suspected the child might have been named after a man named John Page, who also roomed in the Harding home, and whom Al suspected was having an affair with Lucille. The infant Johnny Allen soon acquired the nickname "Buster," after the Buster Brown comic strip character.

Lucille was not an attentive mother. She had no steady home, no steady job, and little idea how to care for a baby. Another of the family's friends, Freddie Mae Gautier, recalled how Lucille's mother, Clarice, once brought Buster over to her house, the child so cold that his diaper was frozen and his legs were blue. Lucille's life was further complicated by her bad taste in men. She had indeed become involved with John Page (whether this happened before or after Buster's birth remained unknown), who proved to be abusive. Page took Lucille and the child to Portland, Oregon, and when her family came down to find her, she was in a hospital recovering from a beating. As Lucille was still a minor, Page was charged with violation of the Mann Act (transporting a minor across state lines) and sent to prison for five years.

At some point, Buster ended up in the care of the Champ family, who lived in Berkeley, California; as with much in Jimi Hendrix's life, there are conflicting accounts over how this occurred. Al had been informed of his son's whereabouts, and two months after he was discharged from the service in September 1945, he headed down to Berkeley to reclaim his son.

Al was understandably nervous when he arrived at the Champ household. "Jimmy wasn't scared or anything," he later wrote in his memoir, *My Son Jimi*. "He was just bashful, and I felt the same way." The Champs had grown fond of the child and were willing to adopt him. Al considered the offer but decided he wanted to raise his son himself. The two returned to Seattle, and Al had his son's name legally changed to James Marshall Hendrix, though he and other relatives continued using the nickname "Buster" for some years before switching to "Jimmy" when he was older.

While still in the service, Al had begun divorce proceedings, but after seeing Lucille in person, he decided to try to reconcile with his wife. The two reunited, but it would be a troubled relationship, with numerous breakups followed by reconciliations, until the couple finally divorced on December 17, 1951. By then, there were more children in the family: Leon (born in 1948), Joseph (1949), Kathy (1950), and Pamela (1951). After the divorce, Al and Lucille made another attempt at reconciliation, which didn't last but did result in the birth of another child, Alfred (1953). Joseph, Kathy, and Pamela were all born with various developmental disabilities and later made wards of the state; Alfred was also born with disabilities and put up for adoption after his birth.

At the time of the divorce, Al was granted custody of Jimi and Leon. He worked at a series of low-paying jobs, and money was always tight—Leon recalled his father having to make ketchup sandwiches on occasion. The two boys would sometimes go to friends' houses to eat or would shoplift food. With no money for childcare, the brothers were left on their own much of the time, especially if their father decided to go out drinking after work. Al's absence eventually attracted the attention of the welfare department, and Leon was put into foster care for a time. The foster home was not far from Al's house, and Jimi visited his brother regularly. There was even a bonus: if he came by at mealtimes, Leon's foster parents would feed Jimi too.

Al and the two boys moved frequently. At one point, Jimi and Leon were sent to live with their paternal grandmother, Nora Hendrix, in Vancouver, British Columbia. It was a pattern that would continue in Jimi's adult life as well—even when he became financially successful, he never purchased his own home and lived in a series of apartments and hotels. Unsurprisingly, the lack of a stable home life made Jimi withdrawn; neighbors remembered him as a shy, ill-dressed boy with an occasional stutter and holes in his shoes. Years later, Leon remembered lying in the backyard with his brother at night, Jimi wondering aloud about the vastness of the universe. It's not difficult to imagine such dreams of outer space reflecting a young boy's desire to escape his circumstances.

But life wasn't entirely grim. Jimi and Leon spent hours exploring the parks in their neighborhoods, including Leschi Park and Seward Park. Leon even recalled sneaking into "underground Seattle," the old city ruins from the Great Seattle Fire of 1898. Jimi also had typical boyhood interests in comic books, movies, and sports; one childhood photo shows him in a football jersey and helmet horsing around with his father, with father and son each sporting big grins. He also had a keen interest in science fiction and drawing; Al's memoir has several examples of Jimi's work.

In the spring of 1953, when Jimi was ten years old, he was enrolled at Leschi Elementary School, where he met Terry Johnson and Jimmy Williams, who would become his closest friends. "We used to hang around together and do our paper routes together," Terry Johnson said in an interview with the author in 1997. "Learning how to swim, and all that stuff." After seeing a film version of *The Three Musketeers* on television, the three friends took on the name for themselves. Another fellow student, Pernell Alexander, was also a close friend. Despite frequently changing schools, Jimi would retain these friendships for the rest of his days in Seattle.

He was also gradually becoming interested in music. Jimi had been given a harmonica when he was around five years old but showed little interest in it. His first exposure to music outside the home came when his maternal grandmother, Clarice, took him to church, where he heard the congregation and choir singing hymns and gospel music. The people in church, he told a family friend, always seemed to be having a good time.

Jimi's early musical education took another step when Al offered boarding to Cornell and Ernestine Benson. Ernestine had great collection of blues records that Jimi listened to, including Robert Johnson, Howlin' Wolf, Muddy Waters, and Bessie

A press ad and ticket for the Elvis Presley concert at Sick's Stadium, Seattle, in September 1957. Hendrix couldn't afford to attend but listened to the show from an adjacent hillside.

Smith. He was particularly impressed with Waters, later telling *Eye* magazine, "I heard one of his old records when I was a little boy and it scared me to death, because I heard all of those sounds. Wow, what is that all about? It was great."

And there was always the radio. Terry Johnson recalled how the music they heard on the radio changed over the course of the decade. "When we were young, we used to listen to Eddie Fisher and 'Ghost Riders in the Sky.' Then we heard '(How Much Is) That Doggie in the Window?' And pretty soon it was the Ink Spots. Then the music on the side started coming in; 'Jim Dandy' and little things like that started easing in. And then pretty soon you started hearing actual rock 'n' roll: Chuck Berry came on, and Little Richard, Fats Domino, Ray Charles."

Jimi became so fascinated by the sounds coming out of the radio that he took one apart, trying to figure out how it worked. He was especially drawn to the guitar, and long before he owned one he would pick up a broom and play it as if it was a guitar, leaving bristles all over the floor. His first real instrument was a ukulele he found when he was cleaning out a garage with his father and brother; it only had one string, but he experimented with it nonetheless. He later acquired a cheap acoustic guitar paid for by Ernestine Benson, though it too initially only had one string. Undaunted, he worked with the one-stringed instrument until he could get a full set of strings. Though left-handed, Jimi learned to play the guitar right-handed as well. His father felt left-handedness was a stigma (he called it "the sign of the devil"), and he didn't complain as much when he saw his son playing right-handed.

Further inspiration came when he heard one of his rock idols in person. On September 1, 1957, Elvis Presley made one of his last live appearances before entering the army the following year at Sick's Stadium in Seattle. Jimi couldn't afford a ticket, so he sat on the adjacent hillside that offered a view of the baseball field. Despite the distance, Jimi was sufficiently inspired by the show that he later drew a picture of Elvis with the song titles of his hits floating in the air around him.

He had a closer encounter with celebrity the next year, when Leon ran an errand for his foster mother. Leon was asked to take some mustard greens to a neighbor, Mrs. Penniman, who was the aunt of one Richard Wayne Penniman—Little Richard. The rock 'n' roller whose first breakthrough smash was "Tutti Frutti" happened to be visiting his aunt, and though the star had at this time given up rock 'n' roll, Leon was nonetheless excited to meet him. When they learned that Little Richard was going to be preaching that evening at Goodwill Baptist Church, both Jimi and Leon made sure they were there to see him.

It all helped fuel Jimi's own dreams of success. "I'm going to leave here, and I'm going to go far, far away," he told Dorothy Harding, a family friend he called "Auntie Doortee," although she wasn't a blood relative. "I'm going to be rich and famous, and everyone here will be jealous."

Jimi's mother was still an occasional presence in his life, but Lucille's health was failing. After years of heavy drinking, she was suffering from cirrhosis of the liver and was often in the hospital. On January 3, 1958, she was married to William Mitchell but was diagnosed with hepatitis and went back into the hospital soon after. Jimi and Leon visited her and were saddened by her poor condition. Lucille was soon released, but on the evening of February 1, she was found lying unconscious outside a tavern and was taken back to the hospital, where she died the next day. It was later discovered she had a ruptured spleen, something that could only have happened from a serious injury, like falling or being hit. It was never determined how the injury occurred.

The brothers were greatly upset by their mother's death but did not attend Lucille's funeral. Years later, Leon and Al had different memories about why they didn't attend. Leon claimed their father was drunk and got lost on the way to the funeral home. Leon also said that Al attempted to ease the boys' sorrows by giving them each a shot of Seagram's 7 whiskey. Al claimed the brothers didn't attend because he didn't own a car at the time, insisting that he gave Jimi bus fare but that Jimi chose not to go.

Jimi became even more withdrawn after his mother's death. He fared poorly in school, and to his embarrassment, he was held back and made to repeat ninth grade. Music took on increasing importance for him, and as he listened to records with his friends, they tried to imitate the sounds they heard with their own instruments. Jimi was quick to realize that something was missing—he was playing an acoustic guitar, but to play rock 'n' roll, he needed an electric instrument. After repeated requests, Al finally agreed to get Jimi a new guitar, and the two went to Myers Music at 1206 First Avenue in downtown Seattle, where Al put money down on a white Supro Ozark. Al also bought himself a saxophone, planning to play duets with his son, but the experiment apparently failed, because he quickly returned the instrument.

Jimi was thrilled with his first "real" guitar. "This was like having five Christmases all rolled up into one," Carmen Goudy, his girlfriend at the time, told biographer Charles Cross. "I think it was the happiest day of his life." He took his guitar with him everywhere, constantly playing it, only grudgingly taking the time to sleep. "It was as if sleeping were only a pause in some long, continuous song he was playing," Leon recalled in his memoir, *Jimi Hendrix: A Brother's Story*. Indeed, he even slept with his guitar as though he couldn't bear to be parted from his instrument for a second.

The first song he learned to play on the electric guitar was "Tall Cool One," a Top 40 hit for the Tacoma band the Fabulous Wailers. Jimi and his friends soon began performing in informal groupings. "Back in those days, when you'd have a party, you'd say, 'Listen I've got a gig coming up, I need a guitar player, you want to play with me?'" said Terry Johnson. "So we'd get a drummer and a guitar player and a piano

Garfield High School, which Jimi attended from 1958 to 1960. *Gillian G. Gaar*

player and we'd go play a private party. That's how we got a little musician's circle in Seattle going so we knew we could play different gigs."

Jimi's first proper gig was a performance with a makeshift band at a local synagogue, Temple De Hirsch Sinai. His flashiness, already evident, didn't go down too well with the other musicians, and he was dismissed after the first set. Jimi's penchant for showmanship would be a recurring problem for him until he got his own band.

For now, he was still learning his craft, and he soon found a more welcoming group of musicians in the Velvetones. The group, which had a revolving membership, was founded by Robert Green (piano) and Luther Rabb (bass) and also featured Jimi's friend Pernell Anderson on guitar. The Velvetones played R & B and blues covers— they were a party band whose purpose was to get audiences to dance. They were skilled enough to land a regular gig at Birdland, a notable Seattle jazz club where Jimi would spend his off hours watching the other musicians play.

Jimi then moved on to a band called the Rocking Kings, which even had a manager, James Thomas. It was at Birdland that disaster struck when his guitar was stolen after he left it at the club following a gig. The loss of the guitar was compounded by Jimi's fear of telling his father. Al was increasingly unhappy at the amount of time Jimi was spending with his guitar. Before it was stolen, Jimi had kept his guitar at Pernell Anderson's house, afraid that his own father might confiscate it. The Velvetones' Anthony Atherton remembered Al saying to his son, "Put that damn thing down; that's not going to get you a job" (an echo of what future Beatle John Lennon was being told by his fearsome Aunt Mimi: "A guitar's all right John, but you'll never earn your living by it.").

Al was indeed very angry when Jimi finally confessed to losing his guitar. But the Rocking Kings eventually chipped in to get him a new one, a white Danelectro

Silvertone with its own amp, purchased from Sears, Roebuck & Co. at a cost of $49.95. Jimi soon painted it red and added the name of his girlfriend, Betty Jean Morgan, to the instrument.

Jimi had met Betty Jean at Garfield High School. He began attending in 1958 and ended up leaving sooner than he intended, skipping school so frequently that he was finally expelled in October 1960. Later, with a touch of braggadocio, he claimed he'd been kicked out because he'd been caught holding hands with a white girlfriend. But he had no white girlfriend—only the faithful Betty Jean, who was black. In a foreshadowing of his dismissal from the army, his school days came to end because of his all-too-apparent lack of interest in attendance.

Al insisted that if Jimi wasn't going to go to school, he'd have to get a job. Al had formed his own landscaping company, and Jimi grudgingly began working for him. There was little choice, as the Rocking Kings weren't making much money. The band, like the Velvetones, was a dance-oriented group, playing the songs of Chuck Berry, Duane Eddy, Fats Domino, the Coasters, and the Pacific Northwest's own garage rock classic "Louie Louie." They managed to land shows beyond the Seattle city limits, playing gigs at the exotic-looking Spanish Castle in the Seattle suburb of Kent (later immortalized by Jimi in "Spanish Castle Magic"), as well as at Seattle's annual Seafair Festival. They also placed second in an "All-State Battle of the Bands" contest.

The group eventually broke up in the wake of a mishap on the way to a show in Vancouver, British Columbia. The band's car broke down before they reached Canada, and though they managed to secure a gig that night in Bellingham, Washington, they had to take the bus back to Seattle the next day. The band's manager James Thomas quickly regrouped the musicians, taking the lead singer spot himself and renaming the band Thomas and the Tomcats.

Men of the 101st Airborne Division at Fort Campbell, Kentucky, where Hendrix was stationed, cross a stream with rifles aloft, September 1962. *Ralph Morse/The LIFE Picture Collection/Getty Images*

It wasn't enough to support himself. At loose ends, Jimi and a friend then tried to join the air force but were turned down. He also considered the army after becoming enamored with the Screaming Eagle patch worn by the 101st Airborne Division. And he proposed to Betty Jean, though he had no means of supporting himself, much less a family.

In the end, the decision was made for him. Jimi had never been much interested in drinking, drugs, or petty crime, but he began a slow drift in that direction. He and a friend broke into a clothing store and were caught when they donated the stolen clothes that didn't fit to a clothing drive at school. Then, on May 2, 1961, Jimi was arrested for riding in a stolen car. He claimed he didn't know the car was stolen but nonetheless spent the night in jail. When he was picked up riding in another stolen car four days later, the punishment was more severe. He was held in juvenile detention for a week, then released pending a sentencing hearing. The hearing took place on May 16, where it was agreed that Jimi would receive a two-year suspended sentence, provided he join the army. He enlisted the next day.

On May 28, the night before his induction, Jimi played a final show with Thomas and the Tomcats. After the gig, he gave Betty Jean a rhinestone engagement ring and asked her to hold his guitar for him. The next day, Al gave him a piece of fatherly advice: "Keep your head up, son." He then boarded a train headed for Ford Ord in Monterey County, California. He could never have imagined that in six years he'd return to Monterey to play what would become known as one of the most important concerts of his career.

⁂

When Jimi left Seattle, he left his childhood behind as well. In the remaining nine years of his life, he only returned to the city on four brief occasions. Seattle became part of his past.

However relieved he may have been to finally leave behind a life without much direction, he was nonetheless homesick. Aside from his little-remembered early years in Berkeley and visits to his grandmother in Vancouver, British Columbia, he hadn't traveled outside Washington State. And as impoverished as his life at home had been, he at least had his family and friends around him—and his guitar.

He wrote his father almost immediately: "I just wanted to let you know that I'm still alive, although not by very much. . . . Although I've been here for about a week, it seems like about a month. Time passes pretty slow even though we do have a lot to do." He also complained about all the expenses army life entailed ("haircut $1, shoe polish kit $1.70, shaving razor, blades and lather $1.70") and asked for a loan to tide him over until payday.

In September he was granted a one-week leave and headed back to Seattle by bus, spending most of the week on the road. He was wearing his uniform when he arrived. "I couldn't have been prouder," Leon later wrote about the moment he saw his

left: An undated photograph of Hendrix playing a Danelectro guitar with his US Army band in the early 1960s.

below: Hendrix onstage with one of his earliest bands, the King Kasuals, in January 1963. *Experience Music Project/1999.883.2*

brother. He was equally impressed with Jimi's present to him: a $5 bill. Jimi also met up with Betty Jean during his leave, promising that they would get married once he left the service. His parting gift to her was a silk pillowcase that he signed "Love forever, always yours, James Hendrix, September 7, 1961."

Back at Ford Ord, Jimi received orders transferring him to the 101st Airborne Division in Fort Campbell, Kentucky. By early November, he was training to be a paratrooper, writing his father that his initial jumps from a 34-foot tower were "almost fun." Being a paratrooper also meant an extra $55 a month in pay, as great an incentive as the chance to get a Screaming Eagles patch. By early January 1962, Jimi was fully qualified as a parachutist with the right to wear the patch. He bought several of them to send back to his family as souvenirs.

Music was again becoming a predominant part of his life. After arriving in Kentucky, Jimi asked his father to retrieve his guitar from Betty Jean Morgan's home and began spending all his spare time practicing, even sleeping with his guitar in his bunk. He'd also begun to meet fellow musicians within the ranks.

One day while Jimi practiced in one of the clubs on the base, a young man passing by the open window on his way home from the movies heard him playing and came in to introduce himself: Billy Cox. "This friend of mine was with me and he said it sounded like a bunch of noise, but I knew better," Billy later recalled. "I heard the uniqueness."

Billy Cox was a bassist, and the two soon formed a band together, calling themselves the Kasuals (later the King Kasuals). The five-piece group played military base clubs in addition to other clubs in and around Nashville, which was only 60 miles from Fort Campbell.

The band proved to be popular, but opportunities were limited since Jimi and Billy were still in the army. Billy was scheduled for discharge in September 1962, but Jimi still had over two years to go.

But by June 1962, James Marshall Hendrix was out of the army. He always claimed that he'd broken his ankle on his twenty-sixth jump from a plane, also injuring his back in the process. But Charles Cross's Hendrix biography, *Room Full of Mirrors*, claimed that Jimi planned a more strategic escape. Beginning in April, Jimi began making repeated visits to the base psychiatrist, claiming that he was having sexual fantasies about his fellow soldiers. Around the same time, he was also caught— certainly deliberately—masturbating. Jimi maintained that he suffered from physical ailments as well, wrapping gauze around his "injured" ankle as evidence.

In interviews promoting his book, Cross said he gleaned this information from army documents that hadn't previously been made public. But a 2007 book, cowritten by Hendrix historian John McDermott and Jimi's adopted sister Janie Hendrix, played down what the two called "rumors" about Jimi pretending to be gay, noting, "Hendrix's official military record makes clear the issues were based on Hendrix's abysmal performance as a soldier." Indeed, official army records posted on the Smoking Gun

An undated promotional photograph of Bobby Taylor & the Vancouvers, with whom Hendrix played in the early 1960s.
GAB Archive/Redferns/Getty Images

website do note Jimi's "unsatisfactory duty performance," citing him for missing bed checks, sleeping on the job, being "an extreme introvert," and noting that he "requires excessive supervision at all times." (The masturbation charge was also noted.) Clearly, Jimi was exploring every avenue to get out of the service.

By the end of May, the army reached its breaking point and Jimi was discharged. He gave various accounts of what happened next. In one interview, he said he stayed in the area to be with girlfriend Joyce Lucas, who lived in nearby Clarksville, Tennessee. In another, he said that he blew all his army earnings on the day he was discharged, buying everyone drinks at a local bar until he was left with nothing but $16. He was also without his guitar, having sold it to a fellow soldier who agreed to loan it back to him whenever he had a gig. In some later interviews, Jimi bragged that he had to sneak back onto the base to steal his guitar to get it back; in other accounts, he said he simply tracked down the soldier he'd sold the instrument to and "borrowed" it again, neglecting to say that this time it would be a permanent loan. He soon sold the guitar to a pawnshop, and Billy Cox helped him buy a new one, an Epiphone Wilshire purchased in Clarksville.

Until Jimi left for England in 1966, there would never be a confirmed chronology of his activities over the next four years. He moved from band to band and town to town without leaving a verifiable record, resulting in numerous contradictory accounts of where he was, whom he was with, and when specific events happened. It is known that he spent his first few months after army service gigging with the King Kasuals, biding his time until Billy left the service and the band could travel more extensively. He also moved in with Joyce Lucas and wrote a letter to Betty Jean Morgan to break off their engagement.

Once Billy was discharged, the King Kasuals landed a job as the house band at the Del Morocco club in Nashville. The band worked steadily but never made very much money. Jimi took advantage of the opportunity to connect with many musicians he admired as they passed through town, watching them play and sometimes asking for tips from the likes of Albert King, B. B. King, and Johnny Jones of the Imperial Seven. In addition to honing his guitar technique, Jimi was also developing his stage presence. When playing with the King Kasuals, his guitar had a 75-foot extension cord, leaving him free to roam through the audience.

At the end of 1962, Jimi left for Vancouver to visit his grandmother. He soon hooked up with a local R & B band Bobby Taylor and the Vancouvers; one of the group's other guitarists was Tommy Chong, later a member of stoner comedy duo Cheech and Chong. In early 1963, Jimi headed back to Nashville, rejoining the King Kasuals. Later that year, he joined another Nashville-based outfit, Bob Fisher and the Bonnevilles, who toured with Motown girl group the Marvelettes and Curtis Mayfield and the Impressions.

He also joined various package tours, playing the Chitlin' Circuit—the name given to the mostly Southern venues that catered to black audiences. Jimi was just another anonymous musician in a backing band, but these tours featured a stellar roster of

below right: Soul singer Solomon Burke onstage at the Apollo in 1964. *Michael Ochs Archives/Getty Images*

below left: Jackie Wilson performs at a dinner for the Motion Picture Pioneers Association at the Playboy Club, New York City, November 19, 1962. *PoPsie Randolph/ Michael Ochs Archives/Getty Images*

R & B acts, including Sam Cooke,
Jackie Wilson, Solomon Burke, Carla
Thomas, and Slim Harpo among them.
It was an invaluable education.

Though ostensibly just a backing
musician, Jimi liked to indulge in some
flamboyant showmanship when he
played, playing his guitar behind his
back or with his teeth, tricks he'd
seen other musicians do. It wasn't
always appreciated. "Five dates would
go beautifully, and then at the next
show, he'd go into this wild stuff that
wasn't part of the song," Solomon
Burke told Charles Cross. Fed up with
Jimi's antics, Burke swapped him for
two horn players from Otis Redding's
band. Jimi didn't fare any better with
Redding, who fired him in less than
a week. While playing with Bobby
Womack, his playing so infuriated
Womack's brother that he threw Jimi's
guitar out of the tour bus window.

Back in Nashville, Jimi entered the recording studio for the first time near the end of
1963. Producer William "Hoss" Allen, a DJ with Nashville station WLAC, was producing
what he recalled as a session for Billy Cox at King Records studio. Billy wanted Allen to
hear what Jimi could do with a guitar, but Allen wasn't impressed with Jimi's extravagent
style. "I thought someone had made a mistake," he recalled when he heard Jimi hit
his first chords. "I had him plugged into the board so I just told the engineer to turn
Jimi's track off. He just played and played for about two hours and I didn't record
a damn thing." Other accounts say that the session was for Frank Howard and the
Commanders, not Cox, and that the song recorded was "I'm So Glad" (written by Cox).

As 1963 came to an end, Jimi met a promoter who promised him work if he
moved to New York City. It was an easy decision to make. The King Kasuals weren't
making much progress, and he was tired of the restrictions he faced when he played
in other people's bands. He tried to persuade the King Kasuals to come with him,
but none of the other musicians were interested. It didn't matter to Jimi; he was
determined to leave. He borrowed a coat from Larry Lee, a fellow musician, to help
ward off the winter chill and boarded a bus headed for Manhattan.

above: Harlem, New York, in the mid-1960s.
The Apollo Theater on 125th Street can be
seen in the distance. *Bettmann/Getty Images*

opposite: Left to right: O'Kelly Isley,
Hendrix, and Ron Isley listen to a playback
at Atlantic Studios, New York, in 1964.
Experience Music Project/1999.260.6

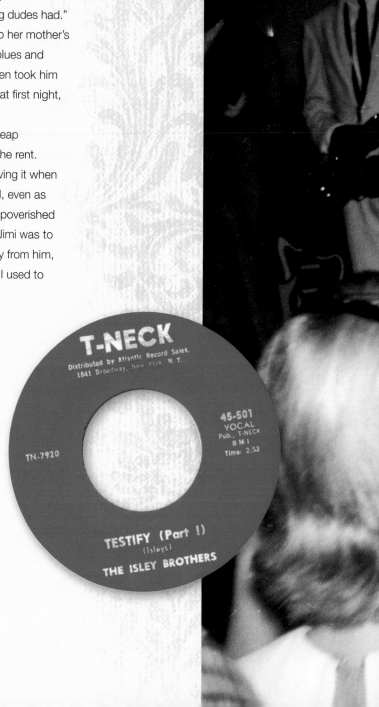

If Jimi Hendrix arrived in the Big Apple with high hopes, they were quickly dashed. The promoter he'd met in Nashville reneged on his promise to find him work, and he was without any other prospects. He did manage to win the Apollo Theater's Wednesday night amateur talent contest, but even in 1964, the $25 prize didn't go far.

As the new year began, Jimi was just another struggling musician trying to make it in New York, making the rounds of Harlem hot spots such as the Palm Café, Small's Paradise, and Frank's. One night as he was trying to get backstage to meet Sam Cooke at the Apollo, he met Lithofayne "Fayne" Pridgon (also called "Faye"), a girlfriend of Cooke's. Fayne had seen Jimi around at parties. "He had processed hair and shiny black pants that showed where the knees bent," she later told *Gallery* magazine. "But he had something about him, a warmth, that none of the other fast-rapping dudes had."

Fayne led Jimi inside to meet Cooke, and afterward the two walked to her mother's apartment. Hendrix was impressed by her mother's record collection of blues and R & B and eagerly devoured the food she prepared for the two. Fayne then took him back to the Hotel Seifer, where she was staying with a girlfriend. "After that first night, I never left. He never left. He just moved in with me," she recalled.

The two lived a hand-to-mouth existence, continually moving from cheap accommodations when they were invariably kicked out for failing to pay the rent. Jimi got in the habit of pawning his guitar to get some money, then retrieving it when he had a gig. Fayne's mother could always be relied on to provide a meal, even as she tried to discourage her daughter's relationship with the perennially impoverished musician. As others had before her, Fayne quickly learned how devoted Jimi was to his instrument—he still slept with his guitar, and if she tried to take it away from him, he'd instantly wake up and tell her, "No, no, no! Leave my guitar alone." "I used to think of my competition not as a woman, but as a guitar," she observed.

Jimi tried to break into Harlem's tight music community but didn't make much headway. "These old fuddy-duddy, rough-dried, ain't-never-beens, they ain't gonna give him a break," Fayne said in the documentary *A Film about Jimi Hendrix*. She tried to help out where she could. She introduced him to her friends, the twins Arthur and Albert Allen, musicians who were temporarily working as drug dealers (later, under the names Taharqa and Tunde Ra Aleem, they'd form the Ghetto Fighters). The twins suggested Jimi could try his hand at dealing drugs himself, but he was uninterested, wanting to stay focused on his music. He later said he had taken a few non-music jobs to help make ends meet but always ended up quitting them before too long.

opposite: The Isley Brothers onstage in 1964, with Jimi Hendrix on guitar. *Experience Music Project/1999.260.4* **inset:** The Isley Brothers' 1964 single "Testify (Parts 1 and 2)"—Hendrix's first recorded appearance.

Jimi soon got a break. When sitting in with a band at the Palm Café one night, he caught the attention of Tony Rice. Rice knew a number of musicians, including the Isley Brothers, whom he knew were on the lookout for a new guitarist. The group had scored hits with "Shout" and "Twist and Shout," the latter of which would find new life on the US charts in 1964 when the Beatles' cover of the song was released as a single, going to No. 2.

Rice tipped off the Isleys about Jimi, and he was invited to audition, though his guitar had to be retrieved from the pawnshop before he could do so. He was quick to make an impression; after playing less than a minute he was told, "Okay, you've got the job." He was also invited to stay at the Isley family home in New Jersey when he had nowhere else to go. The brothers were amazed at how much Jimi worked on his playing. "Jimi would practice phrases over and over again," Ernie Isley said, "turn them inside out, break them in half, break them in quarters, play them slow, play them fast." Sometimes, when asked a question, instead of giving a spoken response, he'd play a short lick on his guitar by way of an answer.

Soon after being hired by the Isleys, Jimi joined them in the studio for his first recording session with the band. They recorded the lively number "Testify (Parts 1 and 2)," which was released as a single in June but failed to chart. Shortly after the session, the band headed out on tour. Jimi was glad to have steady work but was already chafing at the rules for band members, such as being fined if a member wasn't properly attired for a gig.

Once back in New York, Jimi landed some session work with Don Covay in May. The single "Mercy, Mercy," released in September, was drawn from the session. It topped the R & B charts and reached No. 35 on the pop charts—Jimi's first appearance in the pop Top 40. Jimi was fond enough of the soulful number that he later played it with the Jimi Hendrix Experience. The songs also appeared on Covay's album *Mercy!* (1965).

The Isleys headed out on tour that summer, but Jimi quit when they reached Nashville. He later joined a package tour featuring Sam Cooke, Jackie Wilson, and the Valentinos. When the tour reached Memphis, Hendrix sought out Steve Cropper, the guitarist with Booker T. and the M.G.'s, the house band at Stax Records. Cropper was busy in the studio, but Hendrix stuck it out, waiting all day until Cropper came out. Cropper became excited when he learned Hendrix had played on "Mercy, Mercy," later writing in the liner notes of *Drivin' South*, "That was one of my favorite records—that lick that's in there, that funky little intro lick." The two went out to eat then returned to Stax and jammed together in the studio, Hendrix trying to show Cropper how to play the lick, which he "never did quite get."

Jimi is said to have made another visit to Stax at some point. Although Cropper wasn't present, Jimi set up to play for the other musicians, including Roland

An original Rosemary Records pressing of "Mercy, Mercy" by Don Covay and the Goodtimers—another record that featured a young Jimi Hendrix on guitar.

right: A studio portrait of Little Richard's group, the Upsetters, taken in 1965. *Gilles Petard/Redferns/Getty Images* **inset:** Little Richard's Vee-Jay Records single of "I Don't Know What You've Got But It's Got Me," written by Don Covay and featuring Jimi on guitar.

Robinson, who'd later open for Hendrix as a member of the Buddy Miles Express. In Robinson's recollection, the musicians were singularly unimpressed with Jimi's "wild style," and to Jimi's dismay, they laughed and left the room.

At some point during this period, Jimi was left stranded in Kansas City, either by choice or design. He then made his way to Atlanta, Georgia, and secured a new gig with the Upsetters, Little Richard's backing band, calling himself Maurice James. Little Richard had renounced rock 'n' roll for the church in 1957, but he'd returned to playing the devil's music in 1962. He was a demanding bandleader, fining the musicians for such infractions as wearing frilly shirts. "I am the only one allowed to be pretty!" he asserted on one occasion. During his time with Little Richard, Jimi recorded one single with him, "I Don't Know What You've Got But It's Got Me" b/w "Dancing All Around the World." Released in November 1965, the record stiffed on the pop charts but reached No. 12 on the R & B charts.

Jimi was gaining a lot of experience as a sideman, but he had yet to make a name for himself.

CHAPTER 2

FROM THE BIG APPLE TO THE BIG SMOKE

On New Year's Eve 1964, Jimi found himself in Los Angeles. Looking for a place to ring in the new year, he headed for the Wilcox Hotel's California Club, where Ike and Tina Turner were performing. An aspiring singer in the audience named Rosa Lee Brooks caught Jimi's eye, and the two became a couple, spending what she recalled as "three beautiful months together." The two imagined they could become a duo, in the fashion of Ike and Tina Turner or Mickey and Sylvia of "Love Is Strange" fame.

An early promotional photo of Hendrix with drummer Mitch Mitchell (left) and bassist Noel Redding (right). *Bettmann/Getty Images*

They soon had a song they wanted to record, "My Diary," which Rosa Lee said she and Jimi wrote together, though her friend Arthur Lee (later a cofounder of the band Love) claimed he was the sole writer of the song.

Rosa Lee and Jimi arranged to record the song with producer Billy Revis, who had a studio set up in his garage; Arthur Lee also came along to provide backing vocals. Jimi's distinctive guitar can be heard at the beginning of the number, and Rosa Lee provides a strong, warm lead vocal. Told that the single needed a B-side, the session's bass player, a man only recalled as "Alvin," told everyone about a popular dance from Detroit called the "U.T." and suggested they write a track of the same name for people to dance to. The musicians quickly put together a loping track called "Utee," and the single was completed. The record was released in June 1965 but only garnered some local play.

Jimi left Little Richard for a short time in 1965, during which he briefly played with Ike and Tina Turner (at least according to Ike Turner—Tina Turner has insisted that Jimi never played with the group). But he eventually rejoined Little Richard's band and left Los Angeles. Rosa Lee never saw him again, though she did send him money when he later wrote and asked for some cash to get his guitar out of hock.

When Little Richard's tour hit Nashville on July 6, Jimi made his TV debut when the Upsetters backed a duo called Buddy and Stacy on a local TV show *Night Train* which aired on WLAC. The group performed a cover of Junior Walker's hit "Shotgun," and as a left-handed guitarist, Jimi can easily be picked out of the lineup, carefully moving in synchronization with the backing line of musicians. (At time of this writing,

above: Rosa Lee's single "My Diary," which Hendrix may or may not have co-written, depending on whom you believe.

left: Husband-and-wife duo Ike and Tina Turner perform in Dallas–Fort Worth, Texas, 1964. Hendrix briefly played with their band in 1965 (at least according to Ike). *Michael Ochs Archives/Getty Images*

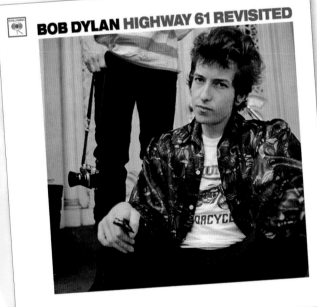

the footage could be found on YouTube.) It may have been during this visit that Jimi sat in with Frank Howard and the Commanders, recording "I'm So Glad," which had some regional success when released as a single; other accounts say the song was recorded at the end of 1963 (see Chapter 1).

By mid-July, Jimi had again left Little Richard's band. Little Richard's brother Robert claimed that he was fired: "[Jimi] was always late for the bus and flirting with girls and stuff like that . . . I was running the road for Richard and I didn't accept that kind of bullshit." Jimi rejoined the Isley Brothers, and soon after, he recorded another single with the group, "Move Over and Let Me Dance." Released in September, the single failed to chart. On July 27, Jimi signed a contract of his own with Sue Records after the label's owner, Henry "Juggy" Murray, saw him playing with the Isley Brothers. As Jimi wasn't a singer, Murray wasn't sure what to do with him.

"How the hell do you record a guy who is a great guitar player without a hit single?" he later said to Hendrix historian John McDermott.

In the end, Jimi never recorded anything for Sue Records, but he was clearly looking ahead to a recording career of his own. In early August, he wrote a lengthy letter to his father, claiming he was already sought-after: "There's a few record companies I visited that I can probably record for." More interestingly, he addressed the subject of his singing voice, which he thought was poor. "Nowadays people don't want you to sing good," he wrote, perhaps in an effort to reassure himself more than his father. "They want you to sing sloppy and have a good beat to your songs. That's what angle I'm going to shoot for." He added that if he later released a record "which sounds terrible, don't feel ashamed, just wait until the money rolls in."

His comments were perhaps prompted by his growing interest in Bob Dylan, who'd released a number of groundbreaking singles that year, including "The Times They Are a-Changin'," "Subterranean Homesick Blues," and "Like a Rolling Stone." Dylan's voice often polarized listeners (author Joyce Carol Oates wrote that his voice sounded "as if sandpaper could sing"). Jimi was fascinated by Dylan's work, an interest not shared by his friends. When Jimi convinced a DJ to play "Blowin' in the Wind" in a Harlem club, there were immediate requests to take it off, and on another occasion, Fayne Pridgon became upset when Jimi spent his last few dollars on Dylan's *Highway 61 Revisited* album instead of groceries. Jimi would later cover Dylan's songs and credited him with inspiring his own songwriting, telling a journalist, "Dylan really turned me on. Not the words or his guitar, but as a way to get myself together."

In the fall of 1965, when he wasn't on the road with the Isleys, Jimi took up residence at the Hotel America on West Forty-Seventh Street. He soon struck up an acquaintance with fellow musician Curtis Knight, lead singer with Curtis Knight & the Squires. After hearing Hendrix play guitar, Knight introduced him

above: Curtis Knight's 1965 single, "How Would You Feel," which included an arranging credit for one "Jimmy" Hendrix.

opposite: Curtis Knight poses with his band, the Squires, featuring Hendrix (left), 1965.
Michael Ochs Archives/Getty Images

to Ed Chalpin, a producer who ran a company called PPX Enterprises Inc. Chalpin produced cheap covers of hit songs for the overseas market and also licensed original material. Chalpin already had Knight under contract, and he offered Hendrix a deal as well.

Jimi later said that he told Chalpin about the contract with Sue Records and was assured that the PPX contract wouldn't interfere with his obligations to other companies. But he didn't get a copy of the contract, and it's doubtful he even read it carefully. "He would sign a contract with anybody who came along that had a dollar and a pencil," Fayne later recalled. So on October 15, 1965, he signed a one-page contract stating that he would "produce and play and/or sing exclusively for PPX Enterprises, Inc., for three years." It was a contract that would plague him for the rest of his life.

Jimi's guitar was again in the pawnshop when Knight introduced him to Chalpin, so Knight loaned Jimi one of his own guitars to tide him over. From October to December 1965, and in February 1966, Jimi recorded a number of tracks with Curtis Knight & the Squires. The first to be released were "How Would You Feel"/"Welcome Home" (the A-side clearly influenced by Bob Dylan's "Like a Rolling Stone") on RSVP Records in April 1966. Curtis Knight was credited as the artist and songwriter, but "Jimmy Hendrix" also received a label credit as the arranger of both songs. A second single, "Hornet's Nest"/"Knock Yourself Out" was released later in the year. Both sides were instrumentals written by Jimi, who received his first writing credit on the label (though he was forced to split the credit with RSVP owner Jerry Simon). Neither single made the charts.

It's also been said that one of Jimi's recordings with the Squires was used as a backing track for Jayne Mansfield's single "As the Clouds Drift By"/"Suey," released in 1967. However, in the book *Ultimate Hendrix*, author John McDermott expressed skepticism about the claim, noting that Chalpin never released those tracks on the plethora of recordings he later issued to cash in on Jimi's participation.

Jimi also played live dates with the Squires, and in November 1965 he signed on for a tour with Joey Dee and the Starliters, best known for their 1961 hit "Peppermint Twist." But he was getting tired of the grind. "I was trying to play my own thing," he later said. "I dug listening to Top-40 R & B but that didn't necessarily mean I liked to play it every night."

At the end of 1965, it seemed he had made little headway in getting to "play my own thing," but he had a premonition that things were about to change. "I had these dreams that something was gonna happen, seeing the number 1966 in my sleep, so I was just passing the time till then," he later told the *New York Times*. At the time, he worried that meant something would happen to his father in 1966. But it was Jimi's own future—and luck—that was about to change.

In January 1966, Jimi joined King Curtis and the Kingpins, both in the studio and on tour. The first track he recorded, "Help Me (Get the Feeling)" (Parts 1 and 2), was used on a number of different releases. It was first released in 1966 with Ray Sharpe singing lead. Later that year, Owen Gray used the same backing track for his own single. In 1967, the track was used for an Aretha Franklin single, though Jimi's guitar part was mixed out. And in 1969, King Curtis released the track, with new overdubs and a new name, "Instant Groove" (also the title track of an album he released that year). In April 1966, Jimi joined the band in the studio again and recorded more material, but the tapes were lost.

above: A promotional shot of King Curtis, with whom Hendrix started playing in early 1966. *Gilles Petard/Redferns/Getty Images*

inset: The original release of Curtis's "Help Me," with Ray Sharpe as the featured vocalist.

opposite: Hendrix performs with Wilson Pickett at an Atlantic Records launch party for Sledge's "When a Man Loves a Woman" at the Prelude Club in Harlem, New York, May 5, 1966. *William "PoPsie" Randolph photograph*

By May, Jimi had left (or been fired by) King Curtis. He picked up some session work with producer John Brantley and recorded a number of tracks later farmed out to different vocalists: "Sweet Thang" by Billy Lamont, "That Little Old Groove Maker" by Jimmy Norman, and "(My Girl) She's a Fox" by the Icemen, all of which were released as singles. Further tracks were also released under saxophonist Lonnie Youngblood's name, with "Go Go Shoes" and "Soul Food (That's What I Like)" released during Jimi's lifetime.

Jimi then went back to working with Curtis Knight & the Squires, although his relationship with Knight became complicated when he got involved with Knight's girlfriend, Carol Shiroky. On learning that Jimi couldn't leave the band because he was using Knight's guitar, Shiroky helped him get his own instrument, a white Fender Stratocaster.

His relationships with women were also becoming more complicated. He argued frequently with Fayne Pridgon, and at one point he only communicated with her via letter. He also took up with Diane Carpenter, a sixteen-year-old prostitute. She was eventually arrested by the police, who sent her home to her parents on discovering her age. By then she was pregnant. She would give birth to a daughter in February 1967, and because the child was black and her clients had only been white men, she believed that Jimi was the father. But by the time her child was born, Jimi was no longer living in the United States.

On May 12, 1966, Curtis Knight & the Squires played the first night of a two-week stand at a new venue, the Cheetah Club. It was sometime during this run that Linda Keith walked into the Cheetah with two friends, Roberta Goldstein and Mark

Kauffman. (Some accounts have this meeting taking place in late June, but Hendrix is not known to have played at the Cheetah after June 3.) There was an audience of around forty people, and the band made little impression on Linda at first. But then she noticed Jimi and became increasingly interested in his playing. "I couldn't believe nobody had picked up on him before because he'd obviously been around," she later told the *Guardian*. "He was astonishing—the moods he could bring to music, his charisma, his skill, and stage presence. Yet nobody was leaping about with excitement. I couldn't believe it."

When the band went on a break, Jimi was invited to sit at Linda's table, and afterward everyone went to Goldstein and Kauffman's apartment, dubbed the "Red House" due to its décor. Jimi was excited when his new friends offered him LSD, a drug he had been wanting to try. ("I looked into the mirror and thought I was Marilyn Monroe," he later recalled of his first trip.) He became even more excited when Linda pulled out Bob Dylan's latest album, *Blonde on Blonde*, which Jimi hadn't heard yet. The two spent the rest of the evening talking and playing records, Jimi providing additional accompaniment with his guitar.

Linda had her own room at the Hilton Hotel, and Jimi became a frequent visitor, though she always maintained they never had a romance, perhaps in part because

Hendrix onstage with Percy Sledge on the night of Percy Sledge's launch party at the Prelude Club. *William "PoPsie" Randolph photograph*

Carl Holmes and his group the Commanders on the set of *Dial M for Music*, CBS Studios, New York, July 1965. Hendrix, weary of playing "other people's music," had left the group a month earlier. *CBS Photo Archive/ Getty Images*

when she'd asked him if he had a girlfriend he'd replied "Many." Instead, she focused her energies on trying to advance Jimi's career in any way that she could.

"I was interested in Jimi's music and desperate for it to be fulfilled," she said in John McDermott's *Hendrix: Setting the Record Straight*. "He needed motivation and direction because, emotionally, he was almost completely lacking in confidence and terribly indecisive. He would muster this sort of false bravado to protect himself, but beneath that hard, external shell lay the real Jimi. He was confused about his ethnic identity and there was a great conflict between his musical roots and desire to play the blues and then wanting to be this sort of middle-class pop star."

Jimi returned to the Cheetah with Carl Holmes & the Commanders, playing from May 27 to June 3. The band planned to tour after the engagement and invited Jimi along, but he declined. "I had all these ideas and sounds in my brain," he told the *New Musical Express* the following year, "and playing this 'other people's music' all the time was hurting me."

During his week at the Cheetah, he'd met musician Richie Havens. The two discovered they were both fans of Dylan, and Havens encouraged Hendrix to check out the music scene where Dylan had launched his own career—New York's bohemian Greenwich Village neighborhood. Havens directed him specifically to Cafe Wha? on MacDougal Street, already a legendary club that had hosted Dylan and Peter, Paul, and Mary, among the notable acts. Jimi duly went down one night and introduced himself to the club's manager, Manuel "Manny" Roth (uncle of future Van Halen lead singer David Lee Roth), who invited Jimi to take the stage that evening if he was ready.

Jimi had no songs of his own, but his selection of blues and R & B covers spiced up with his imaginative guitar solos nonetheless impressed the sparse crowd, and

Roth offered him a steady gig. Jimi quickly put together a band, which, though only together for three months, went through a surprising number of lineup changes. Tommy "Regi" Butler, from Cafe Wha?'s house band, was the first bassist, a position later filled by Jeff "Skunk" Baxter (who later played with Steely Dan and the Doobie Brothers), and then Randy Palmer. Chas Matthews and Danny Casey both served as drummers. While browsing around Manny's Music store in Midtown Manhattan, Jimi spied a young guitarist named Randy Wolfe and invited him to join the band, dubbing him "Randy California" to distinguish him from Randy Palmer (whom Jimi nicknamed "Randy Texas"). Wolfe liked the "California" surname so much he kept it; he would later co-found the group Spirit.

Jimi variously called his group Jimmy James & the Blue Flames ("Jimmy James" after blues guitarist Elmore James, and the "Blue Flames" in homage to Junior Parker's group) or the Rainflowers. Carol Shiroky also recalled this as the time when he began spelling his name as "Jimi."

The band primarily played covers, including Howlin' Wolf's "Killing Floor," Dylan's "Like a Rolling Stone," and a recent hit by the Troggs, "Wild Thing." While hanging out in the Cock n' Bull, another Greenwich Village club, Jimi heard a version of "Hey Joe (You Shot Your Woman Down)" by Tim Rose. In contrast to the more popular, up-tempo version of the song by the Leaves, Rose slowed the number down, and it was this arrangement that Jimi used when he played the song himself. There also were a few originals in the set — "Mr. Bad Luck" was an early version of "Look Over Yonder," later recorded by the Jimi Hendrix Experience. People who heard Jimi play during this period said they recognized fragments of songs resurfacing in his later work.

Now, at last, the leader of his own band, Jimi was free to indulge himself. He could play as outrageously as he wanted to, working in all the moves he'd absorbed from watching other players. And with no temperamental lead singer there to tell him "I am the only one allowed to be pretty!" he began accessorizing his wardrobe with scarves and jewelry. Much of his look was inspired by his friendship with Mike Quashie, "The Spider King," whom he'd met through Carol Shiroky. Quashie performed at the African Room in a black leotard and platform boots, with a spider monkey perched on his shoulder, among other elaborate accoutrements. Jimi also began further developing his sound, using a primitive fuzz box put together for him by a member of underground rock group the Fugs.

Linda Keith was still in Hendrix's corner. When his guitar was stolen after he left it at Cafe Wha? one night (though other accounts say he actually smashed his guitar in anger), she let him use one of Keith Richards's guitars, which was another white Strat. When the Stones arrived in New York City in July, she made sure the band saw Jimi's performance at hip Midtown club Ondine's. Brian Jones was impressed, but the other Stones showed no interest. She took the Stones' manager, Andrew Loog Oldham, down to Cafe Wha?, but Oldham was wary of the situation, fearing to put himself between Hendrix and a potentially jealous Keith Richards. She also brought Seymour

Outside Café Wha?, the legendary
folk club on MacDougal Street, New York,
April 1966, a few months before Chas
Chandler first saw Hendrix perform there.
Jack Manning/New York Times Co./Getty Images

Stein, then in the process of setting up Sire Records, to see Jimi, but Stein was put off
when he saw Jimi smash a guitar during a show.

Linda was frustrated that her attempts to help Jimi weren't paying off. Then one
night everything changed. In late July, the Animals arrived in the United States for their
final tour, and on August 2, when the band was in New York City, the band's bassist,
Bryan James "Chas" Chandler, was spending the evening at Ondine's. He met Linda
while at the club, and when she learned that Chas was planning to leave the Animals
and move into management and record production, she urged him to see Jimi.

Chas made his way to Cafe Wha? with Linda the next afternoon. He already had a
song in mind to record—"Hey Joe"—and when he walked into the club and heard Jimi
playing that very song, the meeting must have seemed preordained. He was instantly
a convert. "I thought immediately he was the best guitarist I'd ever seen," he later
recalled. "You just sat there and thought to yourself, 'This is ridiculous—why hasn't
anybody signed this guy up?'"

After the first set, Linda introduced the two men, and Chas spoke enthusiastically
about what he could do for Jimi. He explained he was still on tour with the Animals but

would come back to New York when the tour was done to finalize their plans to record. Jimi listened politely and nodded in agreement. Though he was pleased that Chas was so interested in his work, he'd heard similar promises before. Who knew if he'd even see Chas Chandler ever again?

So it was back to building up his reputation in the Village. Jimi landed a new gig when John Hammond Jr., playing at another Village club, Café au Go Go, was told he should check out the wild guitarist playing at Cafe Wha?. Hammond went over and was surprised to see Hendrix playing numbers from his own album *So Many Roads* (1965). Suitably impressed, he invited Jimi to play a guest spot with his group, billing the act as "John Hammond and Blue Flame." He also brought along his father, a legendary producer who worked with Billie Holiday and had signed Aretha Franklin and Bob Dylan to Columbia Records, but the elder Hammond wasn't interested in the guitarist.

British R&B group the Animals in early 1966. Bass player Chas Chandler (right) would soon leave the group and become Hendrix's manager. *Doug McKenzie/Getty Images*

Jimmy James and the Blue Flames soon landed their own bookings at Café au Go Go, and Jimi also dropped in at the club when he wasn't scheduled to play, looking to jam with whoever was playing that evening—a lifelong habit. One performer he sat in with was Ellen McIlwaine—who played piano while Jimi played guitar—the only time he was known to play live with a woman also playing an instrument. In contrast to his own shows, McIlwaine recalled his playing "very gently and very sensitive," without flashy tricks. She could nonetheless sense Jimi untapped potential: "Anybody that got hold of him sensed that he'd be very famous."

In September, Chas returned to New York, ready to start working with Jimi, but he couldn't find him. Linda Keith was no longer around to help; after her relationship with Keith Richards foundered, Richards had contacted her father to report that his daughter was hanging out in New York with disreputable people who were using drugs. Mr. Keith wasted no time in flying to New York, tracking Linda down at Café au Go Go, dragging her out, and whisking her back to England.

Jimi rarely had a fixed address, but Chas eventually located him and outlined his plans. He wanted to take Jimi to London, where he would serve as his manager, produce his records, and get him a record deal. He explained that he would co-manage Jimi with Michael Jeffery, manager of the Animals. Jeffery had previously run the Club A'Gogo in Newcastle, England, meeting the Animals when they played there. Though the Animals enjoyed phenomenal success with their 1964 breakthrough hit "The House of the Rising

Sun," the band never felt they'd been suitably compensated by Jeffery, who kept them working constantly while funneling their earnings into an offshore account called Yameta in the Bahamas. But if Chas had doubts about Jeffery's business practices, he was also a new, unproven manager himself and needed all the contacts he could get.

With little happening for him in New York, Jimi agreed to Chas's proposal, though he assumed his band would be coming along as well. Chas said no—it was only Jimi he was interested in. There was then the matter of obtaining a passport. It took a while to track down Jimi's birth certificate, as the original certificate listed his name as Johnny Allen Hendrix, not James Marshall. With birth certificate in hand, they enlisted songwriter Scott English (whose best-known song was "Brandy," the original version of Barry Manilow's breakthrough hit "Mandy") in a bit of subterfuge on Jimi's passport application, saying that he'd known Jimi for years and could vouch for his character.

Finally, they were ready to go.

On September 23, Jimi boarded a Pan Am flight headed for London's Heathrow Airport in the company of Chas and Animals roadie Terry McVay. The party arrived on September 24, with McVay carrying Jimi's guitar through customs so it wouldn't look like Jimi was coming to England seeking work. Jimi was nonetheless held up at immigration until Chas and Tony Garland, who handled press for Michael Jeffrey's acts and had come to the airport to meet them, made a convincing case that Hendrix was merely a songwriter who'd come to the UK to collect his royalties. He was allowed in on a one-week visa.

With that hurdle overcome, Chas wasted little time in spreading the word about his discovery. Before even checking in to a hotel, Jimi was taken to the home of musician

right: Fashion model Linda Keith met Hendrix in New York in 1966. *Trinity Mirror/Mirrorpix/ Alamy Stock Photo*

below: John Hammond Jr.'s 1965 LP *So Many Roads*. Hendrix landed a gig with Hammond's group in Greenwich Village.

and bandleader George "Zoot" Money (who would later join the New Animals, the band formed from the remnants of Chandler's previous band). After introductions were made, Jimi sat down and played a few songs on an acoustic guitar. Money's wife, Ronnie, was so impressed she went upstairs to rouse Kathy Etchingham, a hairdresser and part-time DJ who shared the house with them. Kathy, still sleeping off the previous night's clubbing, said she was too tired to come listen, little suspecting how much her life would change when she finally met Jimi a few hours later. Another musician, Andy Summers (later the guitarist in new wave act the Police), was also staying with the Moneys; stories later claimed that he listened and even jammed with Jimi on that first visit, but he maintained that he stayed in his room and missed seeing Jimi on this occasion.

After checking into the Hyde Park Towers hotel, Chas brought Jimi to the Scotch of St. James that evening. The club was popular with London's hippest rock stars, and Chas knew that an appearance by Jimi would help spread the word about his new find. He arranged for Jimi to get on stage and play for a bit, and Jimi duly excited those in attendance, including the Who's Keith Moon and Chandler's former Animals bandmate Eric Burdon.

Kathy Etchingham later arrived at the club with Zoot and Ronnie Money while Jimi was playing and immediately noticed "an incredible stillness in the atmosphere. . . . People were always getting up at the Scotch and jamming but usually the club carried on around them, everyone talking and drinking. This was different; the whole place seemed mesmerized. Obviously something special was happening."

They sat at Chandler's table, with Jimi joining them after he'd finished playing. Chas hadn't wanted him to play too long, as Jimi's visa didn't allow him to take work of any kind, even if he wasn't being paid. Linda Keith was also there, sitting next to Jimi. When she got up to use the bathroom, Jimi turned his attention to Kathy, flirting with her in a fashion she found both sweet and innocent. Linda wasn't pleased when she returned and found her place had been usurped, and, according to Kathy's later account, got into a fight with Ronnie, who threatened her with a broken bottle. Chas ended up hustling Jimi and Kathy out of the club. Linda told Charles Cross the fight story was "ludicrous," but in any event, Jimi and Kathy did leave together to return to Jimi's hotel, later joined by Chas and other friends.

That wasn't the last the two saw of Linda Keith. According to Kathy's memoir *Through Gypsy Eyes: My Life, the 60s, and Jimi Hendrix*, Linda stormed into Jimi's hotel room the next morning and found the two in bed together.

Kit Lambert and Chris Stamp, co-managers of the Who, 1966. Chandler would initially turn down their offer of a record deal for Hendrix. *Chris Morphet/Redferns/Getty Images*

left to right: Eric Clapton, Jack Bruce, and Ginger Baker of the blues-rock supergroup Cream in October 1966, the same month Clapton and Bruce invited Jimi to sit in on a gig in London. The temperamental Baker wasn't so impressed. *Paul Popper/Popperfoto/Getty Images*

She grabbed his guitar (actually the guitar she'd "borrowed" from her former boyfriend Keith Richards) and threatened to hit them with it. "Oh, man—*not the guitar!*" Jimi cried. Linda paused, then left with the instrument. When she later called and insisted on speaking to Jimi in private, Jimi asked Kathy to leave, assuring her he'd call her later that day. After somehow placating Linda, who agreed to return the guitar, he picked up where he'd left off with Kathy, who would be his primary girlfriend for the next few years.

As Jeffery dealt with Hendrix's immigration issues, Chandler concentrated on the musical side. There was a return visit to the Scotch of St. James for another jam, which drew the attention of Christopher "Kit" Lambert and Chris Stamp, who co-managed the Who and were in the process of setting up their own label. They immediately offered their services, but Chas turned them down, for the moment—he was holding out for a deal with a major record company.

Chas had also run into Eric Clapton at the Cromwellian Club and eagerly told him about Hendrix. Clapton, who'd recently formed the power trio Cream with Jack Bruce and Ginger Baker, suggested that Chas bring Jimi to the band's next show on October 1 at the Regent Street Polytechnic in central London. Jack Bruce later said that he met Jimi at a pub near the Polytechnic on the day of the show and that Jimi asked if he could sit in with the band that night; other accounts have Chas making the same request after the band's first set. In either case, Clapton and Bruce were agreeable, but the temperamental Ginger Baker wasn't pleased to find a stranger on the bandstand. Nor was he taken with Jimi's performance, later dismissing him as a mere "showman . . . Eric is a musician first."

But Clapton was blown away. Jimi had torn into Howlin' Wolf's "Killing Floor" with such force that Clapton left the stage, asking Chandler in passing, "Is he that fucking good?" Jimi had told Chas he was eager to meet Eric Clapton, but now it was Clapton

who became his follower—as he later recalled, after witnessing Jimi's performance, "My life was never the same again, really."

Another club appearance brought an unexpected bonus. Chas had contacted Brian Auger, who headed up Brian Auger and the Trinity, suggesting that he take on Jimi as a guitarist in his band. Auger wasn't at all interested in that idea but did invite Hendrix to jam with the band at their next gig at the London club Blaises. Sitting in the audience that night was French singer Johnny Hallyday; he was so taken by Jimi that he offered him the opening slot on his upcoming tour in France, due to start in a few weeks' time.

It was a great opportunity—a chance to break in a new band away from the media spotlight in London. There was just one problem: Jimi didn't have a band yet. But he and Chas were working on it. They attended auditions for the New Animals and were on hand when a guitarist named Noel Redding, who'd read an ad about the audition, walked in. By then the guitar spot had been filled, but Chas asked if he'd consider switching to bass and auditioning for a different band. Having nothing to lose, Noel agreed, jamming with Jimi, Mike O'Neill on keyboards, and Aynsley Dunbar on drums. Afterward, Jimi invited him out to have a drink. Noel was quick to stress that he wasn't that confident on bass, but Jimi assured him he was fine. Plus, with his frizzy hair, he looked a bit like Bob Dylan. Noel was offered the job.

Although O'Neill was just on hand to jam that day, the idea of taking on David Knights on bass and moving Redding to guitar, was briefly considered. It was quickly decided that a second guitarist would take the spotlight away from Jimi. (Knights would go on to join Procol Harum.) Now it was down to a drummer. Auditioned along with Dunbar were Johnny Gustafson, formerly of the Merseybeats, and John "Mitch" Mitchell, who'd most recently been working with Georgie Fame & the Blue Flames. It came down to Dunbar and Mitchell, and the final decision made by a coin toss. The winner: Mitch Mitchell.

Chas wanted to position the group so that Jimi was seen as the star and needed a name that made that clear. Jimi suggested Jimi Hendrix and the Blue Flames, but Chas said it was too similar to the name of Georgie Fame's group and instead proposed the Jimi Hendrix Experience. Having Jimi front and center also meant that he would be the lead singer. Still embarrassed by how his voice sounded, Jimi initially turned up the volume on his guitar to cover his perceived vocal weaknesses. During sessions, he recorded his vocals while hidden behind sound baffles so he wouldn't be seen.

The band's overall volume had been given a boost thanks to their new powerful amplifiers. When he jammed with Brian Auger and the Trinity, Jimi had taken note of the Marshall amps used by guitarist Vic Briggs. He learned that Mitch had been taught how to play drums by Jim Marshall himself, who had his own equipment

The Jimi Hendrix Experience at the Big Apple Club in Munich, Germany, November 9, 1966.
INTERFOTO/Alamy Stock Photo

factory in Hanwell. Mitch brought Jimi to the factory on October 8 and introduced him to Marshall. Hendrix won Marshall's respect when he said he didn't want free equipment but was happy to pay full price as long as he received quality service. "And that's what we gave him," said Marshall, who would later call Hendrix "the greatest ambassador Marshall Amplifiers ever had." Noel recommended hiring his friend Gerry Stickells as the group's tour manager, and Stickells would work with Jimi for the rest of his career.

Just five days later, on October 13, the Jimi Hendrix Experience made their debut in Évreux, France, on the Johnny Hallyday tour. The band was limited to a fifteen-minute set, playing covers, as they had no original material. The first show didn't generate much good press, and Jimi was described as "a bad mixture of James Brown and Chuck Berry." But Mitch was surprised at the metamorphosis he witnessed in Jimi. "He was a quiet bloke—at least until he got on stage," he wrote in his memoir *Jimi Hendrix: Inside the Experience*. "It was on the first gig that we saw the whole other person, completely different from anything I'd seen before, even during rehearsals. . . . It was like 'Whoosh! This man really is out front!'"

There were subsequent shows in Nancy and Willerupt and a final date at the prestigious L'Olympia in Paris on October 18. By the time of the Paris gig, Chas had devised an introduction for the band that helped whip up excitement. With the band waiting off stage, the show's emcee would step up to announce "Ladies and gentlemen!" followed by the sound of Jimi playing a quick riff on his guitar. "From Seattle, Washington!" the emcee continued, followed by another burst of riffing from Jimi. After a bit of this back-and-forth, Jimi finally strode on stage, holding one hand in the air, "and when the audience suddenly realized that all of this great guitar sound was being played one-handed, they went bananas," Chas recalled. The set list for the Paris show featured "Killing Floor," "Hey Joe," and "Wild Thing" and was recorded by French radio station RTE.

On October 23, the band entered London's De Lane Lea Studios to make their first record. At the moment, Chas only had enough money to record the "Hey Joe" for the A-side. He immediately came into conflict with Jimi, who'd turned his amp up so loud it was making the equipment rattle. When Chas told him to turn it down, Jimi groused, "If I can't play as loud as I want, I might as well go back to New York." Chas had been at the immigration office that morning getting Jimi's visa extended for another three months. Now, in a dramatic gesture, he pulled out Jimi's passport and immigration papers, threw them on the console, and announced, "Well, here you go. Piss off!" If it was a tactic meant to diffuse the situation, it worked: Jimi laughed as he admitted, "All right, you called my bluff!" and got back to work.

Particular about how he wanted the record to sound, Chas overdubbed Noel's bass line himself. For the B-side, Jimi had thought the band would simply record another cover, suggesting "Land of 1000 Dances," but Chas said if Jimi wanted to make more money from his record sales, he needed to write his own material. Jimi

Norwegian, Japanese, Spanish, and Yugoslavian picture sleeves for "Hey Joe." The Yugoslavian pressing wasn't released until 1975. The Spanish pressing was a four-song EP that somewhat ironically promoted Barry Sadler's "Ballad of the Green Beret" on the rear sleeve.

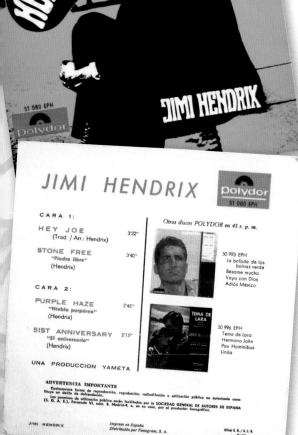

quickly came up with "Stone Free," a rollicking song about the joys of being free of romantic ties—certainly a sentiment that was prominent in his own life.

Chas had gambled everything on recording the single. Money was still tight—Chas had sold some of his guitars to bring in cash, and Michael Jeffery borrowed money from his parents. The next step was signing with a record label. Surprisingly, Chas couldn't even get a meeting with an A&R rep at the Animals' label, EMI. Over at Decca, Dick Rowe—infamous as the man who missed out on signing the Beatles in 1962—also gave a thumbs down to the Jimi Hendrix Experience.

So it was back to Chris Stamp and Kit Lambert and their new label, Track. The two had secured a distribution deal with Polydor Records, giving their label the clout of a major. This was inducement enough for Chandler to sign with Track; a deal with an American label would hopefully follow later.

The Experience made its London debut at the Scotch of St. James on October 25, drawing a packed house of tastemakers. Its next engagement was a four-night stand at the Big Apple Club in Munich, Germany, which began on November 8 with the band playing two shows a night. On the final night, a new element was inadvertently added to their live act. Jimi had gone into the audience while playing his guitar, and on his return to the stage, he broke the instrument when he threw it up on stage ahead of him. In his anger, he climbed onstage, grabbed the guitar, and smashed it—to the crowd's enthusiastic delight. Chas immediately decided to make sure they always had a spare guitar on hand for smashing.

The band was excited as they returned to England. The German shows had been a great success. "That was really the first time we all knew something big was going to happen," Noel said. The buzz continued to build as the band made appearances at various London clubs and other small UK venues. A November 25 date at London's Bag O'Nails drew a dazzling array of famous names: John Lennon and Paul McCartney of the Beatles, Mick Jagger and Brian Jones of the Rolling Stones, Pete Townshend and Keith Moon of the Who, and Donovan, among others.

Record Mirror journalist Peter Jones was also at the Bag O'Nails show and pronounced Jimi "quite amazing" in an article entitled "Jimi Hendrix: Mr. Phenomenon!" that appeared in the December 10 issue of the music weekly. "Visually he grabs the eyeballs with his techniques of playing his guitar with his teeth, his elbow, rubbing it across the stage—but he also pleasurably hammers the eardrums with his expert playing," Jones wrote of the show, adding that Jimi "is going to whirl round the business like a tornado."

Jimi met another person at the Bag O'Nails show who would have a profound effect on his guitar sound: Roger Mayer. Roger was then working at the Royal Navy's Admiralty Research Laboratories and had a keen interest in electronics. He spoke with Jimi after the show and brought along some of the equipment he designed when he saw the band the following month at Chislehurst Caves in Bromley, Kent, on December 16. One device was of particular interest—the Octavia, which, as its name suggests, reproduces the sound of the guitar an octave higher (Jimi tended to pronounce it "Octavio"). It would play a key role in Jimi's next single. Mayer became part of Hendrix's inner circle, working on his equipment and customizing gear, such as fuzz boxes and wah-wah pedals.

On December 13, the band taped an appearance for the UK rock music TV series *Ready Steady Go!*, performing "Hey Joe" with Noel and Mitch miming and Jimi singing a live vocal. The show aired on December 16, the same day as the single was released on Polydor, as Track wasn't quite set up yet. On December 29, they performed the song again on the live TV show *Top of the Pops*, Noel and Mitch again miming and Jimi singing live.

The single received good reviews. "Here's a young man who could make a profound impression on the future," the *New Musical Express* wrote. "It's guttural, earthy, convincing, and authentic." *Record Mirror* was equally positive, writing, "Should justice prevail, this'll be a first-time hit." "Hey Joe" did manage to crack the Top 10, peaking at No. 6—though it was later revealed its performance had received an unorthodox push when the Hendrix camp bought up copies at record stores known to provide sales figures to the entities that compiled the charts; even Kathy Etchingham loyally bought some copies to help boost the record's performance. In a more underhanded move, Michael Jeffery had given away some of the publishing rights on "Stone Free" in exchange for radio airplay.

Everything was coming together for the band. The Experience signed management and recording contracts with Chandler and Jeffery, who would each receive 20 percent of their income; Jimi also signed a separate publishing contract. The band members were put on a salary of £15 a week. Jimi was delighted to have a regular income and spent freely, sprucing up his wardrobe to create a new visual image for himself. Prowling London's trendy used-clothing stores, he found what would become one of his signature clothing items—an antique military jacket, replete with elaborate braiding.

The jacket sometimes brought him the kind of attention he didn't want. When Little Richard was in London in December, Jimi and Kathy went by his hotel to see him. Little Richard was happy to see his one-time bandmate, though he was less pleased when Jimi insisted Little Richard still owed him $50 in salary. On the way home, the couple was stopped by the police, who demanded to know why Jimi was wearing a military uniform. Jimi explained that he meant no offense and was a military veteran himself. The police were unmoved, insisted he take the jacket off, and threatened him with arrest if he was seen wearing it again. Jimi removed the jacket, and the police went on their way.

The final show of the year was a New Year's Eve gig at the Hillside Social Club in Folkestone, Kent. Afterward, everyone went to the home of Noel's mother, Margaret, to usher in 1967. Jimi's simple request to stand next to the fire to warm himself would stick in his mind and provide him the inspiration for a future song. And though he didn't know it, just four days earlier, Jimi had already crafted what would become his signature song.

Hendrix settles into life in London, late 1966.
Cyrus Andrews/Michael Ochs Archives/Getty Images

CHAPTER 3

SUPERSTARDOM

When the expense of living in hotels became too great, Jimi and Kathy moved into a flat owned by Ringo Starr at 34 Montagu Square along with Chandler and his girlfriend, Lotte. Sharing living quarters meant Chas was around as Jimi worked on new material, and he frequently offered suggestions. One day in December 1966, he heard Jimi playing a distinctive riff and immediately recognized its commercial potential. "That's the next single!" he told Jimi. He was just as sure about it when he heard Jimi playing the same riff backstage before the band's show at London's Upper Cut club on December 26. "I said, 'Write the rest of that!'" Chas later recalled. "So he did."

The riff evolved into "Purple Haze," Jimi's breakthrough record and the song that's most associated with him. The distinct opening made use of a musical interval known as a "tritone" (meaning it spanned three whole steps in the musical scale), once denounced during the Middle Ages as "the devil's interval" or *diabolus in musica*—"the devil in music"—and banned from religious songs.

Hendrix and the Experience at the Grand and National Halls, London, December 22, 1967.
Bentley Archive/Popperfoto/Getty Images

The lyrics drew on the imagery of the science-fiction novels that Chas owned, which Jimi had picked up and read, having a longstanding interest in sci-fi himself. Considering the narrator's sense of disorientation throughout the number, it wasn't surprising that "Purple Haze" was seen as a drug song. Jimi always denied that interpretation. "It's got nothing to do with drugs," he said. "It's about this guy—this girl turned this cat on and he doesn't know if it's bad or good . . . he likes this girl so much that he doesn't know what he's in, a sort of daze, I suppose."

The original lyrics were quite lengthy—"a thousand, thousand words" Jimi said in one interview—which Chas insisted he pare down; if the song was going to be a single, it had to be as commercial as possible. Sessions for the track began at De Lane Lea on January 11, then moved to Olympic Studios on February 3. Chas hadn't been entirely happy with the sound quality at De Lane Lea (though the Experience would continue to use the studio in the future when it had no other options) and was looking for a new studio. Olympic was recommended by Brian Jones and Bill Wyman of the Rolling Stones.

opposite: Hendrix and his bandmates take the stage from behind the curtain at the Saville Theatre, London, January 29, 1967. *Chris Morphet/Redferns/Getty Images*

below: Hendrix in the kitchen of his new home at 34 Montagu Square, London, in early 1967. *Petra Niemeier-K & K/Redferns/ Getty Images*

The Jimi Hendrix Experience tune up for and tape the German TV show *Beat-Club* at London's Marquee Club, March 2, 1967. *Both Bob Baker/Redferns/Getty Images*

At Olympic, Jimi also met engineer Eddie Kramer, who would work with Jimi throughout his career and on many of his posthumous releases as well. Eddie immediately instituted changes in the way the Experience recorded. Many British studios at the time were still using four-track machines, but Eddie worked out a way to expand the number of tracks available. He used all four tracks (one for Jimi's guitar, one for Noel's bass, and two for Mitch's drums), then mixed the tape down to two tracks on another four-track recorder, thus leaving two tracks available for Jimi's lead guitar and vocals. With a secure musical foundation to build on, Jimi felt freer to create his own parts. Chas also got Polydor to guarantee payment for sessions at Olympic, freeing him up from worrying about paying the bills.

Hendrix and manager Chas Chandler at London's Marquee Club, March 1967.
Jan Olofsson/Redferns/Getty Images

The Experience was kept busy with a steady stream of club dates in London and around England. There was a second *Top of the Pops* appearance on January 18, with Jimi again singing "Hey Joe" live to a mimed backing track. Club gigs could only provide so much in the way of exposure; TV spots were far more effective in boosting the group's profile. On January 29, the band played its first major London show, opening for the Who at the Saville Theatre, then being leased by the Beatles' manager, Brian Epstein. The buzz had spread about Jimi through London's club scene, but this was the first time a larger audience in the capital was able to see him. Eric Clapton was bowled over by the show, and his Cream bandmate Jack Bruce was inspired to write the song "Sunshine of Your Love" after witnessing the performance. The Experience's set was also filmed and combined with off-stage footage shot two days later to create a promo film for "Hey Joe."

The Experience also made numerous appearances on BBC Radio in 1967, starting with a session for *Saturday Club* on February 13

above: Japanese picture sleeve.

top: The Jimi Hendrix Experience performs "Purple Haze" on *Top of the Pops*, March 30, 1967. *Ron Howard/Redferns/Getty Images*

(broadcast on February 18). BBC sessions were particularly interesting in that they gave acts a chance to preview new material while also performing favorite songs (usually covers) that they never recorded officially. The Experience duly plugged its new single on *Saturday Club* and also unveiled some new songs that hadn't been recorded yet: "Foxy Lady" and "Love or Confusion." On February 22, the band made a live appearance on the BBC Radio show *Parade of the Pops*, again playing "Hey Joe."

When the Experience played the Chelmsford Corn Exchange on February 25, a Dutch filmmaker was on hand to capture the proceedings, including the performance of a somewhat raggedy version of "Like a Rolling Stone" as well as "Stone Free." In the film, Jimi sports his military jacket and plays a right-handed guitar in front of a packed house with audience members jammed up against the small stage, his Marshall speakers looming behind him. A few days later, the band would try to record a studio version of "Like a Rolling Stone," but to Chandler's frustration, he was never able to get a good take. "For some reason, Mitch could never keep the time right," he said.

The "Purple Haze" release on March 1 further helped the band's momentum. Another performance was captured for the cameras the day after the single's release, when the Experience was filmed playing "Hey Joe" and "Purple Haze" at London's Marquee Club for later broadcast on the German television program *Beat City*. Recorded before a small invited audience, the film is more like watching a

above: Hendrix and his Stratocaster backstage at the Finsbury Park Astoria, London, with Cat Stevens (holding gun), Gary Walker, and Engelbert Humperdinck, March 31, 1967. *Pictorial Press Ltd./Alamy Stock Photo*

opposite: Hendrix poses with a copy of "Hey Joe" at the Star-Club in Hamburg, Germany, March 1967. *Conti-Press/ullstein bild/Getty Images*

rehearsal but is nonetheless exciting, especially "Purple Haze." There were also a few promotional dates on the Continent, including an appearance on the Belgian TV show *Tienerklanken* on March 7 and a German radio session in Hamburg on March 18, with the band playing the first night of a two-night stand at the Star-Club following the session. Back in the UK, the Experience appeared on the TV show *Dee Time* on March 27, BBC Radio's *Saturday Club* on March 28 (broadcast on April 1), and another *Top of the Pops* appearance on March 30.

On March 31, the Experience joined a package tour headlined by the Walker Brothers (whose best-known song was "The Sun Ain't Gonna Shine [Anymore]"), also featuring Cat Stevens and Engelbert Humperdinck on the bill. Though it now seems an unusual mix of artists, package shows of the era typically had a roster of varied acts. Such shows also drew a general audience, and Chandler was interested in getting as much exposure for the Experience as he could. He and Jimi took the opportunity very seriously; Noel later pointed to the tour as "our real turning point."

(continued on page 68)

ARE YOU EXPERIENCED

Gillian G. Gaar

Are You Experienced might have been the Jimi Hendrix Experience's debut, but it was a very different experience for listeners on opposite sides of the Atlantic.

It was only a difference of three songs. The UK version included "Red House," "Can You See Me," and "Remember," while the US edition substituted "Purple Haze," "Hey Joe," and "The Wind Cries Mary" for those tracks. But consider the running order. In the UK, the album opened with the sensuous "Foxy Lady"; in the United States, the irresistibly catchy riff of "Purple

Haze" more boldly set the stage for what was to follow (oddly, the US album also spelled the former song "Foxey Lady"). One reason for the varying track listings is that the UK labels tended to not place previously released singles on albums, feeling that the album then gave the buyer more value for money. Conversely, the US labels felt having singles on an album gave more incentive to buy it.

And having all the UK singles on the US album helped make the American edition more robust. "Hey Joe" was a decidedly idiosyncratic

choice for the Experience's first single, though it had the advantage of emphasizing Hendrix's blues roots (check out the deft guitar solo), which, in the UK at least, helped it straight into the Top 10, thanks to the British blues revival. "Purple Haze" is, quite simply, a classic—a perfect blending of rock and psychedelia that evokes the 1960s but is nonetheless timeless (and one of the few songs a rock fan can immediately identify by just hearing its first two notes). And "The Wind Cries Mary" showcases Hendrix's sensitive side, featuring some fancy but subdued fingerwork—Hendrix wasn't the kind of guitar master who felt that volume was mandatory to establish one's skills. "Hey Joe" and "Purple Haze" performed indifferently on the US charts ("The Wind Cried Mary" was the B-side to "Purple Haze" in the United States), so the presence of all these songs on the US version established the breadth of Hendrix's versatility in his native land.

For someone who had only recently begun playing original music, Hendrix proved to be a quick study ("Hey Joe" is the album's sole cover song). "Foxy Lady," almost as much of a signature song as "Purple Haze," burns with confidence, with Hendrix's fine vocal performance belying all his fears that he wasn't a strong singer. Then compare that to "Fire," a rollicking number that Hendrix sings with a teasing braggadocio while a taut instrumental backing ratchets up the energy. (Mitch Mitchell's rapid fire drumming is especially impressive here.) There are some sweet songs that exude an unexpected calm, such as "May This Be Love," but there are also songs of indecision and uncertainty concerning women, such as "Manic Depression" and "Love or Confusion."

The strength of the band should also be mentioned. Hendrix had been playing with Noel Redding and Mitch Mitchell for less than a month when they first went into the studio to record. They quickly honed themselves into a tight unit, providing a powerful base from which Hendrix could operate—no matter how high he soared, they were always there to catch him. The record also benefitted from Chas Chandler's

firm control. He'd had very little money to pay for session time initially, meaning he pushed the group to work as expeditiously as possible. Hendrix may have had more control over the production of his subsequent albums, but on *Are You Experienced*, his excesses were held in check, giving the record a freshness and immediacy not as evident in his later work.

And an early clue to his future excesses comes on "Third Stone from the Sun," the album's longest number (running over six and a half minutes), a meandering track with space-age lyrics best remembered for their proclamation about the death of surf music. It's the album's least satisfying track. But there are plenty of other compensations, such as the title song, another fuzzy slice of psychedelia (with a guitar solo to match), and its lyrical double meaning: in the fade out, Hendrix jokingly assures that "experienced" doesn't mean "stoned."

When Experience Hendrix reissued the album in 1997, the CD included all tracks from the US and UK editions, along with the UK B-sides "Stone Free," "51st Anniversary," and "Highway Chile." "Stone Free" is especially interesting, as it was the first original song Hendrix recorded (released as the B-side to "Hey Joe" in the UK). It's one of his wittiest and most playful numbers, in which he forswears any kind of attachment to a woman who might "keep me in a plastic cage," preferring instead his freewheeling life on the road, which gives him the chance to move on "before I get caught."

There's another odd quirk on the US CD: the version of "Red House" is not the one from the original UK album but a different version originally used on the US *Smash Hits* compilation. The original UK album version now appears on *Hendrix: Blues* (1994).

Are You Experienced was the album with which Jimi Hendrix staked his claim as a major rock artist. And it changed everything about how the guitar could be played, breaking the rules to show there was no limit to the instrument's possibilities. It's a lesson aspiring musicians benefit from to this very day.

(continued from page 65)

The tour's opening night was at the London Astoria. Hanging out with the band and Chas backstage was *New Musical Express* journalist Keith Altham, already a strong supporter of the group. As Chandler wondered how to ensure the Experience made an impression, Altham noted that it had to be something dramatic but different. Just smashing instruments wouldn't work—that was the Who's shtick. "It's a pity you can't set fire to your guitar," he said to Jimi. Though meant in jest, both Jimi and Chas were immediately excited by the idea: why *couldn't* they do that? Gerry Stickells was promptly sent out to purchase lighter fluid.

The Experience's set concluded, fittingly, with the song "Fire" (the song inspired by Jimi's stay at Noel's mother's house). When the moment came, Jimi squirted the instrument with lighter fluid and, after a few tries, managed to set it alight. The crowd went wild, and Jimi heightened the moment by grabbing the guitar and swinging it around his head before a stagehand extinguished the flames with water. Backstage afterward, Jimi received a stern lecture by the security staff for the stunt, and disingenuously claimed that the guitar had short-circuited and he'd merely swung the instrument around in an attempt to put out the blaze. Threats were made to ban him from the venue in the future, but Jimi shrugged it off. His gesture had its intended effect. The media now rushed to cover him, newspapers nicknaming him "the black Elvis," and, more dubiously, "the Wild Man of Borneo." "Purple Haze" began heading up the charts, eventually peaking at No. 3.

Chas was anxious to capitalize on this exposure by getting an album out quickly. Sessions were squeezed in between live dates, and *Are You Experienced* was ready for release by May. First came the single "The Wind Cries Mary," released on May 5, a subdued number that stood in stark contrast to the fierce rock of "Purple Haze." It was inspired by an argument Jimi had with Kathy (whose middle name was Mary)

left: The 1965 Fender Strat Hendrix set alight onstage at Finsbury Park Astoria on March 31, 1967 (see photo, page 65). The guitar sold at auction for $575,000 in 2008. *Peter Macdiarmid/Getty Images*

opposite: A poster advertising the 1967 package tour that featured the Jimi Hendrix Experience alongside Cat Stevens, Engelbert Humperdinck, and the Walker Brothers.

when he had criticized her cooking one too many times and she responded by throwing pots at him and storming out of the flat. Jimi wrote the song, then showed her the lyrics the next day by way of apology. The single reached No. 6.

Are You Experienced was released on May 12 and would reach No. 2 in the UK, kept from the top spot only by the Beatles' landmark *Sgt. Pepper's Lonely Hearts Club Band* album, which was released at the end of the month. The UK and US versions of the album were substantially different. The UK track listing was "Foxy Lady," "Manic Depression," "Red House," "Can You See Me," "Love or Confusion," "I Don't Live Today," "May This Be Love," "Fire," "Third Stone from the Sun," "Remember," and "Are You Experienced?" In keeping with the accepted custom in the UK, the album didn't include any of the band's singles.

The cover shot taken by Bruce Fleming had Jimi positioned in the center, holding his cape aloft, flanked on either side by his bandmates. The front cover featured only the album's title, not the band's name—a precedent set by the Beatles on *Rubber Soul* (1965). The back cover featured short bios of the group. Jimi's was the most extensive and ended with a quote: "I came to England, picked out the two best musicians, the best equipment, and all we are trying to do now is create, create, create music, our own personal sound, our own personal being."

By then, Jimi's management had finally secured an American record deal. The first order of business had been to deal with his previous record company contracts, and Michael Jeffery hired the New York–based law firm Marshall and Vigoda to handle the matter. The firm first tracked down Juggy Murray of Sue Records, who was experiencing financial difficulties by that point and readily agreed to a payout of $750.

Hendrix's managers had also learned about his involvement with Curtis Knight. One night while at a club with Jeffery, the DJ put on "Hornet's Nest" and Jimi said, "Hey, listen to this one. I'm on there somewhere." When Jeffery asked him what he meant, Jimi said the record was from his time with Curtis Knight—yes, he'd signed a contract, but "it doesn't mean anything." Jeffery was dismayed at yet another loose end to tie up. Johanan Vigoda negotiated Jimi's release from RSVP Records for $500 (RSVP's Jerry Simon later said he'd have been happy to sell Vigoda the master tapes themselves, had he been asked to). Neither Jeffery nor Chandler yet knew about Hendrix's contract with Ed Chalpin and PPX. They'd find out soon enough.

In searching for a US deal for the Experience, Jeffery had first approached Atlantic Records' president Ahmet Ertegun. Ertegun had no interest, but someone else did: Mo Ostin, president of Reprise Records (a subsidiary of Warner Bros. Records). Ostin was interested in acquiring more rock acts for the label and was aware of the excitement the Experience was generating in the UK and Europe.

The final contract left Hendrix's management firmly in control. The Warner Bros./Reprise deal wasn't with the Experience but with Yameta, the offshore company that had been set up to handle the Animals' earnings and was now doing the same for the Experience. Under the terms of the contract, Yameta would provide master recordings of Jimi Hendrix and the Jimi Hendrix Experience to Reprise while retaining ownership of them. There was also a soundtrack exclusion, prohibiting Warner Bros. from using or licensing any soundtrack recordings of Hendrix or the Experience. Warner Bros. was also granted the right of first refusal of any non-Experience recordings made by Redding or Mitchell. The label's advance was $40,000, of which Jimi received $8,000. It also provided $20,000 for promotional support.

"Hey Joe" was the first Experience single released in the United States, on May 1. It failed to chart, in part because the band made no US appearances to promote it. Reprise felt confident that it had laid sufficient groundwork for the release of an album, which would come by the end of the summer. By then, Jimi would be generating plenty of excitement stateside.

The Walker Brothers tour ended April 30; Jimi called it "a gas, in spite of the hassles." As spring turned into summer, the Experience was kept busy with live dates and other promotional appearances. On April 10, the band appeared live on BBC Radio's *Monday Monday* program, performing "Purple Haze" and "Foxy Lady." On April 17, they performed "Purple Haze" and "Manic Depression" on the BBC TV show *Late Night Line-Up*. On May 4, the Experience made another BBC television appearance performing "Purple Haze," while a May 10 appearance on *Top of the Pops* saw the group performing "The Wind Cries Mary." Among the live dates, there was a return to the Saville Theatre on May 7. "He is confident and entirely at ease," Penny Valentine wrote in *Disc* about Jimi's performance. "Feeling much more at home with his success."

May 15 was the first date of a hectic European tour that began in Germany. While there, the Experience recorded an appearance for the TV show *Beat Beat Beat* on May 18, performing "Stone Free," "Hey Joe," and "Purple Haze" (broadcast on May 29). Then it was off to Sweden, Denmark, and finally Finland on May 22, where they

Original single releases of "Purple Haze" (Germany) and "The Wind Cries Mary" (Scandinavia).

Hendrix pauses in his dressing room backstage at the Saville Theatre, London, June 4, 1967. *Tony Gale/Alamy Stock Photo*

were greeted by a headline in the *Helsingin Sanomat* that read "New Madman Coming to Helsinki." During the brief visit, the Experience made a TV appearance miming "Hey Joe" and "The Wind Cries Mary." Noel noted the group always felt silly when they had to mime. Mitch agreed: "We used to think 'What the hell are we doing this for?' But obviously it paid off in terms of publicity." They then returned to Sweden and performed "Purple Haze" and "The Wind Cries Mary" for the TV show *Popside* on May 24. There were three more shows in Germany, then the tour ended on May 28.

Back in England, the band performed at a daylong festival called Barbeque 67 in Spalding, Lincolnshire, with Pink Floyd and Cream also on the bill. The "venue" was a building used for cattle auctions and tickets were oversold, resulting in a hot, packed house. Jimi struggled to keep his guitar in tune, and when the audience began to catcall, he shouted, "Fuck you, I'm gonna get my guitar in tune if it takes all night!" The show came to a chaotic ending when Jimi smashed his guitar and amps, which resulted in a blown fuse that shut off the lights. Feminist author Germaine Greer was in the crowd and wrote how the audience was already seeing Jimi as a caricature: "They wanted him to give head to his guitar and rub his cock over it. They didn't want to hear him play . . . and he looked at them heavily and knew that they couldn't hear what he was trying to do and never would." A historical commemorative plaque was later hung on the Red Lion Hotel where the Experience had stayed.

On June 4, the Experience again played the Saville Theatre, but on this occasion, had a surprise for the audience. *Sgt. Pepper's Lonely Hearts Club Band* had just been released on June 1, and before the show began, Jimi arrived in the dressing room with a copy of the album and told his bandmates they were going to open their set with the title song. Noel and Mitch were stunned, but Jimi wouldn't be dissuaded. The musicians listened to the song a few times on a portable record player and quickly worked out an arrangement.

Before they knew it, they were on stage. And as soon as the beginning of "Sgt. Pepper" rang out, the amazed audience leaped to their feet, cheering in astonishment. Paul McCartney and George Harrison were in the audience and were especially impressed. The Beatles had given up touring by that point, and no one would hear an actual Beatle perform "Sgt. Pepper" until McCartney added it to his live show in 1989. Jimi ended the set by swapping the guitar he was playing for a Stratocaster he'd hand-painted. He had taped a poem he'd written on the back of it, which ended with the words "darling guitar please/ rest amen." He then smashed the instrument and kicked the pieces into the audience. McCartney himself was the first to greet the band members when they arrived at the celebratory party held after the show, congratulating them on their performance.

On June 13, the band was on a plane heading for New York in advance of its inaugural date in the United States: the Monterey International Pop Festival, set for the weekend of June 16 to 18 at the Monterey County Fairgrounds—not too far from where Jimi had been stationed at Fort Ord. The festival had its genesis when promoter Ben Shapiro and Alan Pariser, an independently wealthy man with an interest in the music scene, approached the folk-rock group the Mamas and the Papas about headlining a show in Monterey. The group, along with their manager Lou Adler, liked the

opposite: The Experience find the pocket at Monterey Pop, June 18, 1967. *Michael Ochs Archives/Getty Images*

below: Hendrix addresses the throngs at Monterey Pop. *Michael Ochs Archives/Getty Images*

idea. Because they wanted the show to be a charity event, they ended up buying out Shapiro and putting on the show themselves (along with Pariser), expanding the event to three days. (Profits generated by the Monterey Pop films and recordings continue to go to the Monterey International Pop Festival Foundation, "empowering music-related personal development, creativity, and mental and physical health.")

Paul McCartney was on the festival's board of directors and was among those who suggested Jimi be booked for the event. Jimi was excited—if he wasn't returning to the States as a full-fledged star, he was certainly in a more advantageous position than he'd been in when he'd left for England less than a year before.

The band spent two days in New York before leaving for California. A member of the entourage, journalist Keith Altham, recalled that on arrival in New York, Jimi didn't even bother checking into his hotel, instead heading straight for the Colony Record and Radio Center at Broadway and Forty-Ninth, picking up albums by the Mothers of Invention and the debut album by the Doors. The group was billeted at the bohemian Chelsea Hotel. There were later claims that the band moved to the Buckingham Hotel after Jimi was mistaken for a bellhop, but in Mitch's recollection, the move was facilitated because the rooms were infested with cockroaches. Things went better that evening. While dining at the Tin Angel in Greenwich Village, Jimi met some members of the Mothers of Invention. He then took everyone to see Richie Havens at Café au Go Go and ended the night at Steve Paul's The Scene, where the Doors were playing.

The group flew to San Francisco on June 15 and arrived in Monterey (about 110 miles south of the Bay Area) on the first day of the festival, Friday, June 16. The Experience wasn't scheduled to play until Sunday, so they spent their time enjoying the other acts. It was an impressive lineup, including Jefferson Airplane, Ravi Shankar, Laura Nyro, Big Brother and the Holding Company (featuring Janis Joplin), the Animals, Simon and Garfunkel, and Otis Redding, among others. Jimi also participated in the numerous impromptu jams that sprang up among the musicians.

But however relaxed the atmosphere had been, tensions arose when it was time to decide the running order of the acts on Sunday, June 18. Neither the Who nor the Experience wanted to follow the other. "What you *really* mean is you don't want me to go on first," Jimi told the Who's lead guitarist Pete Townshend. "You want to be first up there with the guitar smashing!" Townshend insisted that wasn't the case, and in response, Jimi stood on a chair in front of the guitarist and let forth with a fierce solo, "playing at me, like, 'Don't fuck with me, you little shit,'" in Townshend's recollection. He then abruptly stopped playing and suggested tossing a coin. John Phillips of the Mamas and the Papas did the honors, and Jimi lost. The Who would go on first. Jimi had one final riposte for Pete: "If I'm going to follow you, I'm going to pull out all the stops."

The Who's set climaxed with "My Generation," accompanied by the expected instrument smashing. The Grateful Dead were up next. And then it was time. The Rolling Stones' Brian Jones made the introduction: "I'd like to introduce you to a very good friend, a fellow countryman of yours. A brilliant performer, the most exciting guitarist I've ever heard: the Jimi Hendrix Experience."

Jimi was wearing reddish-brown trousers, a ruffled yellow shirt, a black vest with braiding, a heavy gold necklace, and a colored headband around his head that pushed his hair up even higher. He also wore a white jacket with eyes painted on it and a feather boa, both of which he soon took off. The band members exchanged glances with each other before playing. "It was 'Let's go for it,'" Mitch recalled. "We really gave it everything." The band opened with "Killing Floor" to a good response. The set was a mix of blues songs like "Killing Floor" and "Rock Me Baby," a favored Dylan cover in "Like a Rolling Stone," and the A-side of all of Jimi's UK singles. "Purple Haze" was the penultimate track, after which he announced he was going to do what he referred to as "the English and American anthem combined," adding, "I'm going to sacrifice something right here that I really love, man. Don't think I'm silly doing this because I don't think I'm losing my mind. This is the only way I can do it."

He waved his guitar around to generate some feedback, then went into "Wild Thing." He went all out, playing with one hand, turning a somersault, playing behind his back, and rubbing the guitar against the speaker while bumping and grinding against it. Finally, he laid the guitar down on stage and aggressively coaxed more sounds out of it before spraying lighter fluid on it, kissing it farewell, and setting it alight. A fire marshal watching from the side of the stage became alarmed, but Lou Adler assured him, "It's okay, it's just part of the act." After picking up the guitar and smashing it, Jimi threw the pieces into the audience, and Mitch tossed his drumsticks into the crowd.

The band came off stage to effusive congratulations, but not everyone was enthusiastic. In the dressing room, Michael Jeffery berated Jimi for breaking a microphone. "What the fuck are you going on about!" Chas exploded. "This guy has destroyed America, and the industry is at his feet, and you're giving him hell for breaking a microphone! Piss off!" He duly ejected Jeffery from the room.

The Experience left for San Francisco the next day. Jimi still harbored some bad feelings toward Pete Townshend; when they ran into each other at the airport and Pete jokingly remarked, "I'd love to get a bit of that guitar you smashed," Jimi gave him the cold shoulder. Perhaps he should've thanked him, because going on after the Who had fueled the Experience's desire to up its game. Indeed, Mitch felt the Experience had *won* the coin toss by going on last. The band's set had captured everyone's attention, and the Jimi Hendrix Experience was mentioned in most reviews about the festival. The write-ups weren't always positive. Robert Christgau in *Esquire* dismissed Jimi as a "psychedelic Uncle Tom," and wrote, "I suppose Hendrix's act can be seen as a consistently vulgar parody of rock theatrics, but I didn't feel I have to like it. Anyhow, he can't sing." Others viewed Jimi's antics more favorably. Barry Hansen in *DownBeat* felt that the destruction "had a much more personal, less mechanical feel to it" compared to the Who's set.

opposite: A poster advertising the Fillmore's "Summer Series," featuring Hendrix, Jefferson Airplane, and others, June 1967.

Next on the schedule was a six-night, two-shows-a-night stand at promoter Bill Graham's San Francisco club the Fillmore, which began June 20 (it's been said that the Experience had no other dates booked after its Monterey appearance, but this is untrue— Jimi mentioned the Fillmore engagement during an interview with the Swedish radio program *Pop 67 Special* on May 25, which was broadcast on May 28). On the first night, the band opened for Jefferson Airplane, whose members were so overwhelmed by the Experience's performance that they quickly begged off the rest of the run. They were replaced by Big Brother and the Holding Company, and the Experience became the new headliners. The shows were so successful that Graham gave the band a $2,000 bonus as well as engraved watches for each member. Prior to its final gigs on June 25, the Experience also played a free show at Golden Gate Park.

The band then headed to Los Angeles, where it spent three days at Houston Studios working on its next single, "Burning of the Midnight Lamp." Chas was displeased with the poor sound quality of the recordings, which were never released.

When the band wasn't in the studio, they were enjoying their newfound celebrity. Peter Tork of the Monkees, who'd attended Monterey, invited them to a star-studded party at his home, where they rubbed elbows with Joni Mitchell (a favorite singer of Jimi's), David Crosby, Judy Collins, and Mike Bloomfield. Stephen Stills invited Jimi to come by his house for a jam, and when the noise brought the police, the officers assured the musicians they only wanted to listen: "So me and Hendrix jammed with the sheriff's protection!" Jimi also met Devon Wilson during his time in L.A. Born Ida Mae Wilson, Devon was a beautiful African American who had worked as a prostitute in her teens and now preferred the company of rock stars. She also had a decided taste for drugs and would become one of Jimi's regular companions whenever he was in the States.

The hard partying wore the band down. There was a show at the Earl Warren Showgrounds in Santa Barbara on July 1, and by the time they made their L.A. debut on July 2 at the renowned rock club Whisky a Go Go, they were exhausted. "We were tired and too stoned to care," Noel recalled. "We could hardly stand up and it didn't help to know we had a 10 a.m. flight to New York the next day."

Nor were they able to take a break. They played the first of two nights at the Scene as soon as they arrived, followed by an appearance at the Rheingold Central Park Music Festival on July 5, co-headlining with the Young Rascals. Prior to the latter show, Jimi dropped in to see Fayne Pridgon, arriving at her apartment with Arthur and Albert Allen and bragging about his success, showing them the album cover of *Are You Experienced*. None of them believed he was really a recording artist, as he'd only brought the cover and not the record. "You can have that stuff printed downtown on Broadway," Fayne told him. Jimi had to invite his friends to see his show that night before they believed him.

Noodling and writing. *Ron Raffaelli/Bridgeman Images*

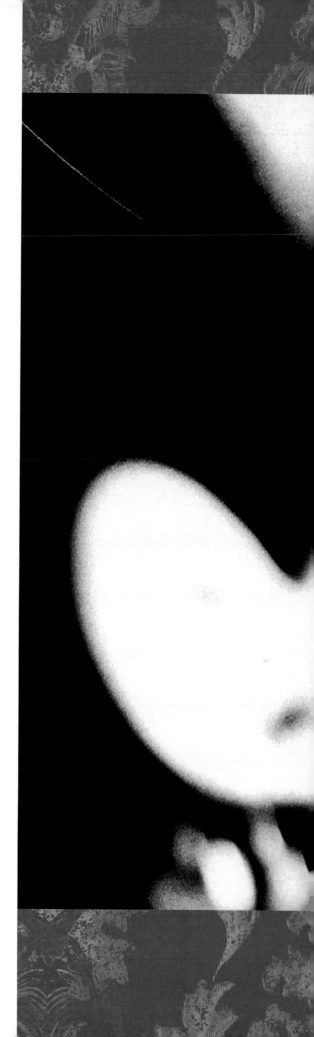

There were further sessions at Mayfair Studios to continue work on "Burning of the Midnight Lamp." The song featured backing vocals from the Sweet Inspirations, who also sang on sessions for Aretha Franklin and Solomon Burke, among others, and would later tour with Elvis Presley in the 1970s. The Experience then headed out on the most unlikely tour of its career—opening for teen pop sensation the Monkees. Jeffery had arranged the booking, reasoning that the Experience had previously played tours with artists it didn't necessarily have much in common with—Engelbert Humperdinck being a prime example—and the Monkees were currently the hottest group in the country, meaning the Experience would get a lot of exposure. Nor did the record company find it an odd bill: Warner Bros. executive Stan Cornyn was quoted as saying, "After all, they both played loud."

The Monkees were also excited to have the Experience on the bill. Micky Dolenz had seen the band at Monterey along with Tork; he'd also seen Jimi when he opened for John Hammond Jr., in the summer of 1966 and in London earlier in the year. The band also hoped that having someone like Jimi on their tour might give them some credibility with a more adult rock crowd. So the Experience joined the tour, along with the Sundowners and Lynne Randell, playing dates in Florida, North Carolina, and New York's Forest Hills Stadium. When the band played in the Southern states, Noel and Mitch came to realize the kind of discrimination Jimi faced as an African American, finding, to their surprise, that there were certain shops and restaurants he hesitated to go into.

Arguably, the only people really enjoying the Experience's set were the Monkees, who avidly watched from the side of the stage. "I remember Mike [Nesmith] and I hiding behind the stage watching him play," Tork told the author in an interview. "And he hit this spot, he did this thing where he didn't play anything for a beat—four beats, just dead silence. And then he came back in and his timing was so exquisite that it made us jump. Most musicians, they don't trust themselves, and they'll rush a break like that just a little bit. But Jimi didn't. Jimi waited until the moment, and then he *hit it*. The timing was exciting and wonderful. And everything, the whole quality of his talent, just—dang!"

But Jimi complained about being in the "death spot," playing immediately before the Monkees, drowned out by high-pitched screaming. After the Experience was moved to the opening spot, things went somewhat better, but Jimi was still unhappy and it showed in his playing, despite Noel's entreaties that a gig was a gig and they should do their best regardless. In the end, after eight shows, the Experience made its final appearance on the tour on July 16. A press release was issued stating that the Experience had been dropped due to complaints from the Daughters of the American Revolution. It was a false claim meant as a joke; the DAR never made any comment on the matter.

The band filled up their unexpected free time with club gigs at Café au Go Go and the Salvation. After the shows, Jimi frequently headed to the Gaslight Cafe to jam with John Hammond Jr.; Eric Clapton joined them on two occasions. Jimi also spent time with his friends, introducing Fayne and the Allen twins to LSD. The twins later took Jimi to meet Frankie Crocker, a DJ with WWRL, which catered to a black audience, hoping he might be interested in playing Jimi's music, but Crocker demurred. Nor did Jimi find much of a welcome in Harlem or former haunts such as Small's Paradise, where his flower-power attire and bell-bottoms were decidedly out of step with the smartly tailored, straight-legged trouser look that he found Uptown.

On August 9, the band played the first of five nights in Washington, DC, moving on to Ann Arbor, Michigan, for a show on August 15 and the Hollywood Bowl on August 18, opening for the Mamas and the Papas. Mitch didn't rate the show highly. "We went down okay, but nothing grand," he said, feeling that most of the audience were there to see the headliners. There was a final US date at the Earl Warren Showgrounds on August 19, and then the band headed back to England.

By then, Ed Chalpin had resurfaced. Hendrix's managers may have settled with RSVP Records, but Chalpin contended that he had merely licensed the material to the label and that he'd signed Hendrix to a binding contract with PPX Enterprises that wouldn't expire until October 1968. Since May 1967, he'd been sending cease-and-desist letters to Warner Bros., Track, and Polydor (which handled the Experience's records in Europe). That summer, he filed suit against them all as well.

Jimi was aware of the growing dispute, but this didn't keep him from sitting in on another Curtis Knight session in July, perhaps in a naïve attempt to make amends. After a press conference on July 17, he'd met up with Toni Gregory, the wife of guitarist Ed "Bugs" Gregory, whom Jimi knew. On learning that Gregory was playing a session with Knight, produced by Chalpin, he decided to drop in. Ironically, Dick Rowe, an A&R rep with Decca Records in the UK, was also at the session—Rowe had previously turned down the chance to sign the Experience.

Purple gaze: Hendrix plays while a fan looks out from the stage during a soundcheck at the Hollywood Bowl, August 18, 1967.
Ed Caraeff/Morgan Media/Getty Images

Jimi played guitar and eight-string bass on a number of songs at the session. Though he later said he felt it was nothing more than a "practice session," Chalpin

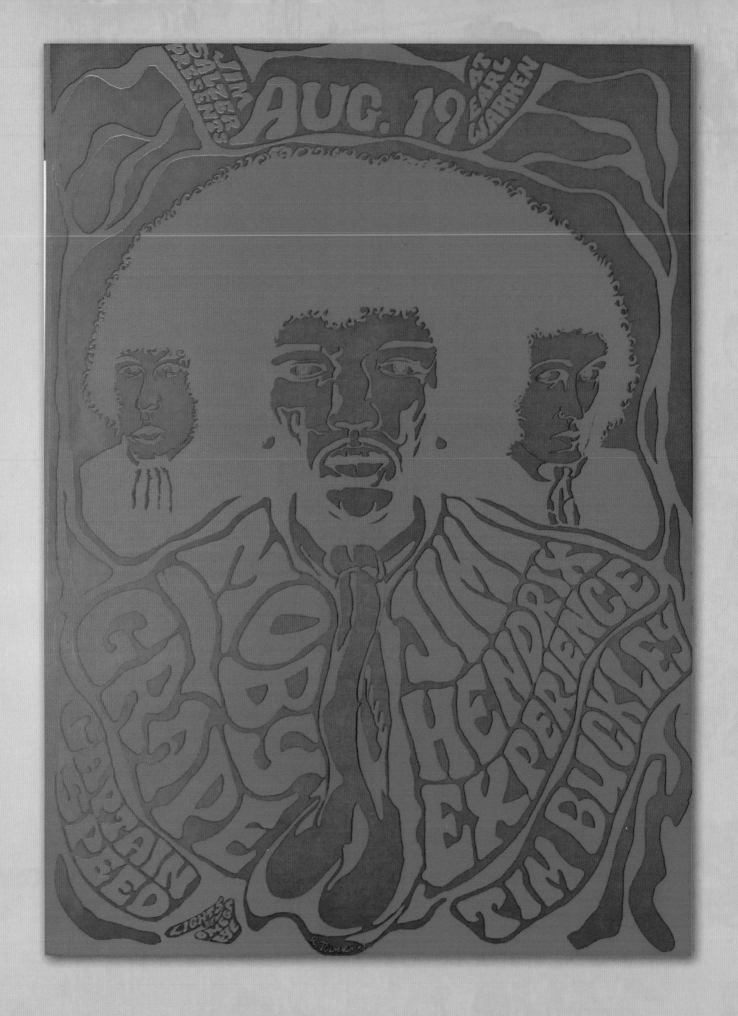

above: The Jimi Hendrix Experience's "Burning of the Midnight Lamp" single.

opposite: A poster advertising the group's performance at Earl Warren on August 19, 1967, on a bill also featuring Tim Buckley, Moby Grape, and Captain Speed.

thought otherwise and claimed to have paid Hendrix in cash for his participation. Incredibly, Jimi turned up for another Knight session on August 8, playing on "Gloomy Monday," among other songs. During the session, he stressed, "You can't use my name for none of this stuff though, right?" "I won't use it, don't worry," Chalpin replied.

What Jimi didn't know was that Chalpin had recovered the master tapes of the Curtis Knight recordings done for RSVP Records from Jerry Simon and was planning to release his own Jimi Hendrix records. Just three days after the August 8 session, London Records released two tracks from 1965, "How Would You Feel"/"You Don't Want Me" as a single in the UK on London Records, credited to Jimi Hendrix and Curtis Knight. (London was affiliated with Decca, explaining Dick Rowe's presence at the July 17 session.)

To Jimi's relief, the single sank without a trace; he had newer records he wanted to promote. On August 16, "Purple Haze" was finally released in the United States. It didn't do much better than "How Would You Feel," peaking at No. 65, but Reprise wasn't worried since it planned to promote the subsequent album heavily. *Are You Experienced* was released on August 23 in quite a different format than the UK version. There was a different running order, as well as different songs: "Purple Haze," "Manic Depression," "Hey Joe," "Love or Confusion," "May This Be Love," "I Don't Live Today," "The Wind Cries Mary," "Fire," "Third Stone from the Sun," "Foxey Lady" (the UK cover spelled the title "Foxy Lady"), and "Are You Experienced?"

(continued on page 86)

Hendrix, Redding, and Mitchell work on *Axis: Bold as Love* at Olympic Studios, London, October 1967. *All Bruce Fleming/Getty Images*

The cover art for the UK "Foxy Lady" single, plus the label for the US edition, with the title spelled "Foxey."

(continued from page 83)

The cover was also dramatically different. Jimi hadn't liked the UK version of the cover, feeling it made him "look like a fairy." Impressed with the cover of the Hollies' album *Evolution*, which featured the band drenched in psychedelic colors, Jimi engaged the same photographer, Karl Ferris, to shoot a new cover. Ferris readily agreed; he'd seen the Experience at the Bag O'Nails in January and liked the music. Jimi invited him to a recording session. "I was totally mind-blown by what I heard there," Ferris recalled. "The sheer power of his psychedelic experimentation was awe inspiring, but when taking a break from playing he was a very nice, unaffected, and a shy kind of a guy." On learning that Karl had lived in Vancouver, British Columbia, Jimi warmed to their shared experiences: "We then started smoking joints and swapping Vancouver stories, and we got on famously."

Ferris found the music "so 'far out' that it seemed to come from outer space. This gave me the idea of the group traveling through space in a Biosphere on their way to bring their unworldly space music to earth." He had the group dress in their best psychedelic finery and held two photo shoots at London's Kew Gardens, a 300-acre garden and park. He used a fisheye lens, shooting from a low angle to draw attention to the size of Jimi's hands. The first picture taken in the sessions was the one used for the cover. The group does look otherworldly—the distortion of the fisheye lens gives the impression they might be peering out of a spaceship porthole. Ferris had wanted to frame the circular photo in gold leaf, but Reprise opted for a cheaper printing process, making the cover yellow with the group picture outlined in orange. The band's name was in swirly purple letters above the picture. If Jimi had hoped the shot wouldn't have him "looking a fairy," he must've

Jimi goofs with a copy of "Hush Now" by Hendrix and Curtis Knight. The record was released in the fall of 1967 by Ed Chalpin's London Records to capitalize on Jimi's continuing success with the Experience. *Mirrorpix/Getty Images*

been disappointed with the *New York Times* review, which said the picture made the band members look "like surreal hermaphrodites." The album reached No. 5 in the United States and went on to sell over five million copies.

The Experience had a new single for the UK as well, "Burning of the Midnight Lamp," released on August 18. They made two TV appearances promoting the single, on *Dee Time* on August 22, and *Top of the Pops* on August 24. There was a slight mishap on the latter show when the backing track for the Alan Price Set's "The House That Jack Built" was mistakenly cued up instead, causing Jimi to joke, "I'm sorry man, but I don't know the words!" The proper backing track was hastily put on. The single's chart performance was something of a disappointment, peaking at No. 18.

⚜☙☯❧⚜

The Experience's first live appearance on its return to England was an engagement at the Saville Theatre on August 27. Though the group was scheduled to do two shows, the second show was cancelled when it was learned that Brian Epstein had died of an accidental overdose. After an appearance at the Nottingham Pop and Blues Festival on August 29, there was a quick European trip to promote the new single from September 2 to 12. The tour began with an appearance on German TV; the band Traffic was also on the program, and the two groups swapped members during their performances as a joke, correctly guessing most people wouldn't know the difference. At a show in Värmland, Sweden, on September 9, the band was nonplussed to find that the opening act was a troupe of trained seals. There was also a performance on the Swedish radio show *Tonarskvall* on September 5.

Back in the UK, the band appeared at a "guitar-in" held at the Royal Festival Hall in London on September 25, sharing the bill with classical guitarist Sebastian Jörgensen, folk guitarist Bert Jansch, and Paco Peña. The show's intention was to display the way different artists played the same instrument.

The group then settled into Olympic Studios for most of October, working on their second album. Jimi, Chas, and their respective partners moved into a new home at 34 Upper Berkeley Street. It was a hectic month that allowed the Experience only five days off. Most of the time, the band was in the studio. Jimi had a backlog of material he'd written, and with the fewer worries about paying studio bills, he could relax and take the time he needed to fully develop the songs.

But the band had outside commitments to meet as well. There were a few live shows, as well as appearances on radio (*Top Gear* on October 6, *Rhythm and Blues* on October 17) and television (*Good Evening* on October 13). There was also a short trip to France, where the group performed at the L'Olympia on October 9, then spent the next few days making promotional appearances on the French TV shows *Dim Dam Dom* (October 10), *Le Petit Dimanche Illustré* (October 11), and *Discorama* (October 12).

(continued on page 92)

AXIS: BOLD AS LOVE

Chris Salewicz

As pop music transmogrified into "rock" in 1967, Jimi Hendrix found himself personally instrumental in helping establish this new form—he was in the vanguard of the zeitgeist.

Boosted by the Beatles' pivotal *Sgt. Pepper's Lonely Hearts Club Band*, released on June 1 that year, albums became icons of the new "underground;" along with their rivals Cream and Steve Winwood's new group Traffic, the Jimi Hendrix Experience was one of the first acts perceived by fans as part of this newly dominant format.

Yet despite cutting-edge cultural attitudes beginning to overtake the thinking of the men running the music business, the Jimi Hendrix Experience's record deal with the Track label—formed by the managers of the Who—was firmly part of the old order. In Tin Pan Alley's tradition of expecting a fast payoff, Hendrix in the UK was required to deliver two long-players in 1967. Accordingly, by the time the groundbreaking *Are You Experienced* was released there in May of that year, the trio already had reentered the studio to begin making its successor.

Recorded in May, June, and October 1967 at Olympic, a four-track, high-ceilinged studio in Barnes in west London, *Axis: Bold as Love* (its enigmatic, trippy title essential to its "alternative" marketing) again had Hendrix manager Chas Chandler at the production controls; Eddie Kramer and George Chkiantz were first and second engineers.

Somewhat to the chagrin of guitarist-turned-bassist Noel Redding and drummer Mitch Mitchell, Hendrix dominated the *Axis* sessions, although the very first recording, made on May 4, 1967, was a Redding composition: "She's So Fine," a song about a hippie girl on which Redding sang lead.

During the recording of *Are You Experienced*, it had become apparent to Chandler that Hendrix had clear and agile abilities at the production console, and on this new LP Chandler frequently gave his client the lead. And as with the tunes for *Experienced*, much of the material on *Axis* had been substantially arranged prior to entering Olympic.

And once brought into the studio, Kramer understood how to make the very most of them. "I would fill the four basic tracks with stereo drums on two of the channels, the bass on the third, and Jimi's rhythm guitar on the fourth," he said. "From there, Chandler and I would mix this down to two tracks on another four-track recorder, giving us two more tracks to put on whatever we wanted, which usually included Jimi's lead guitar and vocals as well as backing vocals and some additional percussion."

In interviews at the time of the record's release—December 1967 in the UK, February 1968 in the United States—Hendrix emphasized how his latest LP was designed to be listened to in stereo. From track one, "EXP," this was utterly evident. Not fully two minutes long, the opener revolved Hendrix's guitar sounds through the stereo effects, playing with vocal sounds and reflecting his fascination with science fiction and his concept of music from outer space.

The jazzy "Up from the Skies" that followed continued this theme and was released in the United States as a relatively unsuccessful single. In fact, a dominant sense of *Axis* was its subtly jazz feel—it's a much looser record than the rougher *Are You Experienced*. A more melodic, meditative album, it features songs such as the gorgeous "Little Wing," in which Hendrix employs the image of a single girl to personify the spirit of the audience at the Monterey International Pop Festival in June that year, the event that broke him into the public consciousness in the United States.

Then there is the definitively psychedelic "If 6 Was 9," the longest track on the record. Alongside Hendrix's recorder and guitar, Graham Nash and Gary Leeds, drummer with the Walker Brothers, stamped their feet, joined by the guitarist and Chas Chandler, for a distinct percussive effect.

Lyrically, much of this second album sprung from within: take, for example, the autobiographical, pessimistic "Castles Made of Sand." With its backward guitar intro, each verse recounted a traumatic biographical event. And "Spanish Castle Magic," a regular part of live shows—although its title suggested that Hendrix had been dallying about

Iberia—recounted a Seattle venue he had found inspiring as a youth. The song features Redding on a Hagstrom eight-string bass, later overdubbed by Hendrix on the same instrument. Hendrix also played jazz chords on piano.

Hendrix almost missed the contractual release date after leaving the master tape of side one in a London taxi, never to be seen again. But with Chandler and Kramer, he remixed the songs during an all-night session at Olympic, making the deadline. *Axis: Bold as Love*, the second album by the Jimi Hendrix Experience, was released in the UK for the 1967 Christmas market to sensational reviews.

(continued from page 89)

The Experience's second album, *Axis: Bold as Love*, was scheduled to be released before Christmas. Final mixes were complete on October 31—and then Jimi lost the master of side one when he accidentally left the tape in a taxi. A new mix was hurriedly completed on November 1, drawing on a rough mix of "If 6 Was 9" that Noel had saved.

The group flew to the Netherlands on November 10, appearing on the TV show *Hoepla* (broadcast November 23) and playing a show that evening in Rotterdam. The group kicked off a UK tour on November 14, opening at London's Royal Albert Hall, running through December 5 and including dates in Wales, Scotland, and Northern Ireland.

The last live date of the year was December 22. The group performed at the "Christmas on Earth Continued" show in London, sharing the bill with Eric Burdon and the New Animals, Pink Floyd, and others. They also recorded an appearance on the TV show *Good Evening* on December 8 (broadcast on December 10) and another radio appearance on *Top Gear*, performing five songs, including "Spanish Castle Magic" and a cover of the Beatles' "Day Tripper."

Axis was released in the UK on December 1 and peaked at No. 5. "Foxey Lady" was released in the United States on December 13, peaking at a disappointing No. 67. Nipping at their heels were Ed Chalpin's releases. Another Knight/Hendrix single, "Hush Now," had been released October 18 on London Records. Further muddying the waters around the release of the "Foxey Lady" single was the album *Get That Feeling*, released on Capitol Records in the United States the same day. The album was credited to Jimi, with his picture (a shot from the Monterey performance) prominently on the cover; the words "and Curtis Knight" were in smaller print below. Chalpin had made an arrangement with Capitol, giving thirty-three tracks drawn from his sessions with Knight and Hendrix to A&R man Nick Venet. Chalpin had hoped a total of four albums might be created from the material, but Venet thought that only eight tracks were worth releasing, admitting to *Rolling Stone* that in remixing the recordings, "We lost some fidelity along the way."

"The record's selling well and nobody is bitching but a few San Francisco types," he asserted in the same article. "We're not saying it is all new material and I think it is valuable to have an artist's early work. If people don't like it, they won't buy it." But he also conceded that there was no information about when the recordings were originally made. "I didn't trust what Chalpin told me, so I didn't put any liner notes on the cover." It was confusing enough to buyers who thought it was Jimi's second album that *Get That Feeling* reached No. 75 on the charts. *Axis* wouldn't be released in the United States until the next month.

Chalpin would cause more headaches for Hendrix in the future, but as the most memorable year in Jimi's life came to an end, he had other things on his mind. On December 20, he was back in the studio to start work on what would be his most ambitious album. But there would be more than a few bumps in the road.

Hendrix thumbs through a copy of *Mad Magazine* #113 while having his hair styled in a motel room. *Rolls Press/ Popperfoto/Getty Images*

CHAPTER 4

YOU GOT ME FLOATIN'

The new year got off to a rocky start for Jimi. On January 2, 1968, he signed an affidavit regarding the Chalpin/PPX lawsuits, insisting that his time with Curtis Knight in the studio the previous summer was a "practice session" and not meant for release. On January 3, the Experience flew to Sweden for a short tour. After checking into their hotel, the three members went out clubbing together. This wasn't a regular occurrence, as Jimi didn't drink as much as his bandmates, but that night everyone got "rotten drunk" in Noel's recollection. Tagging along was a journalist Noel thought was gay. "Perhaps he was putting ideas in Jimi's head, but Jimi suggested we have a foursome," he later said. "I passed on it." But there remained a tension in the air, and Jimi finally erupted and began smashing up his hotel room. The police were called, and Jimi was arrested.

A *Ladyland*-era portrait of Hendrix by David Montgomery, who also took the gatefold cover photograph. *David Montgomery/Getty Images*

The authorities threatened to cancel the shows but ultimately agreed to let them go ahead. Jimi also needed to go to the hospital for injuries sustained to his right hand while breaking up the furniture in his room. As a result, the shows on the tour were shorter, with the last date being January 8 in Sweden. After the show, Jimi met up with Eva Sundquist, a teenage fan he'd met the previous year in Sweden and who had been sending him flowers ever since. Noel and Mitch returned to England on January 9, but Jimi remained in Sweden until his hearing on January 16. He pled guilty and was fined.

Back in England, the Experience fit in three sessions at Olympic Studios. Jimi had been listening to Bob Dylan's recently released album *John Wesley Harding* and decided to record what would become another of his signature songs, Dylan's "All Along the Watchtower," with Dave Mason from Traffic adding acoustic guitar to the track. The sessions were somewhat strained when tensions arose between Chas and Jimi over Jimi's increasing drug use, a problem exacerbated by the large number of hangers-on who were becoming regular fixtures in the studio whenever the band was working. The crack between Hendrix and Chandler would soon widen.

above: Hendrix is led away by police officers after smashing up a hotel room in Gothenburg, Sweden, January 5, 1968. *AP Images*

below: Jimi and his bandmates share a joke with Traffic guitarist Dave Mason (second right), who played with the Experience on its version of Bob Dylan's "All Along the Watchtower." *Michael Ochs Archives/ Getty Images* **inset:** The "All Along the Watchtower" single, with "Long Hot Summer Night" on the B-side.

above: A Barclay Records pressing of "Up from the Skies," the first and only single drawn from *Axis: Bold as Love.*

right: Jimi tunes up in the dressing room prior to the Experience's return visit to the L'Olympia in Paris, January 29, 1968. *Lebrecht Music and Arts Photo Library/Alamy Stock Photo*

Jimi also fit in a January session with Roger McGough and Mike McGear (Mike McCartney, Paul's brother), playing guitar on "So Much" and "Ex Art Student," which appeared on *McGough & McGear*, released later in the year. On January 29, the Experience headed to Paris for another date at L'Olympia, which was also recorded for French radio. Everyone headed for New York City the following day. *Axis* had been released in the United States on January 10, and the Experience's first major US tour was intended to spur sales. The album eventually reached No. 3 on the charts and sold over a million copies. The accompanying single, "Up from the Skies," was released on February 26 but didn't fare as well, peaking at No. 82. The album's success kept everyone happy, and the Experience was quickly becoming a top concert draw.

The band's publicist had prepared a new bio for the media (loping three years off Jimi's age), which featured a Q&A typical of the era for rock musicians, specifying

Jimi's favorite foods (strawberry shortcake and spaghetti), dislikes (marmalade and cold sheets), and hobbies ("reading science fiction, painting landscapes, daydreaming, music"). Jimi would spend most of the year in the United States, and Michael Jeffery would end up closing his London office and relocating to New York during the year.

The band spent a day doing press on January 31. Jimi was happy to talk about the new album. "On the first LP, we were emphasizing sustained notes and the really free scene," he told *Jazz & Pop*. "On this new LP we have now, it's quieter as far as the guitar goes, and it might seem dull to some people, but we're emphasizing the words and the drums. On the next one we're getting together, it's going to be completely out of sight." The band then flew to San Francisco for a four-date stand at the Fillmore. Then, after two shows in Arizona and four more in California, the Experience headed up the coast for Jimi's hometown—Seattle.

Some accounts say that Jimi had passed through Seattle back when he was touring the United States as a sideman, but if so, he didn't contact anyone in his family at that time. Throughout his travels, Jimi had sent letters and postcards to his father, and when he arrived in London in 1966, he had telephoned his father to let him know that he'd moved. But when Jimi called his father collect, Al admonished him, saying he couldn't afford to pay for any long-distance calls. To Jimi's surprise, Al hung up on him, and Jimi had not written or called his father since then.

Then, in May 1967, Leon heard "Hey Joe" on the radio; after the record was played, he was surprised to hear the DJ announce the band's name, the Jimi Hendrix Experience—he hadn't recognized his brother's voice. Later, after the US release of *Are You Experienced*, Al heard his neighbors playing the record and went over to investigate. (In Leon's version, he and his father heard someone playing the album while they were out on a landscaping job.) Al and Leon were amazed to find Jimi's picture on the album cover.

When Jimi arrived in Seattle on February 12, his family met him at the airport. In 1966, Al had married a Japanese woman named Ayako "June" Jinka, who had five children. Al had adopted the youngest, Janie. Jimi spent the afternoon at his father's home, hanging out with his new relatives and old friends. The last time Jimi had seen Leon, he'd given him $5—now he gave Leon a guitar and promised to wire him $5,000 and gave his father money for a new car and a new truck. He also gave Leon some LSD, telling him to hold on to it for him until after the show, when they'd take it together. But Leon couldn't wait and took it all himself before the show even started.

Jimi had been nervous about performing in his hometown, but the show at the Seattle Center Arena (now the Mercer Arena) was a sellout. His family was sitting down front, and his new step-siblings had made a large banner reading "Welcome Home Jimi! Love, your sisters." His performance "wove a spell over the packed house, taking listeners to lands beyond their imagination," recalled DJ Pat O'Day, whose Concerts West company was promoting the show. Author Tom Robbins, then working as a journalist and arts critic, called Jimi "a master stylist; an outrageous exponent of high black showmanship" in a review he wrote for the local underground paper *Helix*. Robbins also noted that Jimi toned down his more outrageous antics ("No copulating with his guitar"), perhaps in deference to his relatives being present.

Janie Hendrix was thrilled by the show. "We were pinching ourselves all night," she told *Goldmine*. "Was this real, or are we dreaming, and is he really up there? It was bigger than life." But she was frightened afterward when autograph seekers besieged Jimi as he was making his way to his limo with Janie. "He would not let go of my hand while he was signing. . . . I remember people were just hanging on the car and throwing their bodies on top and screaming and hollering. That was scary."

After the show, everyone went to Olympic Hotel, the fanciest hotel in town, with Jimi insisting that his relatives avail themselves of room service. The party went on all night, leaving Jimi in no condition for his first engagement the next morning. He'd earlier spoken with O'Day about giving a performance at his old alma mater, and plans were duly made for Jimi to appear at a pep assembly at Garfield High School. But when O'Day arrived at the Olympic, he found none of the musicians awake, let alone ready to perform. Jimi was eventually roused and agreed to get dressed and honor

opposite: Hendrix and his Band of Gypsys see in the New Year at the Fillmore East, January 1, 1968. *Frank Mastropolo/Corbis via Getty Images*

his engagement at Garfield. (Confusingly, other accounts say Jimi spent the night at his father's house playing Monopoly and was driven to his high school by a relative.)

It would prove to be an uncomfortable and awkward event. After being introduced by O'Day, Jimi was overcome by nerves and had little to say. Trying to keep things moving, O'Day asked for questions. One student asked how long it had been since he'd left Seattle. "Oh, about two thousand years," Jimi replied. After a pause, someone else asked how he wrote a song. "Right now, I'm going to say goodbye to you, and go out the door, and get into my limousine, and go to the airport," he said. "And when I get out the door, the assembly will be over and the bell will ring. And when I hear that bell ring, I'll write a song. Thank you very much." He then made a quick exit and was later found hiding in an empty office. He apologized for his behavior: "I just can't face an audience without my guitar."

Jimi and his father, Al Hendrix, backstage at the Seattle Center Arena February 12, 1968.
Experience Music Project/199.29.46

The Experience then flew to California for a show that evening at UCLA. The tour continued all around the country, down to Texas, up to Toronto, along with dates in the Midwest and the East Coast. One of the more memorable dates came on February 25 in Chicago. After the matinee performance, the band returned to the Conrad Hilton Hotel and were met by a young woman named Cynthia Albritton, who had followed their limousine in her car. Cynthia was a music fan who had come up with an ingenious way to meet musicians—offering to cast their erect penises in plaster (hence her nickname, Cynthia Plaster Caster). "Basically, it was a combination of the sixties and wanting to get laid by British rock stars!" she explained in an interview.

When Cynthia and her friend explained their mission, Jimi told her, "Oh yeah, I've heard about you through the cosmos." Both Jimi and Noel agreed to submit to the procedure. As her "assistant" made sure the men were properly aroused, Cynthia prepared the alginate (used to make dental molds). She was still perfecting the technique; although she'd previously cast molds of two friends, Jimi and Noel were the first famous men she cast. The alginate was put in a large vase and then molded over Jimi's erect penis. But she had neglected to lubricate Jimi's pubic hair, which then had to be pulled out one by one after becoming stuck in the mold. To help pass the time while being disengaged, "he was bumping and grinding the mold, fucking it really, because being a mold it was the perfect size for him," Cynthia later told biographer Charles Cross. When the cast of Jimi's impressive member later went on display, it was dubbed the "Penis de Milo." (Noel had an easier time with his casting due to the use of baby oil; he later described his own mold as "a corkscrewed rendition.")

On March 7, Jimi sat for a deposition in New York regarding the Chalpin/PPX lawsuit. Questioned about the various contracts he'd signed, Jimi acknowledged not reading them before signing. Following a tour break, the band entered Sound Center Studios in New York on March 13 and 14. Because Chas was not on the tour, this was the first time Jimi produced himself at a session. The Experience was joined by various other musicians in the studio, including Stephen Stills and Fugs guitarist Ken Pine. It also marked the first time drummer Buddy Miles worked with Jimi in the studio—the two had first met in Canada in their journeymen days as backing musicians. They had also met up at the Monterey International Pop Festival when Buddy was playing in the Electric Flag. They would soon begin working together more extensively.

Shows resumed on March 15 with a gig in Worcester, Massachusetts; footage from the show later appeared in the BBC TV 1968 documentary *All My Loving*. Back in New York briefly on March 18, Jimi engaged in an infamous "jam" with Jim Morrison of the Doors (though a variety of different dates have been given for the event). Jimi had taken to dropping in at the Scene club, looking to jam with anyone who was interested

Diane and Cynthia, the "Plaster Casters of Chicago," pose for a portrait in San Francisco. Hendrix met the pair in February 1968.
Baron Wolman/Iconic Images/Getty Images

and preserving the results on tape. The Doors were also in New York that month, and upon learning that Jimi was a frequent visitor at the Scene, Morrison came by to check him out. Jimi was sitting in with Eire Apparent that night, and Morrison eventually joined them on stage. Unfortunately, he was extremely drunk, and the "performance" ended up being something of a shambles. The set has since been released on various bootlegs (including one titled after a lyric Jimi sang during the jam: *Woke Up This Morning and Found Myself Dead*).

The band flew to Cleveland on March 25, in advance of its performance in the city the next day. It turned out to be an eventful stay. That day, Jimi wound up at a local club, Otto's Grotto, sitting in with the band Good Earth. That same evening, Chuck Dunaway, a DJ with Cleveland station WKYC, was having dinner with Leonard Nimoy, *Star Trek*'s Mr. Spock, and when he learned Hendrix was in town, Dunaway brought Nimoy to the club to meet him. They spent the rest of the evening hanging out together, and Dunaway invited Jimi to come down to the station for an interview the following day.

On the 26th, Jimi fit the radio interview in between the two scheduled concerts, plugging Spirit, a new group featuring his former Jimmy James and the Blue Flames guitarist, Randy California. He also managed to do a little car shopping, buying a new

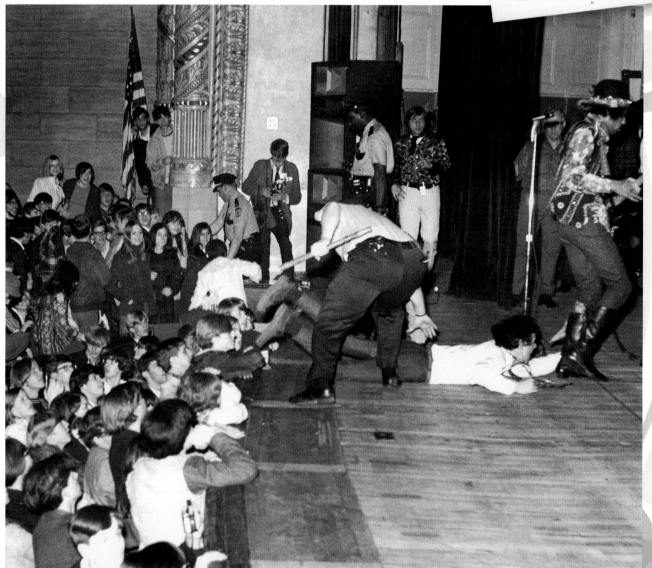

Corvette even though he didn't have a driver's license (after driving it around town, Jimi had the car sent to New York). The second show worked the crowd into a frenzy according to *Plain Dealer* critic Jane Scott, who further described Jimi's antics: "The tall, stove-pipe slim singer in the rainbow-hued jacket and big black hat started making love to his white guitar. He played it with his teeth. He knelt in front of it. He tore off the strings. And he tossed it behind him." Some of the audience rushed the stage, and the police had to push them back—not before one fan had grabbed a souvenir: "'They swung at me, but I got it,' exulted John Paulisin, 15, Cathedral Latin School, holding up a guitar string." After a pause for a false bomb threat, the show resumed, with Hendrix shouting, "Nobody but Jimi burns a house down!" Scott also noted Hendrix's car purchase in her review: "He bought a blue Corvette with all the trimmings at Blaushild's Chevrolet."

Though Jimi largely avoided political statements, he began making the occasional political comment on stage. In Ottawa on March 19, for example, he talked about Vietnam, saying soldiers should change their machine guns for "feedback guitars—that's better than guns." A different kind of politics was in air the following month. On April 4, civil rights leader Dr. Martin Luther King Jr. was assassinated in Memphis. That night, the Experience was playing in Virginia Beach, Virginia, and was scheduled to play two shows the following evening at Newark Symphony Hall in New Jersey. Riots had broken out in cities across the United States in the wake of King's murder, and there was some question as to whether the show would go on. It was finally decided that the band would play the early show and cancel the second. Fearful of attack, the band's white limo driver insisted that Jimi sit in the front seat alongside him as they drove to the gig.

Because Symphony Hall was half full when the Experience took the stage, Jimi invited those who had been brave enough to attend to come down front. Noel recalled the band playing "a load of blues for 45 minutes"; future music journalist Bob Cianci, who attended the concert as a sixteen-year-old, wrote that the band played a short set that included songs the group usually played, such as "Purple Haze" and "Foxy Lady." But King's death was obviously having a profound effect on Jimi; he stood still for the performance, not engaging in any of his signature moves. The last song Cianci remembered was "I Don't Live Today," after which Jimi took off his white Stratocaster and hurled it into the amps. The show was over.

There were other shows on April 6 and 19, then came a break of three weeks. Back in England, April 19 was the release date of Jimi's first "best of" collection, *Smash Hits*. Like Jimi's debut album, both the UK and US versions would have different songs. The UK album featured "Purple Haze," "Fire," "The Wind Cries Mary," "Can You See Me," "51st Anniversary," "Hey Joe," "Stone Free," "The Stars That Play

above and opposite top: Posters for two more shows on the group's 1968 tour, in Denver, Colorado, and Flint, Michigan, with Soft Machine once again on the bill for both concerts.

opposite: Fans invade the stage during a concert at the Public Music Hall in Cleveland, Ohio, March 26, 1968. *CSU Archives/Everett Collection/Alamy Stock Photo*

top: The UK edition of the *Smash Hits* compilation album was released in the spring of 1968. The US edition, with the same cover art but a different track listing, followed a year later.

with Laughing Sam's Dice," "Manic Depression," "Highway Chile," "Burning of the Midnight Lamp," and "Foxy Lady." The album reached No. 4; the US version wouldn't be released until the following year.

Back in New York, where the band members were based, Jimi moved into an apartment below Michael Jeffery's office. The band returned to the studio on April 18 at a facility that had just opened in March: the Record Plant. The new studio was outfitted with a state-of-the-art twelve-track tape recorder rather than the four-track machines found in places such as London's Olympic Studios. Jimi was also delighted to find a familiar face among the staff—Eddie Kramer, who'd been hired away from Olympic. Until he had his own studio, most of Jimi's future recording sessions would be held at the Record Plant.

Though Jimi was glad to be reunited with Eddie again, the sessions became increasingly stressful, with endless retakes and tinkering ruining the focus. Noel told journalist Chris Welch, "There were times when I used to go to a club between sessions, pull a chick, come back, and [Jimi] was still tuning his guitar. Oh, hours it took!"

Chas, who had come to New York to produce the sessions, was also put off by the band's excessive partying, along with the hangers-on such partying attracted. (In a different approach, Jeffery took acid, hoping it would help him better relate to his client.) By May 8, a disgusted Chandler had left the sessions. Jimi continued as producer, but it was a turning point for the band. Chas had provided direction, but left to his own devices, Jimi found it harder and harder to wrap up a project.

The trial over the Chalpin/PPX lawsuit began in May, and ultimately, a settlement was worked out with Warner Bros. PPX would receive a percentage of all of the Hendrix recordings from Warner Bros. in the United States and Canada through 1972, and the Jimi Hendrix Experience was required to provide Capitol (who had been releasing the Curtis/Hendrix albums) with a new album. Chalpin's suits against the overseas labels were still pending and would not be settled until after Jimi's death.

The settlement also brought Jimi's relationship with Yameta to an end. Warner Bros. bought out his contract, contingent upon the delivery of an album (meaning Jimi's next album would come out on Reprise, not Capitol; the album to be released as part of Jimi's settlement with PPX would come out later). Jimi also received a royalty increase. Jeffery would continue as Jimi's manager, with the two now bound to Warner Bros. until 1972. A new publishing company, Bella Godiva Music Inc., was also set up for Jimi.

The seeds of a new idea were sown at this time as well. Jimi enjoyed his nightly jams at the Scene so much that Jeffery suggested he buy his own nightclub (one track recorded during the sessions, "Voodoo Child," even originated from a jam started earlier in the evening at the Scene). Another venue where Jimi had liked to

In bed at the Drake Hotel, New York City, April 1968. *Roz Kelly/Michael Ochs Archives/Getty Images*

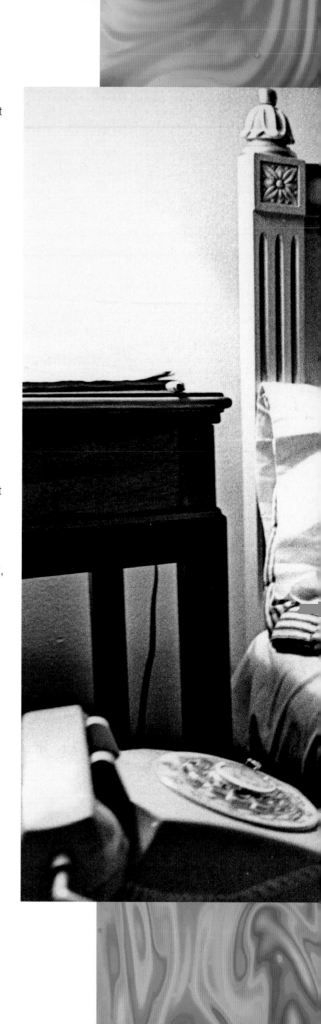

drop in for a jam, the Generation Club at 52 West Eighth Street, had recently closed. Jeffery suggested they purchase the space and add a small recording studio to the club, allowing them to easily record live performances.

There were also a few scattered live gigs. On May 10, the Experience shared the stage with Sly and the Family Stone at the Fillmore East in two sold-out shows. *Billboard*'s reviewer said that even the constant equipment problems "couldn't diminish the excitement generated by the powerful piercing sounds." But a writer with the *East Village Other* was put off by Jimi's excessive theatrics, writing, "The great Jimi Hendrix Experience blessed the stage of the Fillmore last Friday but what a drag it was that Hendrix was so penis oriented that night. The greatest musician in the world really doesn't have to hump his guitar. Playing with his teeth is cool, but 'doing' his guitar is a little out of the question and kind of silly. The strange thing was that the audience responded to this the most. Closest thing to mass hysteria I've ever seen."

A week later, the band was off to Hallandale, Florida, to play the Miami Pop Festival on May 18 and 19. (One of the promoters was Michael Lang, who would later organize the Woodstock festival.) Prior to the first show, the band was offered "something to perk you up" by one of the crew. "Through foolishness, Hendrix and I accepted," said Mitch, thinking they were being given speed. They soon learned it was some kind of hallucinogen, and Mitch was disconcerted about the out-of-body experience he had while playing. "We'd been spiked and badly at that," he said in his memoir. The second day of the festival was rained out and the event cancelled. As Jimi was being driven away in a limo, the pounding rain inspired him to start writing the lyrics for "Rainy Day, Dream Away."

There was a quick jaunt to Europe, with a total of nine shows performed in Italy and Switzerland from May 23 to 21. On June 5, the Experience was back in London, taping an appearance for the Dusty Springfield TV special *It Must Be Dusty!* The band performed "Stone Free" and "Voodoo Child," but the highlight came when Dusty joined Jimi on the song "Mockingbird" (an R & B take on the lullaby "Hush, Little Baby").

By June 10, the band was back at the Record Plant, where they would spend most of the summer. These sessions for the future *Electric Ladyland* album saw numerous guests sitting in, including Buddy Miles, Steve Winwood, Al Kooper, Dave Mason, and Jack Casady, bassist with Jefferson Airplane. Jimi also played many of the bass parts, which irritated Noel, who played bass on only five of the album's eventual sixteen tracks (though he was also given his own number on the album, "Little Miss Strange").

Mitch recalled that the sessions "seemed to take forever." Money was being wasted, he felt, on "stupid things" like having limos on call twenty-four hours a day. "Jimi wanted more freedom in the studio and more control, which was fine, but someone should have had more overall control," he said. "There was far too much wasted time and energy. It wasn't that I didn't enjoy all the partying; I did, but it was

Hendrix onstage at the Woburn Music Festival on July 6, 1968—his only British live performance of the year. *Michael Putland/ Getty Images*

no way to work." The sessions finally came to an end on August 28.

※※※※※

Work on the album was interrupted when the Experience returned to England on July 4 in advance of what would be their only UK performance in 1968, an appearance at the Woburn Music Festival in Bedfordshire on July 6. Michael Jeffery also arranged for them to appear at his new club, Sgt. Pepper's, in Majorca, Spain, on July 15 and 18. Keith Altham wrote a review of the first night for the *New Musical Express*: "Jimi Hendrix literally brought the roof down on the opening night, by the simple expedient of ramming the neck of his guitar up through the low ceiling tiles [at the end of 'Wild Thing']. Amid thunderous applause, the Experience exited in a shower of plaster and debris after a series of brilliantly electronic histrionics!" Altham concluded, "The Experience rolls along the motorways of the mind and the airways of the imagination."

Regular touring commenced on July 30 with a show in Baton Rouge, Louisiana. Afterward, Jimi was taken to a local blues club where he sat in for a jam. Tensions were higher elsewhere in the South; after their show in New Orleans on August 1, the band was threatened with arrest for trying to start a riot. The authorities in Texas were equally hostile. "Every time we set up, the fire department, police department and mayor's office were all there saying 'You can't do this, we don't allow *that* kind of stuff in our town,'" sound engineer Abe Jacob recalled. "They all thought Hendrix was going to burn the house down." He didn't, though he did smash his guitar and amps to bits at the end of his show in Houston on August 4.

On August 23, the Experience played at the Singer Bowl in Queens. An August 2 show at the Bowl headlined by the Doors had ended in violence, with the audience throwing chairs and rushing the stage, so the atmosphere was edgy. Happily, there

Jimi and a friend at a birthday party for Howard Solomon, owner of Greenwich Village's famed Café au Go Go, in August 1968. *Jay Good/Frank White Photo Agency*

inset: A poster advertising the Jimi Hendrix Experience's "two big shows"—at 3:00 p.m. and 8:00 p.m.—at the Atlanta Municipal Auditorium, August 17, 1968.

below: Hendrix and Joan Baez chat backstage at Steve Paul's the Scene on the night of a benefit concert to raise funds for refugees displaced by the Biafra War, August 29, 1968. *Bettmann/Getty Images*

were no mishaps. The Experience took the stage after opening sets by Soft Machine, the Chambers Brothers, and Big Brother and the Holding Company, and the set went off without disruption. The few who tried to storm the stage were quickly subdued.

While the reviews were good, the guitar-smashing antics were beginning to bore the critics. The *Village Voice* described the violence of the finale, with Jimi "charging his equipment, guitar neck first, carefully deflecting so as not to really bust the speakers or his axe, then squatting obscene across the axe, merry-go-round-round-round-round-round. For what? He's a genius—what's he need that corn for?" The *New York Times* had a similar sentiment: "Apart from his furious finale, Mr. Hendrix continues to be one of the most compelling performers working these days. His blues wailing and his guitar virtuosity are unparalleled, and his extroverted showmanship is a brilliant form of total musical theatre. But, again, why tear the theater down?" By 2:00 a.m., Jimi was back at the Record Plant, pushing to finish *Electric Ladyland*.

"All Along the Watch Tower" was released on September 4 in the United States, reaching No. 20. Two days later, Jimi returned to Seattle, this time playing the Seattle Center Coliseum (now Key Arena). The show got a mixed review from the *Seattle Times* critic, who called Jimi's performance "less than great. It was good" and felt that opening act, Vanilla Fudge, had "outclassed" the headliners.

After the show, Jimi and Leon drove around town with their friends, arriving back at Al's house at a late hour. Their father was furious, as he'd invited a number of people over to meet his famous son, and they'd been kept waiting. To Jimi and Leon's amazement, Al even took off his belt and threatened to give them a whipping. The brothers stared at their father, then burst out laughing. Al grumbled but put his belt back on.

The next night, the Experience was playing in Vancouver, British Columbia, and Jimi invited his family to attend. Everyone rode in Al's car, though the excitement of the day was spoiled when they stopped in the town of Mount Vernon for lunch and were left sitting at a restaurant table when the staff refused to serve them. Eventually, a young girl recognized Jimi and asked for his autograph, after which the family was finally served.

In Vancouver, they stopped at the home of Jimi's Aunt Pearl for a turkey dinner, then everyone headed for the Pacific Coliseum, where Jimi dedicated "Foxy Lady" to his beloved grandmother Nora. Jimi also complained to his aunt that day about constantly being on tour. He was tired.

After a final Pacific Northwest date in Spokane, Washington, the tour headed back to California, where the Experience headlined at the Hollywood Bowl on September 14. During the show, excited fans rushed down the aisle and jumped in the moat in front of the stage during the show—at one point Mitch stopped playing his drums to help people out of the moat, giving one of them his towel to dry off. The *Los Angeles Times* called the show "one of Hendrix's best appearances locally. . . . He heads one of the best trios in rock music, a trio dominated by his screaming guitar and dry husky voice. But his dominance is made possible by the solid underpinning of Redding and Mitchell on bass and drums, a freely interacting rhythm section which would stand out in any rock combo, whatever its size."

The *Los Angeles Free Press* hailed him as "the Chuck Berry of the acid generation." The band played until 12:30 a.m., when management threatened to turn the sound off if they didn't quit.

Following a show in Sacramento the next evening came a much-needed break. The rigors of the road were exhausting. In his memoir, *Are You Experienced?*, Noel described the disturbing litany of coping mechanisms for the touring musician, starting with the need to bring yourself down after an exciting show:

A few stiff drinks and a sleeper sped you on your way. But plane time would come long before the sleeper wore off, hence the leapers. But the flights are terribly boring when you're up, so a creeper rounds off the edges and a lot of drink takes a bit of the cotton wool out of your mouth. But booze makes life a bit grim, so "just a bit" of acid makes you feel all tingly and good. But it's hard to concentrate on acid, so a quick sniff of coke brings the brain briefly to attention while you smoke some grass or hash to take the nerviness out of the coke. Then, as you're beginning to feel a bit tacky by the time the flight's over, the hotel is found, and it's gig time: a bath, a snort of methedrine and a big tobacco joint puts you on stage. Repeat as necessary.

Jimi hated having to put his sessions on hold to go on the road, and he felt the final mixing of *Electric Ladyland* had been rushed before going out on tour. Increasingly, he was getting little creative satisfaction doing live shows. "He used to always say that people were only coming to see him burn his guitar, and he was bored with that," said Gerry Stickells. "Most nights it took forty-five minutes just to convince Hendrix to go on, then when you got him on, he didn't want to come off. Every night he'd say 'Give them their money back. I don't feel like playing tonight. We'll do it tomorrow,' then he would go on and we would have to scream at him to stop."

A home had been rented for the group on Benedict Canyon Drive in Los Angeles, and Jimi spent time just relaxing and not even entering a recording studio. "We partied for days doing some crazy shit," Buddy Miles remembered. Jimi had another new Corvette he raced around the winding roads in the hills surrounding L.A., totaling his car on one occasion but escaping with barely a scratch himself. Jimi was a notoriously poor driver, and although he admitted he had bad vision, he refused to wear glasses. After the crash, Jimi simply went out and bought another Corvette the next day. There was a more serious incident when Jimi physically assaulted one of the women hanging around him. The woman needed stitches and Jimi was forced to pay an out-of-court settlement.

When Jimi invited Leon to come down and join him, his brother eagerly accepted the offer, taking full advantage of his status as the brother of one of the biggest rock stars in the world to hit the clubs and party every night. Nonetheless, Leon was concerned about his brother's state of mind. Despite his success, Jimi didn't seem happy. Jimi told Leon he wanted to fire his manager and hire his brother to work for him. "It was easy for me to see that the lifestyle was taking a toll on him," Leon wrote in his memoir. "I thought back to the excited phone calls I used to receive from him back in 1966 after he arrived in New York City and how he was truly happy in those days. Now that he was more famous than he'd ever expected to be, that joy was almost gone."

Electric Ladyland was released in the United States on October 16 and in the UK on October 25. The albums had the same running order but strikingly different covers. Following a session on August 7 at the Record Plant, the Experience went to Central Park, where photographer Linda Eastman (who would marry Paul McCartney the following year) took pictures of the group sitting on the park's "Alice in Wonderland" statue. Some young children also sat with the band members, making the pictures especially sweet. In one photo, Jimi looks pleased and happy, holding a young boy in his lap.

Jimi wanted one of the pictures from this shoot for album cover. Instead, the UK played off the album's title: Jimi had explained that "Electric Ladies" was his nickname for groupies, so why not picture him surrounded by adoring women? When Jimi didn't show up for the photo shoot, the photographer changed strategies and offered the women extra pay to disrobe. When a shot of the nude women was displayed over the full cover of the double album's gatefold sleeve, it created an immediate controversy. Distribution was hampered as some shops refused to carry the album, while others packaged it discreetly in a brown paper bag. Jimi himself was unhappy with the picture and was photographed biting a copy of the offending album. Despite the controversy, it went to No. 6 in the UK. An accompanying single, "All Along the Watchtower," was released in the UK on October 18, peaking at No. 5.

In the United States, a heavily saturated color headshot of Jimi was used for *Electric Ladyland*'s cover. The album topped the charts—the only No. 1 record Jimi had during his lifetime. Despite its success, Jimi was unhappy with more than just the cover. He thought the sound mix was "cloudy" and complained that being on the road had left him unable to oversee things properly. For his part, Chas was unhappy with the production credit reading "Produced and Directed by Jimi Hendrix," neglecting to mention his own contributions.

Following Jimi's releases like a shadow, Ed Chalpin also tied his next Hendrix-related record to *Electric Ladyland*'s release, issuing *Flashing: Jimi Hendrix Plays, Curtis Knight Sings* on October 8. At least the title let buyers know this wasn't an Experience album.

It was at this moment, while the band was in Los Angeles, that Chandler told Jeffery he was done—he was quitting. He wanted to be back home in England with his pregnant wife, and Chandler would soon sell all his managerial interest in Hendrix to Jeffery.

While the Experience spent most of October in Los Angeles, there were also a few live dates. On October 5, the band played Honolulu, getting a largely positive review from the *Honolulu Advertiser*: "With all the fury of a violent hurricane, the Jimi Hendrix Experience uncorked a frenzied assortment of funky electronic

(continued on page 118)

ELECTRIC LADYLAND

Jaan Uhelszki

In 1968, after two blockbuster albums full of sex, guitars, and science fiction compressed into neat three-minute songs, Jimi Hendrix decided he wanted to make the album that he wanted. After his resounding success as a recording and touring artist, he believed he deserved it, and for the first time he could actually afford to spend a little extra time in the studio.

Despite his flashy, fashion-forward rock star image and thrilling stage performances, the real magic for Hendrix came from the sounds he created—massive, unruly, psychedelic, and vaguely frightening, simultaneously tribal and futuristic. Hendrix saw music in almost messianic terms: "Our scene is to try and wash people's souls," he once explained. "We're in the process of tryin' to make our music into a religion. It's already spiritual anyway, and we want it to be respected as such. We call our music Electric Church Music. It's like a religion to us."

His goal was to push the needle a little closer to the godhead—to that same cosmic destination for which musicians such as John Coltrane, Sun Ra, and even Jim Morrison aimed: the place where physics met metaphysics, soul met body, and sounds melded into light. He often said that this third album—*Electric Ladyland*—was about breaking through all limitations.

But even given his spiritual bent, Hendrix did enjoy the spoils of the rock wars: the bigger-than-life blondes, the silver-speckled Corvette, the free-flowing drugs, and the groupies whom he claimed he named his album after: "Some groupies know more about music than the guys. People call them groupies, but I prefer the term 'electric ladies.' My whole *Electric Ladyland* album is about them," he explained in 1968.

In all honesty, *Electric Ladyland* wasn't about groupies at all: it was about Hendrix and his vision . . . at the expense of everything and everybody else.

His backing band, Noel Redding on bass and Mitch Mitchell on drums, and his producer Chas Chandler, all felt to some degree neglected, if not abused, during the recording, which began at the Record Plant in New York City. On the seventeen tracks, Hendrix handled most bass duties himself. He also brought in a plethora of outside musicians, often scooping them up from clubs, such as the night he recorded the fifteen-minute slow-burning blues jam "Voodoo Child" with Jefferson Airplane's Jack Casady and Traffic's Steve Winwood on bass and organ, respectively.

On the opposite end of the spectrum, they found Hendrix's obsessive studio perfectionism, which sometimes resulted in forty takes of a song, equally irritating. At the forty-third take of "Gypsy Eyes," a song about Hendrix's mother, producer Chandler imploded, explaining to his friend and client that he couldn't take it anymore. Not only was he quitting the project and going back to the UK, he was done being Hendrix's manager, as well, selling off his interest to his partner Mike Jeffrey.

Chandler's sudden departure shocked the Hendrix camp, but, as the guitarist explained in 1968, "My initial success was a step in the right direction, but it was only a step, just a change. Our records will become better, purely from the point of view of recording technique."

Hendrix felt his recordings under Chandler were far too hurried, and he knew that eventually he could wear down his producer. Now he was in total control, as noted in the credits: Produced and Directed by Jimi Hendrix. He would be the one to determine the balance of perfectionism and impulsiveness in his recordings.

Eight months and an entire ocean separated the first and last sessions for *Electric Ladyland*, but spiritually the gap was even wider. Pulling away from the more poptastic "Come On (Let the Good Times Roll)," "Little Miss Strange," and "Crosstown Traffic" (all produced by Chandler), Hendrix plunged into deeper sonic waters, letting his unruly, restless muse be his guide. Ethereal masterpieces such as the astonishing thirteen-minute "1983 . . . (A Merman I Should Turn to Be)" established Hendrix as not only the greatest guitarist of his day, but as a musician for the ages.

Hendrix thoroughly enjoyed his new freedom, but he also demonstrated on *Ladyland* that he was well aware of what was happening on Planet Earth. "House Burning Down," an urgent blast of gritty funk metal, was a thinly veiled commentary on the late-sixties riots plaguing African-American communities in Watts and Detroit. The guitarist had rubbed shoulders with the politically radical Black Panthers, and it was starting to show.

As the album progressed, it became clear that one disc could not contain his growing ambition. "I plan to have more instruments and longer tracks on the next album, 'cause you just can't express yourself in two minutes in every song," Hendrix announced in 1967. "I want to make it a double LP, which will be almost impossible; it's a big hassle, the record producers and the companies don't want to do that. I'm willing to spend every single penny on it."

And he almost did. Despite the obstructions, complaints, and astronomical costs, Hendrix triumphed. *Electric Ladyland* is the complex masterwork he envisioned.

(continued from page 115)

soul sounds in their Island debut before a charged-up, sell-out crowd at the Honolulu International Center arena." But the paper's critic took exception to their performance of the "The Star-Spangled Banner": "an instrumental which Hendrix manipulated to musically desecrate everything for which the anthem stands . . . I think it was an un-American, unfortunate, unfunny spoof that spoiled an otherwise stand-out rock show." It was a reaction that would become increasingly common as Jimi played the song more frequently.

Then came a three-night stand at San Francisco's Winterland Ballroom, with two shows a night and the Buddy Miles Express as the opening act. There were a few special guests. Jefferson Airplane bassist Jack Casady sat in with the band during the second show on opening night, and flautist Virgil Gonsalves and organist Herbie Rich, both from the Buddy Miles Express, joined the Experience on the second night. "Hendrix puts on a great show," Ralph Gleason wrote in the *San Francisco Chronicle*. "It's pure theater, with flamboyant costumes, dramatic and sexual gestures, symbolism involving the guitar and the crashing, swirling hurricane of sound that characterizes the rock music." Mitch even arranged for Buddy Miles to play a few songs with the Experience so he could go out in the audience and watch his band play. "It was a revelation," he said. The show was professionally recorded, but due to sound problems with amps, the recordings weren't released during Jimi's lifetime. Jimi frequently had sound problems when he played live because the high volume at which he played sometimes burned out his equipment.

Jimi spent the rest of the month in Los Angeles's TTG Studios. He initially worked with Eire Apparent, another act managed by Michael Jeffery who had opened a number of shows for the Experience, and produced their debut album, *Sunrise*, on which he also performed. Jimi immediately butted heads with the studio's engineer, Jack Hunt, a "by the books" employee whose strict adherence to a schedule wasn't at all to Jimi's liking. Jimi refused to work with Hunt when the Experience began recording, asking instead for another engineer, Angel Balestier—to Hunt's great displeasure. In spite of Jimi's involvement, *Sunrise* failed to make much of an impression on its release. "It was never really finished according to my standards," Jimi later said of the record.

The Experience began recording just six weeks after *Electric Ladyland* had been released, and with few finished songs to work on, the band spent their time jamming endlessly. Jimi told Balestier that he wanted every second of the sessions to be captured on tape, and once again Noel found himself frustrated by sessions where little work got done. The rift between him and Jimi was growing and was clearly evident to those around them.

An increasing number of people dropped in on the sessions. Some, including Stephen Stills, Buddy Miles, and well-known studio musician Carol Kaye, came by to jam. Others—such as Lou Reed, Ike Turner, Sonny Bono, Ricky Nelson, and familiar faces from Hendrix's early career such as Billy Preston and producer Bumps Blackwell (who'd produced Little Richard's work in the 1950s for Specialty Records)—just wanted to hang out. But there was also a never-ending stream of casual acquaintances and young women. The barrage of hangers-on was a further distraction, but it seemed that Jimi couldn't say no to anyone who wanted to hang out.

At another live date on October 26 at the Bakersfield Civic Auditorium, the power was cut during the final number when the auditorium's manager, Charles Graviss, felt the show was about to get out of hand and was fearful that Jimi might light his guitar on fire (Graviss had previously cut the power when the Jefferson Airplane played the venue). What happened next is in dispute. Photographer Ron Raffaelli, who was backstage, said Hendrix and Graviss began arguing and that he stepped between the two men to keep the fight from becoming physical. Graviss and police officer Mac Anderson maintained that Hendrix punched Graviss. Jimi was arrested, but Graviss quickly decided to not press charges, and the band was escorted out of town.

Following the Bakersfield show, there were two more sessions at TTG Studios on October 27 and 29, then the band's L.A. sojourn was over. On October 30, "Crosstown Traffic" was released as a single in the United States, peaking at No. 52.

The Jimi Hendrix Experience's "Crosstown Traffic" b/w "Gypsy Eyes" single, a #37 hit in the UK in late 1968.

The band then relocated to New York, where Jimi began working with another of Jeffery's acts, Cat Mother and the All Night Newsboys, and produced their album *The Street Giveth . . . and the Street Taketh Away*. The only known session date is November 6 at the Record Plant, though other sessions were held on other unknown dates. Jimi was again disappointed with his work, saying of the band to an interviewer, "They are presentable enough, but not as good as I wanted them to be." Nonetheless, the band's single "Good Old Rock 'n' Roll" peaked at No. 21, with the album reaching No. 55—decent enough for an unknown group.

The Experience played thirteen shows between November 1 and December 1; the schedule was arranged to be easier on the band, with most shows on the weekends. Jeffery also began exploring the possibility of booking the Experience on the *Ed Sullivan Show*. According to one of Jeffery's associates, it was proposed that Jimi

perform with an orchestra while the Vienna Ballet danced to his music. Jeffery soon turned the offer down, and Jimi never performed on the top-rated variety program.

Meanwhile, the Generation Club had finally been purchased for the proposed nightclub/studio. When Jimi and his manager showed up at the nearest police station to apply for a liquor license, Jimi began to give out autographs to the officers once they recognized him. He was less happy to learn from Jeffery that to fund this new venture, he would need to go back on the road in January.

Jimi spent his twenty-sixth birthday playing a show in Providence, Rhode Island, and afterward the band celebrated with a party at Cafe au Go Go. Another birthday celebration was held following the next night's show at New York's Philharmonic Hall, which was billed as "An Electronic Thanksgiving," also featuring harpsichordist Fernando Valenti and the New York Brass Quintet.

After the December 1 show in Chicago, Jimi remained in New York to celebrate the Christmas holidays, while Noel and Mitch returned to London. Noel had started a new band, Fat Mattress, in which he played guitar, and he began working on the group's first album at Olympic Studios. Whatever thoughts Jimi had about what the new year might bring, he couldn't have anticipated just how tumultuous 1969 was going to be.

Hendrix onstage during his three-night stand at the Winterland Ballroom, San Francisco, in October 1968. Tapes from these shows were eventually issued as *Live at Winterland. Mira/Alamy Stock Photo*

CHAPTER 5

CASTLES MADE OF SAND

Once Chas resigned as Jimi's manager, Jimi understandably no longer wanted to share a flat with him and enlisted Kathy Etchingham to find a new home. There were some difficulties at first, as potential landlords anticipated trouble if Jimi Hendrix was a tenant. Eventually, a friend found an ad for a flat at 23 Brook Street in London's tony Mayfair neighborhood. "It cost us £30 a week, which at the

Jimi plays a Gibson SG at Falkoner Centret, Copenhagen, Denmark, January 10, 1969.
Jan Persson/Redferns/Getty Images

time was a lot of money," Kathy said. "But it was a great place to live because it was central but there were no neighbors." There was also no front door bell, which made it easier to maintain some privacy.

Kathy had begun renting the flat the previous summer, and she and Jimi had gone furniture shopping together during one of his brief trips to England. But he'd spent most of 1968 in the United States, not returning to London and Brook Street until January 2, 1969. He liked the decorating Kathy had done, telling her, "This is my first real home of my own." The two also liked the flat's location. Oxford Street wasn't far away, and the couple was within walking distance of their favorite music clubs. Jimi was also pleased to discover that he was living next door to the former home of classical composer Frederic Handel at 25 Brook Street.

After a month's break, the Experience got back to work, making an appearance on the TV show *A Happening for Lulu* on January 4. The band played "Voodoo Child" without incident. Two minutes into playing "Hey Joe," however, Jimi abruptly stopped and announced, "We'd like to stop playing this rubbish and dedicate a song to the

opposite: The Jimi Hendrix Experience kicks off 1969 with a performance of "Voodoo Child" on *A Happening for Lulu. Ron Howard/ Redferns/Getty Images*

below: Hendrix and girlfriend Kathy Etchingham at the flat they shared in Mayfair, London, in early 1969. *Trinity Mirror/Mirrorpix/ Alamy Stock Photo*

above: Drummer Buddy Miles's debut solo LP, *Expressway to Your Skull,* recorded around the same time as his guest performances on *Electric Ladyland.*

opposite: A striking poster for Hendrix's concert in Stuttgart, Germany, on January 15, 1969.

Cream, regardless of what kind of a group they may be in," in reference to the fact that the supergroup had recently split. The band then went into Cream's "Sunshine of Your Love," much to the consternation of the TV crew, who argued amongst themselves about pulling the plug. Since the show was going out live, it was decided to just let the band finish, though there was a quick fadeout after the group's performance. It was the last time the Experience would appear on the BBC.

On January 5, Jimi went to Polydor Studios to record a quick guitar overdub for the Eire Apparent track "Rock 'n' Roll Band," released as a single that spring. A European tour then began on January 8 in Gothenburg, Sweden. Jimi would have a number of notable encounters on the tour, beginning with the opening night when Chas Chandler showed up. Jimi asked him if he'd consider being his manager again, but Chas turned him down. Chas was unimpressed with the show: "It was a dire concert. You could just see there was trouble in the band. There was friction, it wasn't together, it just didn't work." A film crew accompanying Jimi on the tour compiled footage for a proposed TV special, but the band's performances were desultory—Jimi seemed more engaged when he was jamming in his hotel room.

The next night, when the band was in Stockholm, Jimi reconnected with Eva Sundquist, dedicating the evening's show to her. (Nine months later, Sundquist gave birth to a son she claimed was Hendrix's.) The tour moved on to Denmark, then Germany. The day after the band's show in Düsseldorf on January 12, Jimi met Monika Dannemann in the hotel bar, and she accompanied the group to their next date in Kohn. Monika returned to Düsseldorf on January 14; she was destined to have a more fateful encounter with Jimi the following year.

The tour continued with dates in France, Austria, and a final show on January 23 in Berlin, a performance that degenerated into a brawl when the audience tried to take the stage and trash the band's gear. With almost a month until the next show, Jimi returned to New York to produce four tracks for the Buddy Miles Express album *Electric Church*. (Jimi had previously written liner notes for the band's album *Expressway to Your Skull*.)

Jimi also continued overseeing the nightclub project, which was about to change direction. Jeffery had hired Jim Marron of the Scene to assist, but in Marron's view, there was no point in opening a club since there were already four other clubs in the immediate area. And with the club scene then overseen by the Mob, it was hard to get established. He suggested that they refashion the former Generation Club into a dedicated studio. Hendrix and Jeffery agreed, and Eddie Kramer, who'd recently left the Record Plant, was hired to design what would become Electric Lady Studios. Marron would become the studio's manager.

Back in London, the Experience returned to Olympic on February 14 to record a studio version of "The Star-Spangled Banner." But the sessions were plagued with frustrations, and tensions among the band members that were more readily

opposite and above: Reaching for the sky during the Experience's two shows at the Royal Albert Hall in Kensington, London, February 18 and 24, 1969. *Both David Redfern/ Redferns/Getty Images*

overlooked on stage could not be ignored within the confines of the studio. Noel, in particular, was irritated at again having to sit around for hours waiting for Jimi or Mitch to show up, only to endure endless rounds of retakes. And without a firm hand at the helm, Jimi began to lose his sense of musical direction. Though he would record hours of material from February 1969 through August 1970, he never released another studio album in his lifetime.

On February 18, the Experience played their first show in London in fifteen months at the prestigious Royal Albert Hall; when the first show sold out, a second date was added on February 24 (with Noel's band, Fat Mattress, added to the latter show). Jimi again tapped his former manager to come by and oversee things, but when Chas turned up for a rehearsal on February 18, he found "a shambles," with neither the equipment nor recording gear working properly. Jimi's reported drug use also marred his performance on the first night, though Chas also cited Noel's and Mitch's "lifeless" playing as being more damaging. After additional rehearsals, the Experience rallied for

the second show; Jimi rammed his guitar into a speaker at the end of the encore and then tossed the guitar's neck into the crowd. And he was still eager to jam at the party held at the Speakeasy following the event.

Hendrix, Redding, and Mitchell share a laugh sometime in 1969. *du Vinage/ullstein bild via Getty Images*

On March 13, the Experience flew to New York, planning more session work in advance of its next US tour. A few days later, Kathy flew out to join Jimi at his invitation. She was appalled at the size of the entourage that now followed Jimi everywhere—"the loudest, nastiest bunch I had ever come across," she said. She was no stranger to drug use but was put off by the constant parade of drug dealers, prostitutes, and pimps through their room and was equally alarmed at "how relaxed Jimi seemed among them all, a king presiding over a court of fools." When she caught sight of a gun in the bag of one drug dealer, she fled for the safety of London. It was the beginning of the end of her relationship with Jimi.

There was certainly no shortage of other women willing to keep Jimi company. Devon Wilson was always around and always ready to do drugs with him, to the dismay of his friends. He also hung out with New York friends such as the Allen brothers. "Jimi loved to party and get laid," Albert Allen said. "We would go to

fat mattress

above: The 1969 self-titled debut LP by Noel Redding's new band, Fat Mattress.

top: A poster for Hendrix's show at the Philadelphia Spectrum on April 12, 1969, with Buddy Miles—soon to join Jimi's new-look band—also on the bill.

after-hour clubs, night spots uptown, parties at hotels or just spend money shopping. He loved to do that."

But he also spent time in the studio, working on the Buddy Miles Express record, as well as his own songs—both at the Record Plant and another New York studio, Olmstead Recording Studios, when the Record Plant was fully booked. On March 18, Lonnie Youngblood, with whom Jimi had recorded back in 1966, came by to play with him. He also recorded with different combinations of musicians from the Experience and the Buddy Miles Express.

"Crosstown Traffic" was released as a single in UK in April, peaking at No. 37. The Experience's US tour began the same month, with an April 11 date in Raleigh, North Carolina. The tour continued through June 1, with Noel doing double duty as the Fat Mattress was the tour's opening act. The Experience began running into trouble when performing "The Star-Spangled Banner." When playing the song in Houston on April 19, a police officer demanded that booking agent Ron Terry end the show. Terry refused, and the next night in Dallas, the band was confronted by, in Terry's words, "five imposing Texans" blocking entry to their dressing rooms, one of them announcing, "You tell that fucking nigger if he plays 'Star-Spangled Banner' in this hall tonight he won't live to get out of the building. . . . We'll start a riot, and if he don't make it out of the building, that's just the way it fucking goes." Everyone was unnerved by the threat, but Jimi played the national anthem regardless, without incident.

Recording sessions were dropped in during tour breaks. While in Memphis on April 18, Jimi met up with Billy Cox and asked Billy to join him in New York. Billy duly packed up and headed east, joining Jimi at the Record Plant on April 21. Billy was surprised to hear that his longtime friend now felt at a creative standstill: "He just felt that he couldn't think of anything new." But their first jam went well, and Billy was excited about the prospect of working with his one-time bandmate again.

Billy also got an introduction to the efforts Jimi would make to find new people to record with. One night during a session break, the two headed for the Scene, where Jimi struck up a conversation with Al Marks, manager of a band called the Cherry People, whom Jimi had previously met at the Monterey International Pop Festival. He asked if the band's drummer, Rocky Isaac, could come by the Record Plant later that night, around 3:00 a.m. Marks readily agreed and accompanied Isaac and the band's guitarist, Chris Grimes, to the studio, where Isaac played drums, Grimes played tambourine, and Marks played maracas on thirty-one takes of "Room Full of Mirrors." Isaac had difficulty keeping proper time, causing Jimi to ask in some exasperation, "Man, do you know how to play drums? What's going on?" At the end of the session, he gave the two men $100 each, telling Isaac, "Man, I would practice a bit if I was you!" Despite his dissatisfaction with Isaac's drumming, Jimi invited the musicians back for another session on April 24.

On April 26, the Experience played the Los Angeles Forum. When the sold-out crowd threatened to get out of control, both Jimi and Noel pleaded for calm. "C'mon, let's act like we have some sense," Jimi said at one point. "It's groovy to get high, but let's act like we have some sense while we do it." The following night, the band hit the Oakland Coliseum, closing the show with a twenty-minute version of "Voodoo Child," which also featured the Jefferson Airplane's Jack Casady.

After the show, Jimi received a note left for him by Diane Carpenter, whom he'd known in New York not long before he'd left for England. Jimi got word to her to follow his limo to the airport, where they met up and talked as he waited for his flight. To his astonishment, she pulled out a photograph of a little girl and said, "This is your daughter, Tamika. She's two years old." Jimi noted that the girl seemed to have his eyes but otherwise made little comment about the subject. The following year, Diane would try unsuccessfully to get Jimi to take a blood test to confirm that he was the father.

He did complain to Diane about constantly having to tour to bring money in. His unhappiness was such that on May 2 he refused to fly to Detroit for a show that night. When he finally agreed to do the show after much persuasion, he flew to Detroit on a private jet. The next morning, the band flew to Toronto. Everyone had been warned about carrying any drugs through customs, and Ron Terry even examined Jimi's travel bag before they left their hotel. Still, upon arrival in Canada, a small glass vial with white powder and a small pipe stained with resin were found in Jimi's luggage. After testing the substances, Jimi was arrested for possession of heroin and hashish.

Terry, who was carrying one of Hendrix's bags, was also arrested. The authorities were persuaded that canceling that evening's show might result in a riot, so the two were released on $10,000 bail and ordered to appear in court on May 5. Despite the unexpected developments, the Experience turned in good performances, both in Toronto and in Syracuse, New York, the following night. Hendrix and Terry spent the night

Hendrix's mugshots, taken following his May 3, 1969, arrest on drug charges at Toronto International Airport.
Alamy Stock Photo

METRO. TORONTO JAMES   M. HENDRIX   2199/69 MAY 3/69

A poster for the Experience's show at the Fillmore East on May 10, 1969, set to also feature the "Joshua Light Show."

partying with three airline attendants they'd met, then turned up hungover for the arraignment in Toronto the following day. Charges were dropped against Terry, but Jimi was ordered to return to Toronto for a hearing on June 19.

When Michael Jeffery heard the news, he immediately went into action. Some later speculated that Jeffery had arranged the bust so he could strengthen his hold over Jimi. This was an absurd theory, since the Experience generated most of its money through live performances, and a drug conviction would have seriously impeded the band's ability to tour. Jeffery quickly had the Experience's PR manager, Michael Goldstein, do some heavy-duty damage control, and Goldstein leaned on his media contacts to bury the story, bribing one Associated Press editor with a case of liquor. As a result, news of the bust didn't break for nearly a month.

The tour continued, with Jimi heading back into the Record Plant on his days off. On May 7, he dropped into the Scene and invited Stephen Stills and Johnny Winter to come back to the Record Plant and record. On May 14 and 15, pianist Sharon Layne was invited to the sessions, becoming one of the few female musicians to ever play with Jimi. But despite all the studio activity, he was still not close to finishing another album.

On May 18, the Experience played a sold-out show at Madison Square Garden, a coup for any performer. There was another Seattle show on May 23 at the Seattle Center Coliseum; the *Seattle Post-Intelligencer* critic noted that "the audience never got very turned on by the Fat Mattress" but found the Experience "as good as ever." Jimi's brother Leon wasn't able to attend; after being arrested for burglary, Leon entered the army on a plea bargain and wasn't granted leave to come to the show.

In a nostalgic mood after the concert, Jimi asked a backstage fan to drive him and his girlfriend around Seattle. The three spent the rest of the night visiting the many places Jimi had lived, the boarded-up clubs he'd once played, and his high school. Jimi never failed to talk about Garfield High School during his Seattle shows, even though he'd dropped out.

After a May 25 date at the Northern California Folk-Rock Festival, the band headed for Honolulu for two shows scheduled on May 30 and 31 at the Waikiki Shell in Honolulu's Kapiolani Park. Jimi cut the first show short after about forty minutes, complaining about a hum in the sound system and walking off stage. To the dismay of the promoters, he refused to come back on, so a make-up show was hastily scheduled for June 1. The remaining shows went off without further incident.

Jimi then flew to Los Angeles, where he and Eddie Kramer mixed tracks for a proposed live album from the Experience's second Royal Albert Hall show and the recent L.A. and San Diego dates; the album was later scrapped. At Jimi's hearing in Toronto on June 19, a trial date was set for December 8. It was nerve-wracking to not have the matter settled, and Jimi faced the very real prospect of serving prison time.

The future of the Experience was also very much up in the air. While in Toronto, Jimi had told an interviewer that he wanted to work with different people at his sessions. Earlier in the month, he'd done an interview with Jerry Hopkins for *Rolling Stone*, in which he'd mentioned that Billy Cox was going to be the group's new bassist, and that he had been working with the Allen twins on songs. But he didn't talk to his bandmates about these plans.

On June 20, the Experience played the Newport Pop Festival in Northridge, California. It was a day after the hearing in Toronto, and Jimi was in a bad mood. It was a poor show, further marred by fights in the audience. "We hope we're not playing to a bunch of animals," Jimi finally complained. "Just lay back, because you are really making us uptight, and it's a bad scene trying to get us uptight when we're trying to give you some good feeling, and all this other crap."

Jimi nonetheless felt bad enough about his performance that he appeared at the festival again on June 22 in an unannounced guest appearance, playing for over two hours with Buddy Miles, Tracy Nelson of Mother Earth, Eric Burdon, and Brad Campbell of Janis Joplin's Full Tilt Boogie Band, among others. He performed such numbers as "Hear My Train a Comin'" and "We Gotta Live Together," and the audience was delighted. *Image* magazine wrote of his performance, "He seems to know the instrument and its nearly limitless possibilities better than any electric guitarist who ever lived."

Jimi seemed to invest more energy into his impromptu performances than his regularly scheduled gigs. In Denver on June 28, in advance of the Experience's appearance at the Denver Pop Festival, he called up two musician friends to ask what they were up to. On learning that they were booked to play a wedding that evening, Jimi turned up at the reception to sit in with them. The reception was held in a public park, and when people realized who the guest guitarist was, a crowd quickly gathered, causing Jimi to beat a hasty retreat.

The Experience was booked to play the festival on June 29. On arriving for a preshow press conference, Noel was surprised when a reporter told him he'd heard he was no longer in the band. This was news to Noel, and it didn't set the stage for a good show. There had already been problems at the festival; the previous night, police had used tear gas against a mob trying to gain entry, and gate crashers were a problem on June 29 as well, as they filled the stadium to capacity. Many fans were unruly, throwing rocks and fighting. By the end of an otherwise good set by the band,

right: "We hope we're not playing to a bunch of animals." The Jimi Hendrix Experience at the Newport Pop Festival, Devonshire Downs, California, June 20, 1969. *Vince Melamed/ Michael Ochs Archives/Getty Images*

below: A poster for the 1969 Newport Pop Fest shows the extent to which Hendrix towered over his peers in 1969.

ALBERT COLLINS
ALBERT KING
BOOKER T. & THE MGS
BRENTON WOOD
BUFFY ST. MARIE
BYRDS
CHAMBERS BROS.
CHARITY
CREEDANCE CLEARWATER
EDWIN HAWKINS SINGERS
ERIC BURDON
FLOCK
FRIENDS OF DISTINCTION
GRASSROOTS
IKE & TINA TURNER
JETHRO TULL
JIMI HENDRIX EXPERIENCE
JOE COCKER
JOHNNY WINTER
LEE MICHAELS
LOVE
MARVIN GAYE
MOTHER EARTH
POCO
RASCALS
SOUTHWIND
SPIRIT
STEPPENWOLF
SWEETWATER
TAJ MAHAL
THREE DOG NITE

Jimi stunned everyone by announcing, "This is the last gig we'll ever be playing together!" The audience was now openly rioting and trying to climb on the stage, so the police unleashed tear gas once again. The tear gas hit the band as well, and the musicians were rushed into a rented truck at the side of the stage, coughing, their eyes burning. As the truck slowly navigated through the grounds, the crowds outside pounded on the cargo hold while the band cowered inside. "How could this nightmare have emerged out of all the good feelings and music?" Noel later wondered.

The Jimi Hendrix Experience had played their first show two years and eight months ago, in October 1966. It had been a wild ride, with incredible highs and lows, but now it was over. The original lineup of the Jimi Hendrix Experience would never play on the same stage again.

Noel left for London the next day. "It was the end of the world as I'd known it for three hectic years," he later wrote, though he put on a brave front for the press, telling *Disc and Music Echo*, "I was planning to leave Hendrix this year anyway, because I was getting very bored." Jimi returned to New York City, but he soon relocated to Boiceville, a town 4 miles southwest of Woodstock. Michael Jeffery had a home in Woodstock proper (Bob Dylan and his manager, Albert Grossman, also had homes in the area), and it was thought that by getting away from the hustle and bustle of Manhattan, Jimi could relax free from distractions and get down to work completing his long-awaited fourth album.

With Billy Cox's help, Jimi tracked down Larry Lee, one of the guitarists he and Billy had played with back in Nashville, and invited Lee to come out to Boiceville. The plan was to expand the band and add a rhythm guitarist, leaving Jimi free to focus on lead. He also invited Jerry Velez and Juma Sultan to join him. Both men were percussionists—Velez had met Hendrix when they jammed together at the Scene, while Hendrix had met Sultan, a member of a Woodstock collective called the Aboriginal Music Society, when he was visiting Jeffery. Jimi had wanted a conga player in his group to give the sound a different feel, but unfortunately he asked both Velez and Sultan to join at different times. Not wanting to turn either of them away, Jimi wound up with an additional conga player he didn't really need. It was a sign of the disorganization that plagued the group as well as Jimi's own indecisiveness over what kind of a band he really wanted.

Jimi wouldn't perform a full live show for another month and a half, giving him time to pull the band together, but he did make two TV appearances in July. On July 7, he appeared on the *Dick Cavett Show*, performing "Hear My Train a Comin'," backed by the show's band. During his interview by Cavett, Jimi came across as soft spoken with a tendency to ramble. He didn't mention the dissolution of the Experience

The Japanese edition of *Smash Hits*, released in 1969 with its own unique cover art.

but did address such topics as his on-stage destruction of instruments ("It's nothing but a release, I guess") and what he meant by the term "electric church," a phrase he'd been using to describe his music ("Everything is electrified nowadays. . . . We plan for our sound to go inside the soul of the person, actually, and see if they can awaken some kind of thing in their minds, 'cause there's so many sleeping people"). He also elicited laughs when Cavett asked how disciplined he was; did he get up every day and work? "Oh, I try to get up every day," Jimi deadpanned.

Three days later, he was a guest on the *Tonight Show*, where comedian Flip Wilson was hosting in place of the regular host, Johnny Carson. It was a less successful appearance, marred by Wilson's attempts to sound hip (overusing the phrase "I can dig it!") and, again, by Jimi's tendency to ramble. Asked about his comments that he regarded performing as a "spiritual experience," Jimi's replied, "It's a thing that I don't know—after going to church for a few times and getting thrown out of there because you've got tennis shoes on with a blue and black suit, brown shirt, the works, and then after politics tell you this hogwash about this and that, you know, you decide and say, 'Well let me get my own thing together,' you know, and so music is my scene." The short interview was followed by a performance of "Lover Man," with Cox on bass and Ed Shaughnessy, from the *Tonight Show*'s band, on drums. To Jimi's frustration, his amp blew just as he started his solo. Repairs were quickly made and the ad hoc group completed the song, but it was an unhappy experience.

On July 30, *Smash Hits* was released in the United States, more than a year after its UK counterpart. It also had a different roster of songs, featuring "All Along the Watchtower," "Crosstown Traffic," "Remember," and "Red House" in place of "51st Anniversary," "The Stars That Play with Laughing Sam's Dice," "Highway Chile," and "Burning of the Midnight Lamp." It reached No. 6 on the charts and went on to sell over two million copies. "Stone Free" was released in September as a tie-in single, but it failed to crack the Top 100.

In late July, Jimi suddenly put the new band on hold and went to New York City. He met up with Deering Howe, a friend of Chas Chandler's whom Jimi had gotten to know the previous year when renting Howe's yacht for the day. Deering was flying to Morocco to join Stella Douglas and Colette Mimram, whom Jimi also knew. The two women ran a clothing shop that Jimi frequented; their clients included the likes of Miles Davis, Andy Warhol, and Janis Joplin. Located at 321 East Ninth Street, it was named the Nudist Colony, though no one ever got around to putting the name on the outside. Deering suggested that Jimi join him on the trip, and he agreed, asking his manager to clear his travel plans with the Canadian authorities (his drug trial was still pending).

Jimi spent about a week travelling through Morocco with his friends. "We had a wonderful time," Stella told Hendrix researcher Steve Roby. "We took Jimi to the restaurants, we walked through the streets of Morocco, we stayed in the best hotel in town." Jimi loved taking in the sights and eating new and exotic foods. When everyone was relaxing by the hotel pool one day, he entertained them by playing his guitar. Stella recalled him playing Ravel's "Boléro": "He played it in like a hundred different versions. The song is repetitious, but his version was so wonderful." On another evening, when the group visited a nightclub only to find it empty, they nonetheless began dancing "all together, like kids dancing."

One night Jimi had his fortune told and became upset when the tarot card reader drew the death card. His friends assured him the card usually just symbolized the end of something in one's life (it was a shame they didn't interpret it as relating to the breakup of the Jimi Hendrix Experience), but Jimi insisted on taking it literally and fixated on the idea. "Sometimes it would be 'I'm going to die in three months,'" Colette later told Charles Cross. "And sometimes it would be that he was only going to live for 'six months.' But he kept repeating that he was going to die before he was thirty." Stella claimed that story was overdramatized. "Jimi said that he could die young, but I have lots of friends that have said that and they're now in their fifties and sixties," she told Roby.

On Jimi's return flight to the States, he changed planes in Paris, where, according to Cross's book, he met film actress Brigitte Bardot and delayed his return for two days in order to have a tryst with her. He finally made it back to Boiceville, and Mitch Mitchell soon joined the group, appalled by the unfocused state of things. "The band was grim and the house was grim," he said. "It was probably the only band I've ever been involved with that simply did not improve over that length of time."

One problem was getting all the percussionists to work together. Velez admitted that he and Sultan "overplayed," and Sultan disliked Mitchell, saying he was "drunk most of the time" and "didn't know the concepts that Jimi was moving to." With the music not coming together, Jimi became so irritated at one point that he threw his guitar across the room. "Rehearsals, as I remember they called them, consisted of getting stoned and talking about how great it was going to be," said Gerry Stickells. "The fact that they kept adding people to the lineup proved to me that it wasn't together."

Nor was the house as isolated as had been hoped. Once word got out that Jimi Hendrix was in town, uninvited guests began to turn up. Claire Moriece, who'd been hired as a cook, remembered one young woman showing up and promptly telephoning her father in Texas, "bragging that she was with a big star—and he sent the cops! I had to pretend Jimi wasn't home." There were other kinds of recreation

Billy Cox (left) and Jimi Hendrix rehearse, possibly for their appearance at Woodstock, August 1969. *Experience Music Project/1996.36.22.4*

going on as well; as Velez recalled, "On the coffee table downstairs there would be every drug imaginable available." And there were hassles with the local police. One visitor to the house told *Rolling Stone*, "Once a cop stopped me on the highway and started bragging, 'Hey, I just stopped Jimi Hendrix for the second time today.'"

But Billy Cox insisted that it was also a "very productive" time for Jimi. "He had broken away from the Experience and was able to place his focus on creating new ideas or tightening up 'Izabella' with small, intricate things that no one else would know except for those of us who had to play them. We weren't just jamming."

"Dolly Dagger," about Devon Wilson, was another song written when Jimi was inspired by a bass riff he heard Billy playing one day. Jimi also enjoyed dropping in for jams at the Tinker Street Cinema in Woodstock. Eventually even Billy got tired of the constantly ringing telephone: "They never let him have any peace."

The band's first gig was on the closing night of the Woodstock Music & Art Fair, held August 15 through 17 in Bethel, New York. The festival was originally planned

above: The view from the stage: Woodstock Music & Art Fair, August 18, 1969. *Barry Z Levine/Getty Images*

opposite main: Hendrix stalks the Woodstock stage while turban-wearing Billy Cox looks on. *Henry Diltz/Getty Images*

opposite inset:: Hendrix and Janis Joplin receive top billing on this poster for the Woodstock Music & Art Fair, a "three-day peace and music festival."

to take place in Woodstock itself, but when the producers (including Michael Lang, who'd co-produced the 1968 Miami Pop Festival) couldn't find a suitable location, they decided to keep the name and look for another site. At each possible site, they were met with opposition from the local residents who didn't want crowds of hippies streaming through their neighborhoods. Finally, they made arrangements to lease a farm in Bethel, 61 miles southwest of Woodstock. The delay in finding a site meant there was no time to fully set up, and on August 13 it was decided to focus on getting the stage built instead of erecting a fence.

Without a fence, Woodstock inadvertently became a free festival; advance sales aside, most attendees didn't buy a ticket. The producers had expected around fifty thousand to show up, but the area was flooded by hundreds of thousands of people. At its peak, the crowd was estimated to be around four hundred thousand.

Jimi's friend Richie Havens opened the festival at 5:00 p.m. on Friday, August 15. The impressive roster included the Who, Janis Joplin, Sly and the Family Stone, Joan Baez, and Santana, among others. By the time Jimi and the band arrived at the site, rain had turned the farm into a field of mud. Jimi was scheduled to close the festival, but it was running behind, meaning it wouldn't end as planned on August 17 but on the morning of Monday, August 18. Due to the delays, Lang suggested moving his spot up so that Jimi would play at midnight on the 17th, but for some reason his offer was rejected. The musicians had to wait all night before going on. According to Leslie Aday, who worked for Dylan's manager, Albert Grossman, Jimi seemed ill, and she suspected he'd been inadvertently dosed with drugs. "He seemed very nervous and didn't think he could pull it off," she said. "He didn't feel the band knew the songs well enough or had had enough rehearsal. He was stressed out."

The band finally took the stage at 9:00 a.m., cold and tired. The majority of the attendees had left by then ("It was horrible to see people packing up and leaving as we came on," said Mitch), and a much smaller crowd between twenty-five to forty thousand remained. The group was mistakenly introduced as the Jimi Hendrix Experience, and Jimi was quick to make a correction in his opening remarks. "Dig, we'd like to get something straight. We got tired of the Experience . . . it was blowing our minds too much. So we decided to change the whole thing around and call it Gypsy Sun & Rainbows. For short, it's nothing but a band of gypsies."

The band opened with "Message to Love" and went on to play a two-hour show, the longest show Jimi ever played. If the band was not as tight as the Experience, neither was the show the disaster that Jimi had feared. It's best known for his iconic performance of "The Star-Spangled Banner," which some interpreted as a comment on the Vietnam War—though whether to interpret it as a pro- or anti-American statement provoked much debate. Jimi also wore an outfit that would become iconic: a white leather jacket with long fringe and beads from the Nudist Colony boutique and a red bandana around his head.

After the show, Jimi left with Leslie Aday, and the two caught a ride on a helicopter and checked into a local hotel. "He was unhappy with his performance and just wanted to get away where no one could find him," said Aday. But Jimi was quickly tracked down, and his room was soon full of "people getting high who were not there in Jimi's best interests," as Aday put it. She later found him passed out on his bed, still holding a cigarette that was burning a hole through the sheets.

❦❦❦

Hendrix now took his musicians into the studio, working at the Hit Factory in New York. The full Hendrix-Cox-Lee-Velez-Sultan-Mitchell lineup of Gypsy Sun, and

Hendrix and his new band, for now known as Gypsy Sun and Rainbows, at a benefit show in Harlem, New York, September 5, 1969. *Experience Music Project/1996.36.31.1*

Rainbows would play just one more show on September 5, a benefit for a Harlem-based community organization known as the United Block Association. Jimi was added to the bill (which also featured R & B singer Big Maybelle and other local acts) on the recommendation of the Allen twins, who hoped to get him more exposure to a black audience. "Sometimes when I come up here I hear people say, 'He plays white rock for white people,'" Jimi told the *New York Times* at a press conference held at Frank's Restaurant in Harlem two days before the event. "Well, I want to show them that music is universal, that there is no white rock or black rock."

Tensions plagued the day. Jimi gave Mitch a ride in his Corvette to the gig, held on Lenox Avenue between 138th and 139th Streets. When he parked and a group of kids surrounded the car and made off with his guitar, the Allen twins tracked down the culprits and retrieved the instrument. According to Gerry Stickells, the white people in Jimi's entourage had to keep a low profile and set up quickly when it was time to play, "because people were throwing stuff and spitting on us." Carmen Borrero, Jimi's date for evening, was also harassed. "They saw Jimi with what they thought was a 'white bitch,' and they threw stuff at me," Borrero, who was Puerto Rican, told Charles Cross.

The event ran late, and by the time Jimi took the stage, it was nearly midnight and most of the crowd had left. A few bottles and eggs were thrown at the start (according to Mitch, the egg throwers were caught by the Allens, "who proceeded to beat the shit out of them"), but the show went well after that. "He started playing like he never had before and blew everyone's mind, had everyone on their toes," said Arthur Allen. Chris Hodenfeld, covering the event for *Circus* magazine, agreed:

> He was slow at the beginning, starting with a ripped version of "Fire." He said, "This music might sound loud and funky, but that's what's in the air right now, isn't it?" And then "Foxy Lady," which charred the first six rows of packed standing fans. Then the "Star Spangled Banner," which sounded like feedback violins shot through with dissonance. . . . He wasn't coming off with his Madison Square Garden image of a huge-loined desperado whumping and jacking-off his axe tiredly, and then retiring to his den of lions, while the pimply boys and girls in the crowd leave with their images working overtime, but almost feeling cheated. No, in Harlem, he was right down in it there, honest and true blue/black. "Red House" never sounded bluesier. To finish it all off, he announced the Harlem National Anthem, and wah-wahhed off into "Voodoo Child (Slight Return)."

Hendrix, drummer Mitch Mitchell, percussionist Juma Sultan, and bassist Billy Cox perform on ABC-TV's *The Dick Cavett Show*, September 9, 1969. *ABC Photo Archives/Getty Images*

JIMI'S GUITARS

Dave Hunter

The gear of all major guitar heroes attracts some attention, but the equipment used by Jimi Hendrix, and his Fender Stratocasters in particular, has drawn more intense analysis than most.

Hendrix played several Strats during his short time at the top, and he famously also used a Gibson Flying V and SG. His supposed preference for later-'60s CBS-spec Strats over early to mid-'60s Strats with pre-CBS (i.e., pre-1965) specs remains a hotly debated issue. Certainly the last Stratocasters the world saw him playing were CBS-era models with large headstocks, modern logos, and maple fingerboards. Among these, the white Strat played at Woodstock in 1969 and the black Strat played at the Isle of Wight in 1970 are the instruments he was most photographed with.

In the early days, however, around the time of *Are You Experienced* and his inflammatory performance at the Monterey Pop Festival in 1967, Hendrix was usually seen playing one of a handful of pre-CBS or transition-era Stratocasters with small headstocks and "spaghetti" or transition logos. Hendrix played two Strats at Monterey: a black mid-'60s model with characteristic rosewood fingerboard and small headstock and a guitar at the center of what is possibly the most legendary "Hendrix moment" of all—the Stratocaster that Hendrix doused in lighter fluid and lit on fire at the end of his performance of "Wild Thing," a transition-era '65 Strat, also with the early-style small headstock. This incalculably famous Hendrix Strat was photographed far less than his later instruments for the simple fact that he wasn't

yet as big a star at Monterey as he would be from that moment forward—and also because by the end of this climactic moment the guitar was charred and smashed to pieces. Seen little before the Monterey appearance, it had recently been customized by Hendrix, who painted approximately half of the Fiesta Red body white and adorned it with floral graphics. Otherwise, the standard late-'65 Stratocaster carried a short-lived combination of features, including a fatter, new-style gold logo with black outline on a small headstock and a rosewood fingerboard with pearloid inlays. Another '65 Stratocaster, a sunburst model, was also played, burned, and it was smashed by Hendrix at the London Astoria and later given to Frank Zappa, who left it to his son, Dweezil, upon his death.

While pre-CBS Stratocasters have attained far greater status as collector items, many Hendrixphiles believe Jimi preferred post-'65 guitars for tone-based reasons. One theory is that he found the extra wood in the larger post-CBS headstocks to increase sustain. Another holds that the slightly weaker single-coil pickups of the late-'60s Stratocasters added up to a bigger sound when injected through his 100-watt Marshall stacks (this might sound contrary to reason, but the theory itself is sound: weaker pickups prevent the signal from breaking up too early in the signal chain, so a little more fidelity is maintained through to the output stage of a large amp). Also frequently discussed is his

preference for right-handed Strats played upside down, when left-handed Strats did exist. Among other observations, much is made of the fact that restringing the right-handed guitar with the low E back on top, and thus wound around the tuner post that was now furthest from the nut, created a change in the vibrational characteristics of that string. Perhaps the best authority on these theories is the tech who worked with Hendrix live and in the studio and had hands-on experience with Jimi's guitars. British effects guru Roger Mayer not only built and modified many of the pedals that Hendrix used, but also worked as an all-round right-hand man and even helped select and set up many of the star's guitars. What does he have to say about the wide headstock/ greater sustain theory? "No, Jimi wouldn't have considered that," Mayer told this writer for *Guitar Rigs: Classic Guitar and Amp Combinations*. "All the guitars that we used were bought out of necessity; there weren't that many Stratocasters around [in London] in those days, and they were very expensive. Also, in the 1960s nobody paid much attention to whether pre-CBS Fenders were any better than CBS Fenders. They were all about the same. I can't see a slightly bigger headstock making any difference anyway." Of course, the final word in all of this is that the Strats Hendrix played are iconic simply because he played them—and whatever Strat Jimi wailed on, it was sure to make a heavenly sound.

After the show, Jimi heard a man calling out, "Man, I'm going home right now and practice on my guitar!" He was less amused on returning to his car to find that he'd been given a parking ticket.

On September 9, Hendrix returned for a second appearance on the *Dick Cavett Show*. He'd originally been scheduled to appear on August 18, but his appearance was postponed due to his Woodstock performance running so late. Cox, Sultan, and Mitchell joined him in performing a medley of "Izabella"/"Machine Gun," then Jimi was interviewed. When Cavett asked him about his rendition of "The Star-Spangled Banner," pointing out that playing the national anthem "in any unorthodox way" would naturally result in criticism, Jimi was surprised: "Unorthodox? It isn't unorthodox! I thought it was beautiful." Later, he admitted to being tired. Asked if he'd ever had a nervous breakdown, he replied, "Yeah, about three of them since I've been in this group—since I've been in this business."

Meanwhile, Gypsy Sun and Rainbows was falling apart. In late August, Michael Jeffery had shown up at the Boiceville house and offered Velez and Sultan separate recording deals while his chauffeur shot at targets outside—both men viewed it as a tactic of intimidation. Jeffery also wanted Jimi to tour, but Jimi felt the band wasn't ready. So Jeffery arranged for auditions to be held at the Salvation in New York in early September, against Jimi's wishes. When bassist Roland Robinson of the Buddy Miles Express showed up for an audition, he quickly realized Jimi's own band members didn't know they were being replaced, which made the atmosphere increasingly uncomfortable. Jimi finally lashed out in anger: "Just leave me the fuck alone! Let me play with the people I want to play with and I'll make you all the goddamn money you want!"

Soon after, Hendrix, Cox, Lee, Sultan, and Mitchell played a proper show on September 10 at the Salvation. It was a performance marred by technical problems and marked the last time any configuration of Gypsy Sun and Rainbows ever played in public. A new round of recording sessions began on September 15 at the Record Plant, but after the first session, Lee left, soon followed by Velez. By the end of the month, Cox and Mitchell had left as well. Lee, Sultan, and Velez each suspected that Jeffery didn't want the group to succeed, as he didn't find the band's music very commercial.

In another curious incident during this period, Jimi was said to have been kidnapped at the Salvation, then rescued by Jeffery. In later years, there was speculation that Jeffery himself had arranged the "kidnapping" as a means of intimidating Jimi, while another account had it that Jimi had been hanging out with Salvation club co-owner Bobby Woods. When Woods turned up murdered, Hendrix was "detained" by Woods's gangster associates, who wanted to make sure he didn't know too much about their business operations.

Gypsy Sun and Rainbows perform at the Salvation club, New York City, September 10, 1969. *Jay Good/Frank White Photo Agency*

But in 2011, Jon Roberts told quite a different story in his book *American Desperado*. Roberts, who was born John Riccobono and had family ties to the Gambino family, was also a co-owner of the Salvation, where he'd met Jimi. He became friendly enough with Jimi to invite him to his home on Fire Island on occasion "so he could get away from it all. . . . He was suffocating from these hangers-on."

According to Roberts, Jimi was at the Salvation looking to score drugs when he was approached by two young men ("not Mafia but wiseguy wannabes") who recognized him and lured him out of the club on the pretext of getting drugs. Jimi was then spirited out of the city. "I don't know if they wanted money or a piece of his record contract, but they called Jimi's manager demanding something," Roberts wrote. "Next thing I knew the club manager called me and said Jimi had been taken from our club by some Italians." Through their connections in the nightclub underworld, Roberts quickly tracked down the "kidnappers." "We reached out to these kids and made it clear, 'You let Jimi go, or you are dead. Do not harm a hair of his Afro.' They let Jimi go. The whole thing lasted maybe two days. Jimi was so stoned, he probably didn't even know he was ever kidnapped. Andy and I waited a week or so and went after these kids. We gave them a beating they would never forget."

By the end of September, Hendrix was living back in New York City in an apartment at 59 West Twelfth Street and asked Devon Wilson to move in with him. In search of a new musical direction, he reached out to Billy Cox and Buddy Miles, who joined him at Juggy Sound (formerly owned by Juggy Murray, who had signed Jimi to his Sue Records label in 1965) and the Record Plant. Jimi also began working with producer Alan Douglas (Stella Douglas's husband).

Douglas had produced artists such as Duke Ellington and Charles Mingus for United Artists Records. Hendrix's first session with Douglas was on September 30, when he recorded a number called "Woodstock" that also featured Stephen Stills, Buddy Miles, and John Sebastian. Douglas later edited take number five, retitled it "Live and Let Live," and issued it on *You Can Be Anyone This Time Around*—a spoken-word album by Timothy Leary (the psychologist and former Harvard University instructor who promoted the use of psychedelic drugs) released in 1970.

Jimi asked Alan if he could help him get more organized in the studio. Alan agreed, but when he tried to reign in Jimi's excesses, he found it difficult: "That's why we got nowhere near what we should have gotten out of those sessions," he later said. "Most of it was jamming because they couldn't get the tunes together." He could sense Jimi was bored playing rock and did manage to get him involved in a proto-rap record,

above: The proto-rap song "Doriella Du Fontaine" was recorded by Hendrix and Buddy Miles in 1969 but not released until 1984.

right: A late-1969 German pressing of Hendrix's "Let Me Light Your Fire" single (also known as "Fire").

"Doriella Du Fontaine," by the Last Poets, with Jimi on guitar and bass and Buddy Miles on organ and drums. The track was later released on a 12-inch single in 1984, credited to Lightnin' Rod.

Alan also tried to set up a recording session with Jimi and Miles Davis, which was canceled when Davis demanded an advance payment of $50,000. By early December, Alan ended his relationship with Jimi; Michael Jeffery had become increasingly irritated at the growing influence Alan seemed to have over Jimi, and Alan himself was frustrated at the lack of progress being made in the studio. Alan would go on to play a much larger—and more controversial—role in Jimi's posthumous career.

On December 6, Jimi flew to Toronto for his trial. Unbelievably, when he was stopped at customs, an unidentified capsule was found in his guitar case and he was taken into custody. Its contents couldn't be identified, so Jimi was released and the charges were dropped. The trial began on December 8. Jimi's defense was that fans were always approaching him and giving him gifts, and that he hadn't known he'd been given drugs. He admitted to using drugs but downplayed how much he used them. Some of his answers were admittedly implausible—when asked about the metal tube with the hash, he said he thought it might a pea shooter, which made people in the courtroom laugh. Chas Chandler and Sharon Lawrence, a friend who

With managers Chas Chandler (center) and Mike Jeffery (left). *Jay Good/Frank White Photo Agency*

was also a journalist, testified on his behalf. On December 10, the jury announced a not guilty verdict, and a relieved Jimi called it "the best Christmas present I could have."

Jimi returned to New York rejuvenated, and recording sessions continued at the Record Plant with Billy Cox, Buddy Miles, and a rotating cast of guests. The Allen twins had added backing vocals to a version of "Room Full of Mirrors" in November, and in December Jimi had girl-group singers the Ronettes add backing vocals to a version of "Earth Blues."

There was also a new project on the horizon. Jimi still hadn't completed the album he was required to give Ed Chalpin as part of the settlement for the US lawsuit. Neither Jimi nor his manager wanted to hand over a studio album, so they decided to make a live record. Four shows were duly booked at the Fillmore East for New Year's Eve and New Year's Day. The Hendrix-Cox-Miles lineup would play under the name Band of Gypsys, a name Jimi had been toying with over the previous year.

Jimi spent Christmas at Deering Howe's home with Carmen Borrero as his date and gave her diamond earrings and a diamond ring as gifts. The ring was meant to be an engagement ring, but Borrero told Charles Cross she recognized that marriage wasn't really an option for Jimi. "That marriage would have been with three people: Jimi, Devon, and I."

And then it was New Year's Eve. The second set of the evening began at twelve, with the crowd counting down to the midnight hour and a recording of Guy Lombardo's version of "Auld Lang Syne" filling the theater. The song's melody was then picked up by the Band of Gypsys, who jammed on it while the audience members rattled the toy tambourines left on each seat. "Happy New Year, everybody!" Jimi called to the crowd, as he welcomed in the last year of his life.

Hendrix celebrates his acquittal with sisters Lynne and Debbie Bailey, December 10, 1969. *Bettmann/Getty Images*

CHAPTER 6

THE WINK OF AN EYE

January 1, 1970, found the Band of Gypsys back on stage for their second night at the Fillmore East. The engagement was well received—promoter Bill Graham called Jimi's work "the most brilliant, emotional display of virtuoso electric guitar playing I have ever heard." "It appears Hendrix is finding where he should be at, and he might well emerge as the greatest of the new blues guitarists," *DownBeat* magazine's critic wrote. "I can only hope that he learns that it is not necessary to amplify to or past the point of distortion." And Jimi had more plans for the Band of Gypsys. After the final show, he told Al Aronowitz of the

K. B. Hallen, Copenhagen, September 3, 1970. *Jorgen Angel/Redferns/Getty Images*

of the *New York Post* that he wanted to take the band "back to the blues" and have Buddy Miles do more of the singing.

But by the end of the month, the Band of Gypsys was no more. In late January, Jimi got into a fierce argument with his manager when Jeffery wanted to fire Buddy Miles and reunite the Experience. When Jimi refused, Jeffery threatened to tear up their contract. Jimi backed down; as much as he complained about his manager and talked about leaving him, he never took any serious steps to do so. He also undoubtedly felt conflicted, as he wasn't entirely happy with Buddy's presence in the band himself. Buddy was used to being the leader of his own group, and Jimi didn't like being challenged. "Jimi truly loved Buddy," Billy Cox said, "but *he* was the star. *He* was the boss."

In this fraught atmosphere, the Band of Gypsys came together to play what would be its final show, an appearance at the Winter Festival for Peace at Madison Square Garden on January 28. Despite his dislike of the group, Jeffery had nonetheless arranged for the performance to be filmed for a possible TV special. When Jimi showed up backstage, he seemed unwell. "When I saw him, it gave me the chills," Johnny Winter later told *Guitar Player*. "It was the most horrible thing I'd ever seen . . . it was like he was already dead." He watched as Jimi made his way to a couch and put his head in his hands: "He didn't move until it was time for the show."

Buddy Miles would swear that Jeffery had given Jimi LSD to deliberately sabotage the show and the band, but that hardly seems likely given that Jeffery had put up $6,000 to film the performance. Jimi himself said that it was Devon Wilson who had dosed him. Nor was there any shortage of intoxicants backstage, and Jimi was becoming increasingly reckless in his drug use. "Drugs were not only screwing him up, they were destroying the environment he needed to create," said Electric Lady Studios manager Jim Marron. "Hendrix sat through many paternal lectures about his drug use from all of us, but I doubt it had any long-term effect."

The show ran late, and the band didn't take the stage until 3:00 a.m. Following another argument with Jeffery, Jimi sent out one of the crew to get lighter fluid so he could burn his guitar, but the delivery was intercepted by Gerry Stickells. It was a wise decision, as Jimi was so intoxicated that he ran the risk of setting himself on fire. Billy and Buddy weren't sure Jimi would even make it through the set, and their fears were confirmed as the band staggered through the opening song, "Who Knows." The band then played "Earth Blues," only for Jimi to abruptly stop playing and announce, "That's what happens when earth fucks with space. Never forget that." He then stopped playing and sat on the drum riser until he was helped offstage.

After this debacle, Jeffery fired Buddy—an action Buddy always believed was solely Jeffery's doing. Certainly there was no love lost between the two, but those

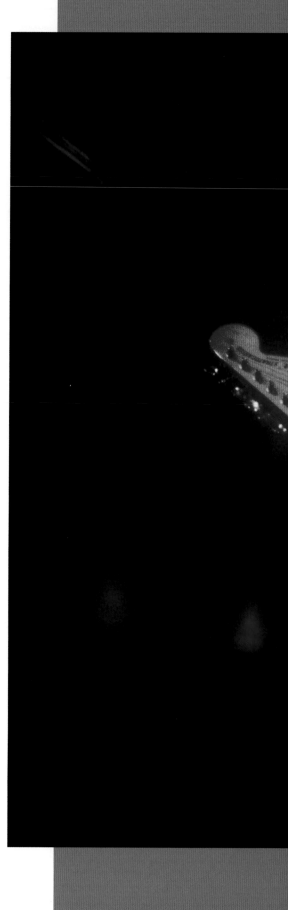

Mid-solo at the Felt Forum, New York City, January 28, 1970. *Walter Iooss Jr./Getty Images*

who worked for Jeffery insisted that his focus remained on business and that he would not have fired a musician without Jimi's tacit approval, which, given Jimi's disinclination to be the bearer of bad news, seemed likely. In any case, it was a dispiriting end to the band, and Billy Cox soon returned to Nashville.

Now Jeffery could get underway with what he'd wanted to do all along: reunite the Jimi Hendrix Experience. Noel and Mitch were agreeable, a press release was sent out, and the three musicians came together for an interview with *Rolling Stone* on February 4 in New York City. Jimi called the Winter Festival for Peace concert "like the end of a big long fairy tale" and explained his performance by saying he was "very tired." But he also didn't sound completely committed to the reunion, saying that he still wanted to "have time on the side to play with friends. That's why I'll probably be jamming with Buddy and Billy; probably be recording, too, on the side, and they'll be doing the same."

The interview turned out to be the full extent of the Experience's "reunion." On reflection, Jimi decided he had no wish to play with Noel again and persuaded Billy to return to New York. Sadly, no one thought to inform Noel of this decision, and he also returned to New York in March to wait for rehearsals to start. He finally learned he'd been kicked out of the band when he contacted Mitch at his hotel after days of waiting for a call, only to be told that Mitch was off rehearsing with Jimi. Jimi never apologized, but he did drop by sessions for Noel's solo

album *Nervous Breakdown*, playing on the track "My Friend." The song, and Noel's album, remain unreleased.

Jimi was also working with Eddie Kramer in preparing the *Band of Gypsys* album, and work was completed on February 19. Jimi hoped it would resolve the ongoing legal situation with Ed Chalpin. Then, in March, he learned some news that stunned him: Kathy Etchingham had gotten married.

Since Jimi now spent most of his time in New York City, he'd fallen out of touch with his one-time girlfriend. Kathy knew he saw other women, which bothered her less than the sycophantic hangers-on that surrounded him. She had no wish to be a part of such an entourage, and as she hadn't heard from Jimi in months, she assumed their relationship had run its course.

Now, he called not only to ask if it was true she had married, but that he was also returning to London to see her. Kathy met him at the airport and was surprised when he took her hand on the ride into town and asked, "This is just a spur of the moment thing, isn't it. It's not serious, is it?" Kathy was taken aback at how "completely devastated" he was by the news. Jimi had expected her to be "waiting for him, the good little woman keeping the home fires burning. . . . I realized that in his mind I had let him down just like his mum and dad had before me."

Jimi tried to persuade her to come back to New York with him, assuring her, "All those people I was hanging out with have gone." But Kathy refused, not wanting to get caught up again in the "mayhem and madness" of Jimi's life. To her relief, he eventually seemed to accept her decision.

Jimi found time for a little session work as well, coming by Island Studios on March 15, where Stephen Stills was recording his self-titled debut album (released in November 1970). Jimi played lead guitar on "Old Times, Good Times" and played on two other tracks that as of this writing have yet to be released. On March 17, he joined Arthur Lee at Olympic Studios, where Lee was working on Love's *False Start* album. Jimi played guitar on the track "The Everlasting First"; the album was released in December. He then returned to New York.

March also saw the US release of *Band of Gypsys*, which reached No. 5. The UK release followed in June, with the album reaching No. 6. The US album cover was straightforward, featuring a color-tinted shot of Jimi in performance; the UK version was decidedly odd, featuring puppets created by artist Saskia de Boer—there was a Jimi Hendrix puppet, a Brian Jones puppet, a Bob Dylan puppet, and a puppet of British DJ John Peel. The cover drew numerous complaints, resulting in Track reissuing the album with a new cover, though the new design was just as odd in its own way—it was a picture of Jimi performing at the 1970 Isle of Wight Festival, not a

(continued on page 162)

BAND OF GYPSYS

Harvey Kubernik

Following his appearance at Woodstock in August 1969, Jimi Hendrix developed song demos and recordings with bassist Billy Cox and drummer Buddy Miles. The trio subsequently recorded a live album that was commercially issued to settle a contract dispute and legal battle with a former producer that dated back to a contract Hendrix inked in 1965.

Band of Gypsys is a live disc culled from four historic concerts at the Fillmore East in New York City—two on New Year's Eve 1969 and two on New Year's Day 1970. They were initially housed in the Capitol Records' April 1970 *Band of Gypsys* LP, which featured six songs from the two January 1, 1970, concerts, including "Machine Gun," the album's dramatic centerpiece.

The revolutionary impact Hendrix, Cox, and Miles had upon the boundaries and definitions of rock, R & B, and funk can be traced to the results captured over the course of two evenings.

Band of Gypsys challenged and surprised the guitarist's wide following with its extended arrangements and vibrant mix of rock and soul. Nonetheless, the album proved to be a runaway commercial success, and sadly, with his death in London in September 1970, would become the last album Jimi Hendrix personally authorized for release.

"We decided that we couldn't do any songs that had already been released," explained Cox. "We wanted to give them something different. So we went at the project in a joyous, creative posture and ultimately developed the repertoire of the Band of Gypsys."

With the anticipation of the sold-out Fillmore audience heightened to fever pitch, Hendrix led his trio through a scintillating seventy-five-minute opening performance. None of the eleven songs presented had yet to grace an Experience album. In the place of signature songs such as "Purple Haze" and "All Along the Watchtower" were confident renditions of "Power of Soul" and "Hear My Train a Comin.'" Hendrix generously extended center stage to Miles, providing a showcase for "Changes" and a charged rendition of the Howard Tate R & B hit "Stop."

"We had rehearsed 'Changes' and a few others for Buddy," Cox offered. "All of the songs we performed had been rehearsed. We didn't look at it as Buddy's part of the show. We were all there to give. We were all there to help and material went on whether it was written by Jimi or not." Hendrix's scalding version of Elmore James's "Bleeding Heart" is the set's only other cover, underscoring the new band's emphasis on the blues. As the Fillmore audience roared with approval, the Band of Gypsys left the stage confident that they had validated Hendrix's new music before his loyal followers.

"After the gigs were finished, Jimi was quite relieved. "We were on big time," Cox told me in a 2015 interview published in *Record Collector News* magazine.

"After the first set, when we walked off, I remember Jimi, who was smiling, telling me and Buddy, 'it's gonna be all right now.' We felt the concerts went well. I might add that in previous gigs with the Experience, Jimi had used a fuzz face [tone control pedal] and a Wah-Wah pedal, then at Woodstock he used a fuzz face, Wah-Wah pedal and Uni-Vibe, but at the Fillmore East he used a fuzz face, Wah-Wah pedal, Uni-Vibe and Octavia and it was incredible. In fact you could hear all of it kicking in on 'Machine Gun.' It was incredible. There were people in the audience with their mouths open," Cox marveled.

"I was 14 going on 15 when I caught Jimi and The Band Of Gypsys at the early show at the Fillmore East on January 1st, 1970," recalls writer Michael Simmons. "A kids' choir called The Voices

The British and American editions of *Band of Gypsys* had strikingly different cover art. While Hendrix's US label, Capitol, opted for a portrait of the artist, Track Records in the UK used a set of surreal mannequins of Hendrix, Bob Dylan, Brian Jones of the Rolling Stones, and British deejay John Peel.

of East Harlem opened. Their soaring voices were the perfect way to greet the new decade and I thought it was cool that Jimi embraced the notion of community here in New York—one of his hometowns along with Seattle and London. He emphasized his guitar playing that night and disregarded stage shtick. We—the audience— were witnesses to Jimi's evolution as an artist and it was thrilling. Personally, I was glad—picking with his teeth or with his axe draped behind his back was getting old.

"I later learned that Fillmore boss Bill Graham had encouraged him to just play. And yet he was very personable and relaxed and yapping about that New Years' Day's football scores. Most importantly, I've never seen a guitarist— or *any* musician—who could equal him in technique or feel or presence. I have friends who got to see Coltrane and Monk. My mother—a jazz singer who dated Charlie Parker's pianist Al Haig—saw Bird. But I saw Hendrix and he set a standard in rock that—for my taste—has never been surpassed. Awww Jimi—though we hardly knew ye, you remain the greatest."

"*The Band of Gypsys* turned the world upside down," underscored Cox in our 2015 conversation. "Jimi was at his peak then. He had done [earlier] albums and then I came on board with a lot of the things we had. He called them 'patterns,' but they're just riffs. We played around with them and a lot of times he'd say, 'If people heard us play this stuff they'd lock us up.' But we were completely free musically.

"So with the *Band of Gypsys*, Jimi was at his peak. Buddy Miles! Oh man! What a guy. No restraint. The *Band of Gypsys* was a trend-setting group. We didn't know that. But it has been said that the *Band of Gypsys* inspired reggae, free-form rock, portions of rap. Jimi wrote about 90 percent of that stuff. And Buddy had 'Them

Changes.' We did some stuff that we put together that we enjoyed which had a rhythm feel to it."

"The Band of Gypsys concerts, along with Bob Dylan's 1965 Newport Folk Festival electric performance," suggests Dr. James Cushing, a radio host on KEBF-FM in Morro Bay, California, "represent possibly the most courageous actions ever taken by a rock star at the highest level of fame: to book a series of concerts in a famous venue on a high-stakes weekend and use them to debut and record a whole new band and a whole new set list.

"Jimi Hendrix, Billy Cox and Buddy Miles are clearly demanding to be heard as artists, not as mere entertainers, and this seriousness elevates the music to the level of jazz improvisation," reinforced Cushing in a discussion printed in *Record Collector News* magazine. "For a certain kind of person, *Band of Gypsys* is the best Hendrix album; the risks the group takes are as high as their accomplishment."

Reissues of the *Band of Gypsys* album on compact disc included three extra songs recorded during the Fillmore East shows and additional material has been released on later albums, including 2016's *Machine Gun: The Fillmore East First Show 12/31/69*, fully documenting the debut of Jimi Hendrix's short-lived but eternally influential group.

(continued from page 159)

Band of Gypsys show. In the United States, the single "Stepping Stone" was released to accompany the album in April, but it failed to chart.

The *Woodstock* film also had its debut in March, running just over three hours and featuring three songs from Jimi's set: "The Star-Spangled Banner," "Purple Haze," and "Villanova Junction." With a $600,000 budget, the film went on to gross over $50 million, making it a remarkable success. The soundtrack, which featured the same three songs, was released on May 27 in the United States, topping the chart, while in the UK, the album was released in June and reached No. 35.

Work on Electric Lady Studios was continuing. Michael Jeffery secured a loan from Warner Bros. to help finance the project, which would eventually top $1 million. Jimi went back on the road to keep money coming in but mostly did shows on the weekends, sometimes including a Thursday or a Monday, which gave him a little breathing room. Mitch Mitchell was back, and Billy Cox was persuaded to return as well. Even Buddy Miles was around; the Buddy Miles Express opened for Jimi at the Los Angeles Forum on April 25 and at Cal Expo in Sacramento on April 26.

The band wasn't officially the Jimi Hendrix Experience, though they were sometimes billed that way. Jimi seemed relieved to put the group behind him. "I'm not sure how I feel about the Experience now," he told Keith Altham in April. "Maybe we could have gone on but what would have been the point of that—what would it have been good for? It's a ghost now—it's dead—like back pages in a diary. I'm into new things and I want to think about tomorrow, not yesterday."

The group was booked into stadiums and other large halls but returned to a smaller venue for one night, the Village Gate, on May 4. The occasion was a benefit concert for Timothy Leary, who'd been convicted of marijuana possession. Noel Redding was also on the bill, and it was the last time Jimi shared a stage with his former bandmate.

On May 30, the band played two shows at the Berkeley Performance Center in Berkeley, California. It was a turbulent time in the college town, where students held frequent protests against the Vietnam War. Tensions were further heightened by the recent events at Kent State University, in Kent, Ohio, on May 4, when the Ohio National Guard fired on a crowd of student protesters, killing four and wounding nine.

Demand for tickets was fierce, but the venue only held three thousand. When the doors opened, those without tickets tried to force their way inside or climbed on the roof in an attempt to gain entry. To mollify those outside, engineer Abe Jacob, who was overseeing the recording of the show from a remote sound truck, opened

above: Print ads for two May 1970 performances, for one of which the band was still advertised as the "Jimi Hendrix Experience."

opposite: Hendrix, studio manager Jim Marron (standing), and producer Eddie Kramer (seated, center) work the board at Electric Lady Studios, June 17, 1970. *Fred W. McDarrah/Getty Images*

the doors of the truck to allow everyone to hear the show. Despite what the *San Francisco Chronicle* called the "Hassle Factor" of the gate-crashers, the reviewer was impressed with Jimi's performance: "His playing appears effortless, even to the point of locking his right hand into a fixed position on the guitar's neck (he is, of course, left-handed), and then playing for what seems to be 30 seconds or a minute varying only his finger-work, not his hand position. By using the electronic variations available he is able to vary his sound from oily to icicle, his technique from blues to steel to flamenco, and the shimmering shattering high notes slice through the brain like those of no other musical instrument."

When the tour reached Memphis on June 9, Jimi invited Larry Lee from Gypsy Sun & Rainbows to hang out backstage. But Jimi was anxious to get back to New York and start recording at his new studio. Jimi's first known session at Electric Lady was on June 15, with Billy and Mitch also on hand; Steve Winwood and Chris Wood from Traffic came by to jam as well.

The studio was designed to provide the most comfortable environment possible for Jimi rather than be an "antiseptic box," as Eddie Kramer put it. The curved walls were covered with white carpet, with a bank of colored lights that could be changed to suit Jimi's mood. "We were trying to create a womblike environment for Jimi, which the sophisticated theater lighting system complemented," Eddie explained. The staff also maintained a tighter control over who gained entry to the studio, helping keep out the hangers-on—except for Devon Wilson, who insisted on being present if Jimi was recording. Jimi occasionally put his foot down, telling Devon she couldn't come in.

Jimi spent as much time as possible at Electric Lady over the next two months, and from June 15 to August 26, there were twenty-four sessions at the venue, which was becoming a second home to him. He worked at a tremendous pace, both creating new material and reviewing the stockpile of songs previously recorded. There was such a surfeit of material that he planned on making his fourth studio record a double album.

Live shows continued. Summer was festival season, and Jimi played the Atlanta International Pop Festival (actually held in neighboring Byron, Georgia) on July 4 and the New York Pop Festival on Randall's Island, New York, on July 17. Randall's Island was across the East River from Manhattan, and the three-day event was poorly managed and plagued by infighting. Several local organizations demanded a share of the profits, and an estimated third of the audience gate-crashed the show. Quickly tiring of the chaos, Jimi and the band tried to leave, but according to Gerry Stickells, they were held at knife point until they agreed to go on. Radio interference during the set didn't help Jimi's mood, and at the end he told the audience, "Fuck you, and good night." Jimi's set was recorded and filmed, with some footage included in the documentary about the festival, *Free* (also known as *Freedom*). Capping a frustrating day, the boat taking everyone back to Manhattan got stuck in the mud.

An unused Robert Crumb—designed ticket for the July 19, 1970, Aquarius Benefit for the Children's Day Care Center at Stanford University's Frost Amphitheater. Jimi did not make the show due to a scheduling conflict.

On July 25, the band performed in San Diego, then flew up to Seattle for what would be Jimi's last hometown show. He spent the day at his father's home, though their time together was marred by an argument. His brother Leon wasn't there; he'd been convicted of larceny and was in prison, but his sister, Pamela Hendrix, who had been placed in foster care in the early 1950s, unexpectedly turned up at Al's home. Jimi hadn't seen his sister since she was a baby. Jimi also telephoned Betty Jean Morgan, who was now divorced and living with her parents.

The concert was held at Sick's Stadium, where Jimi had heard Elvis play back in 1957. He invited many family members and friends to the show, leading a caravan of thirteen cars. Although it was raining, the show went ahead anyway. *Seattle Times* reviewer Janine Gressel later wrote that Jimi "seemed somewhat ill at ease, perhaps put off by the chill and drizzle," but that "the spark and fire of his music were there." Still, she added, the acoustics of the stadium were poor, and that "sitting on wet grass and mud is a horrible way to watch even as dynamic an attraction as Jimi Hendrix," further suggesting that the show should've been called off due to the weather.

Afterward, Jimi asked three female relatives and friends to accompany him on a drive around town, once again going by his old haunts. They even tried to find Greenwood Cemetery, where his mother, Lucille, was buried, in the neighboring town of Renton. Unable to find it in the dark, the party eventually returned to Seattle.

The next day, most of the band and crew flew to Maui. Jimi stayed in Seattle for an extra day to spend more time with his family, then flew out on July 28. The Hawaii trip was meant to be a working vacation, for Michael Jeffery had arranged for the band to appear in the film *Rainbow Bridge*. Jeffery had begun work on the project as a means of getting more money out of Warner Bros. He arranged for an advance from the company to fund the film in exchange for giving Reprise the rights to the soundtrack.

The film's director was Chuck Wein, whom Jeffery had tapped to work on the proposed TV special about the Madison Square Garden concert the previous January, a plan that had fallen apart in the wake of the disastrous performance. The minimal plot was about a model from San Diego journeying to Maui, where she mixes and mingles with members of the counterculture. Hendrix's business associates rolled their eyes at Wein's new age affectations, saying, for example, that the success of the film *Easy Rider* was because one of its scenes had been shot near a Native American burial ground, which imbued the movie with mystical "high-energy."

For his part, Wein, who'd previously worked with Andy Warhol, insisted the film was a serious venture. "*Rainbow Bridge* was prophetic in many ways," he told John McDermott. "We were talking about environmental issues way before it came into vogue. The people in the film weren't all stoned-out space cadets and surfers: what we were documenting was an alternative lifestyle that Hendrix's predominantly New York-based associates couldn't relate to."

Jimi was uninterested in whatever Wein thought the film was trying to say, but he finally consented to participate, filming some scenes and agreeing to have the band play. For the concert sequence shot on July 30, an outside stage was set up on the slopes of the volcano Haleakalá, and locals were invited to attend. Wein seated everyone according to their astrological sign and began what he called the "Rainbow Bridge Vibratory Color/Sound Experiment" by having everyone chant "om."

The band performed two sets. The wind made recording difficult, and Mitch's drum parts weren't properly recorded—he had to overdub his entire performance later in the studio. Though each set ran nearly an hour, only about seventeen minutes of the band's performance ultimately appeared in the film.

Two days later, on August 1, the band flew to Honolulu and played a show at the Honolulu International Center. "It's going to be loud," Jimi warned the crowd. "It will get louder. It will get loudest." "He wasn't kidding," wrote Wayne Harada in *Billboard*. "The audience of hip and young folk dug it. Hendrix appeared, looking like a Madam Butterfly in his Kimono-sleeved outfit with psychedelic oranges and greens, and his music was equally colorful: emphatic, trance-like, piercing, ranting, riveting." After the show, Jimi begged the promoter, Tom Hulett, to take him out for a meal, having tired of the vegetarian fare served on Maui. On learning that Hawaiian singer Don Ho was appearing in town, Jimi asked to see him, and Hulett drove Hendrix, *Rainbow Bridge* star Pat Hartley (who'd first seen Jimi when he was performing in Little Richard's backing band), and Hulett's wife to the club. After the show, Ho joined the group and drank with them until dawn. Jimi had just given his last US concert.

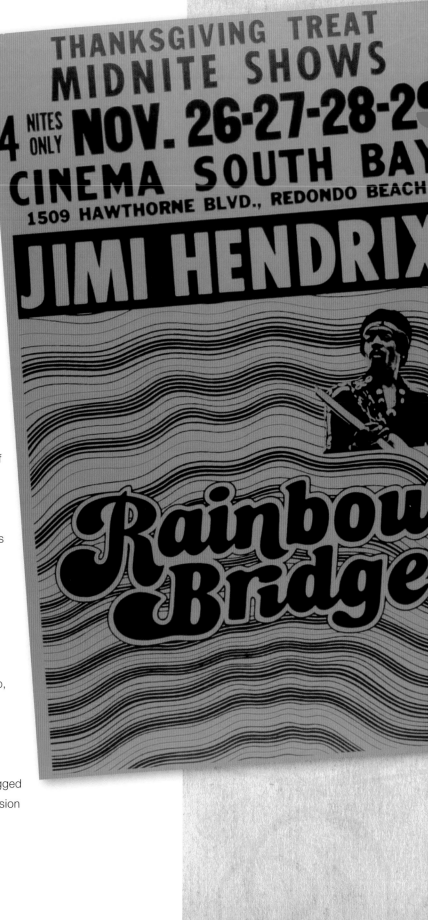

Jimi then returned to Maui. After cutting his foot earlier in his trip, he now exaggerated its severity and told Jeffery he wasn't able to travel. Jimi enjoyed the laid back atmosphere of Hawaii, and the distance also kept his drug connections at bay. Yet he was unable to relax entirely. One evening he'd suggested to Wein and Hartley that they commit suicide, a comment Wein shrugged off. According to biographer Charles Cross, on another occasion

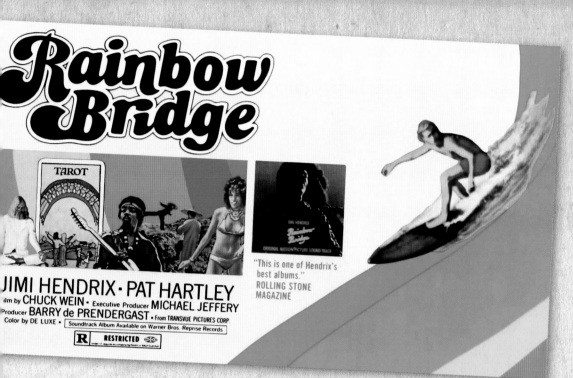

Rainbow Bridge

TAROT

"This is one of Hendrix's best albums."
ROLLING STONE MAGAZINE

JIMI HENDRIX · PAT HARTLEY

film by CHUCK WEIN · Executive Producer MICHAEL JEFFERY
Producer BARRY de PRENDERGAST · From TRANSVUE PICTURES CORP
Color by DE LUXE · Soundtrack Album Available on Warner Bros. Reprise Records

R RESTRICTED

above and opposite: A poster for *Rainbow Bridge,* described by Hendrix biographer Harry Shapiro as "an antidote to *Easy Rider,*" and a print ad for a midnight screening of the film.

Jimi morosely told Melinda Merryweather (a local who was also appearing in *Rainbow Bridge*), "Next time I go to Seattle, it'll be in a pine box." Other times he seemed fine and, as he did whenever he had spare time, ventured out to local clubs looking for a jam.

Jimi returned to New York the second week of August, and on August 14 he was back working at Electric Lady. He spent the remainder of the month focusing on the songs he wanted to include on his next album, recording additional overdubs (bringing in the Allen twins to provide backing vocals on "Dolly Dagger") and preparing final mixes. On August 22, he recorded his last song, "Belly Button Window," sung from the perspective of a child in the womb, which Hendrix said was inspired by the upcoming birth of Mitch Mitchell's first child. On August 26, he and Eddie Kramer cut test pressings of "Dolly Dagger" and "Night Bird Flying" at Sterling Sound. Jimi planned for the two songs to be his next single.

That evening, he attended the official opening party at Electric Lady Studios. A tape playing his proposed new single, as well as "Ezy Ryder" and "Straight Ahead," was played throughout the evening. He was scheduled to leave the next morning for a short European tour, and to Eddie he seemed frustrated at having to once again put his recording projects on hold. Noel was at the party and spoke to Jimi, who told Noel that he'd see him back in England. Later that evening, Jimi met up with Colette Mimram and Devon Wilson. Colette had planned to accompany Jimi on tour but couldn't sort out her passport details. Devon was eager to go to Europe herself, but Jimi put her off.

As he climbed the stairs leaving the studio, he ran into a young woman sitting on the steps. It was Patti Smith, then twenty-three years old and just starting her own career as a writer and performer. Jimi asked what she was doing, and Patti confessed that although she'd been invited to the party, she was too nervous to go in. Jimi understood—he told her he often felt shy at large gatherings too. Patti watched him leave: "I pictured his back, the embroidered vest, and his long legs as he went up the stairs and out into the world for the last time," she later wrote

(continued on page 170)

above: The full bill for the Isle of Wight festival, featuring headline performances across three nights, August 28–30, by Chicago, the Doors, and Hendrix.

left: Hendrix, Mitch Mitchell, and Billy Cox onstage at the Isle of Wight Festival, August 30, 1970. *Rolls Press/ Popperfoto/Getty Images*

(continued from page 167)

in her memoir *Just Kids*. Four years later, Patti would record "Hey Joe" as her first single, and she would return to Electric Lady to record her debut album, *Horses* (1975).

Hendrix performs at the K. B. Hallen in Copenhagen, Denmark, September 3, 1970.
Jorgen Angel/Redferns/Getty Images

When Jimi arrived at London's Heathrow airport on August 27, he was met by an *Evening Standard* reporter who asked him about his upcoming appearance at the Isle of Wight Festival. "The more there are the better," he said. "I really dig this festival scene." He checked into the Londonderry hotel and spent the evening at the Speakeasy, where he met Angie Burdon (then separated from her husband Eric Burdon), who was with a friend. He brought both women back to his hotel.

The next morning, Kathy Etchingham received a panicked phone call from Angie. Jimi, she said, had "gone mad," throwing her and her friend out of his bedroom and refusing to let them retrieve their clothes. Could Kathy help? Kathy rushed over and found the living room of the suite in disarray, the furniture destroyed. Jimi was in bed, shivering though the heater was on, complaining that he was still cold. Kathy gave the women their clothes and stayed with Jimi for a bit, putting a cool cloth on his head to calm him. She was saddened to see her one-time boyfriend in such a condition. "All the sweetness and gentleness had disappeared: the drugs and the stress had changed him beyond recognition."

After spending the rest of the day doing interviews, Jimi rebounded. A friend, Karen Davis, came by his suite along with her friend, Danish model Kirsten Nefer, who was in London filming an appearance in the movie *Universal Soldier*, starring George Lazenby. The three stayed up late talking. The next morning, Kirsten returned to her flat for a bath, only to soon find Jimi and Karen on her doorstep. The three spent the rest of the day together, and Jimi asked the women to attend his performance the next day, arranging transportation for them.

Jimi and the band arrived on the Isle of Wight on August 30 at 7:30 p.m., and Kirsten and Karen waited in his dressing room to meet him. The festival was scheduled to run August 28 to 30 but ended up featuring acts on August 26 and 27 as well, and it didn't end until the morning of August 31. The Doors, Joan Baez, Miles Davis, the Who, Melanie, and Leonard Cohen were a few of the other acts who shared the bill.

Jimi opened his set with a squalling version of the UK national anthem "God Save the Queen." The performance was marred by constant interference from radio transmissions, and Jimi was relieved when it was over. Afterward, he asked Kirsten and Karen to meet him in Denmark, assuring them he would make their travel arrangements.

Jimi flew to Sweden on August 31, playing a show in Stockholm. Backstage, he was confronted by Eva Sundquist, who'd given birth the previous year to a child she claimed

was Jimi's. She'd been trying to contact him ever since but hadn't received a response. Nor would she on this occasion, because Jimi refused to discuss the matter. On September 1, the band performed in Liseberg. Chas Chandler was in attendance and was dismayed by the show, describing Jimi as "wrecked. He'd start a song, get into the solo section and then he wouldn't even remember what song they were playing at the time. . . . It was a disastrous concert, it was really awful to watch." After the show, someone spiked Billy Cox's drink with acid. The effect was profound, and he became increasingly paranoid over the next few days.

The tour moved to Denmark on September 2. Jimi had a worsening cold and had unaccountably taken a large number of sleeping pills, even though he needed to be awake to do more interviews. When Kirsten and Karen arrived, Jimi asked that Kirsten sit by him while he spoke to reporters. He remained agitated throughout the day, and before the evening's show, he refused to come out of his dressing room. "I can't tune my guitar, what am I going to do?" he complained to Kirsten. "I don't want to go on." When he did, the show was a shambles, and he left the stage after three songs.

The next day, in Copenhagen, Jimi arrived at his hotel to find loud construction work going on outside. Kirsten suggested they go to her mother's house, where Jimi slept the rest of the day. That evening, he ate a home-cooked meal and was so taken with the friendly family

left: The view from behind the stage at the Open Air Love & Peace Festival. *Feddersen/ullstein bild/Getty Images*

inset: A poster for the Open Air Love & Peace Festival, held on the Isle of Fehmarn, Germany, September 4–6, 1970. Hendrix's set on the second night would prove to be his final live performance.

atmosphere that he asked Kirsten to marry him. The Danish press arrived, and in the photos accompanying the story of his engagement in *SE og HØR*, he looks relaxed and happy, smiling broadly. For her part, Kirsten didn't take Jimi's proposal too seriously, later telling author Tony Brown she thought his desire to get married was merely "wishful thinking."

The concert that evening went well, but by the next morning, September 4, Jimi's mood had changed again. Kirsten had arranged to take time off from her film work

At Fehmarn, Hendrix performed one of his party pieces—playing guitar with his teeth—for the last time in front of a live audience.
Michael Ochs Archives/Getty Images

to accompany Jimi to Germany, but now he told her, "No, a woman's place is in the house." "I was damn furious," she later recalled. On the way to the airport, Jimi asked her to change her mind, but Kirsten was still angry: "I said most likely you go your way and I go mine, buddy. This is what we did." She returned to London, while Karen Davis stayed with the entourage.

The band played a show that night in Berlin. The next day, everyone traveled to the Isle of Fehmarn, where the band was scheduled to play on September 5 as part of the three-day Open Air Love & Peace Festival. When the weather turned bad, Gerry Stickells refused to let Jimi play and the performance was pushed back a day.

By Sunday morning, the festival was on the verge of falling into chaos. Hell's Angels were providing security, which turned out to be extremely heavy handed. There were reports that the onsite buildings had been vandalized and the ticket proceeds stolen, and when Jimi's entourage arrived, Stickells was hit by a board. Billy was becoming increasingly distressed, saying he feared they wouldn't get off the island alive. "The feeling was, let's do the gig and get the hell out," Mitch recalled.

When the band took the stage, they were met by loud heckling. Jimi tried to apologize for not playing the previous day, but he was clearly irritated as well: "I don't give a fuck if you boo, long as you boo in key, you mothers." Things improved as the band played, but as the set went on, fights began breaking out. After performing "Voodoo Child," Jimi ended the show, saying, "Thank you, goodbye, peace." The band then raced for the safety of their helicopter. Hell's Angels stormed the stage and set it on fire. Jimi's career as a concert performer had come to an end amidst scenes of violence more common to a war zone.

The band returned to London the same day. After the previous damage Jimi had caused, the Londonderry wouldn't take him back, so he checked into the Cumberland Hotel in Great Cumberland Place. Despite their argument, Kirsten turned up to see Jimi on September 8, arriving at his hotel just as he was receiving a call about Billy's deteriorating mental state. The two visited Billy at his hotel to try to help him, and later that evening they joined Karen Davis and went to see Michelangelo Antonioni's latest film, *Red Desert*. Billy was in no better shape the following day, so it was decided to send him back to the United States to his parents' home in Pennsylvania. There was talk of taking on a replacement, but the group decided instead to cancel the rest of the tour.

With nothing else on his schedule, Jimi was free to return to New York. But he remained in London, seemingly at loose ends, with no clear idea of what to do next. His lawyer, Henry Steingarten, was dealing with the paternity suit Diane Carpenter had filed and tried to reach him. Ed Chalpin was also trying to reach Jimi regarding an upcoming hearing in London over his lawsuit against Track and Polydor. Jimi didn't respond to any of their messages.

On September 11, Jimi did a final interview with Keith Altham, one of his longtime supporters, for *Record Mirror*. He sounded uncertain about what he wanted to do next, talking about sticking with a three-piece band, or forming a larger band, or maintaining two separate bands. "I just hate to be in one corner," he explained. "I hate to be put as only a guitar player, or either only as a songwriter, or only as a tap dancer, or something like this." He sounded like a man adrift.

Devon Wilson had also tracked him down via phone; she'd heard stories of Jimi's "engagement" and called to demand an explanation. Kirsten overheard one of her phone calls when she was visiting Jimi, hearing him yell, "Devon, get off my back, for Christ's sake!" Embarrassed, Kirsten left the room.

Kirsten's work on *Universal Soldier* was scheduled to continue on September 14, and when she left that morning, Jimi told her to call him that night. Kirsten did so but was unable to reach him. She left a message and continued to phone the hotel over the next few days, but she never heard from Jimi again.

Jimi spent the evening of September 14 with Alan Douglas, who was in London with his wife, Stella, along with Devon Wilson and Colette Mimram. The two discussed future recording projects, and Alan later recalled Jimi saying he wanted to end his relationship with Michael Jeffery. Jimi accompanied Alan to the airport the next morning.

Hendrix talks to Stephen Clackson of the *Evening Standard* at the Londonderry Hotel on August 28, 1970. *Evening Standard/ REX/Shutterstock*

Monika Dannemann, Hendrix's girlfriend at the time of his death. *Keystone Pictures USA/ Alamy Stock Photo*

That night, September 15, he turned up at Ronnie Scott's Jazz Club. Eric Burdon's new band, War, had a weeklong residency at the club, and Jimi dropped by hoping to jam. But he was clearly under the influence of something. Eric described him as being "well out of it . . . he was wobbling too much to play." The band's road manager, Terry McVay, discouraged Jimi from getting up on stage; Eric suggested he come back the next night.

Jimi wasn't alone when he had come to Ronnie Scott's. He was with Monika Dannemann, the German woman he'd met in Düsseldorf the previous year. It's unclear how he reconnected with Monika, who was staying at the Samarkand Hotel, but she would be Jimi's companion over the next few days.

According to Chas Chandler, Jimi stopped by his flat on September 16 and again asked if Chandler would consider managing him. He also spoke of bringing his current recordings from New York to London to work on at Olympic Studios. "He wanted to use that studio again because he really felt that's the way to put it right," Chas recalled. During their conversation, Hendrix called Eddie Kramer in New York, asking him to send the tapes over. "Jimi, don't be crazy," Eddie told him. "We've built this beautiful studio for you. You'll be here Monday." After a pause, Jimi replied, "Yeah, you're right. I'll be back on Monday and we'll get it together." Chas remembers Jimi saying he still wanted to bring his tapes to London. Chas explained that he was going out of town for the weekend and promised to speak with Hendrix when he returned.

Next on the schedule was a birthday party for one of Jimi's friends, Judy Wong, at the flat where his *Rainbow Bridge* costar Pat Hartley lived. Jimi brought Monika along and told Judy they were planning to get married—he'd evidently proposed marriage to Monika as impulsively as he'd suggested it to Kirsten Nefer. "I have no idea if he really intended to [get married]," Judy later said. "I only know what he told me." Following the party, the group went on to Ronnie Scott's, and Jimi finally sat in with War, accompanying the band on "Mother Earth" and "Tobacco Road."

🎶

Jimi and Monika awoke late the next day, September 17. In the early afternoon, Monika photographed Jimi in the hotel's garden; the pictures were later published in her book, *The Inner World of Jimi Hendrix*. Jimi wears dark trousers and a purple shirt, with a blue jacket and a long scarf tied around his neck. He seems relaxed, if a bit tired, posing with his black Fender Stratocaster. In a few shots, he's sitting at a table set with a teapot and teacups, the guitar resting on a chair next to him. In one picture, he playfully offers to put sugar in the teacup that's placed in front of the guitar.

The two then went out to do some shopping. While at Kensington Market, Jimi ran into Kathy Etchingham and asked her to call him at his hotel that night. Kathy said she might, knowing that she wouldn't—she had moved on with her life. While driving back to the Cumberland, Jimi spotted Devon Wilson, Colette Mimram, and Stella Douglas walking down King's Road and had Monika stop the car so he could speak with them. They invited Jimi to a party that night at the home of Pete Cameron, a music publisher.

Monika then continued driving back to the Cumberland Hotel. En route, their car came alongside another car driven by Phillip Harvey, son of Lord Harvey of Prestbury, a prominent member of Britain's Conservative party. Phillip had two young companions with him, Penny Ravenhill and Anne Day, and when Penny recognized Jimi, Phillip suggested she roll down the car window and invite Jimi to join them for tea. She did so, and Jimi impulsively agreed to the invitation, saying he first had to go by his hotel to check his messages.

At the Cumberland, Jimi called Gerry Stickells and arranged to sign contracts the following day for an upcoming tour. Stickells recalled Hendrix being anxious to get back to New York and continue working on his album. After the call, Mitch Mitchell arrived at Stickells' and phoned Jimi at the Cumberland himself, saying that he and Ginger Baker would be picking up Sly Stone at the airport later that night and inviting him to come by the Speakeasy for a jam. Jimi eagerly agreed, saying he'd be at the club by midnight.

Jimi and Monika then left the Cumberland and followed Phillip's car back to his home at 4 Clarkes Mews. It was around 5:30 p.m. They spent the next several hours together, drinking tea and wine, smoking hashish, and dining on the vegetarian food the women prepared. As the hours passed, Phillip noticed Monika become more and more irritated, which he attributed to jealousy—when Anne Day picked up a guitar and sang a song that earned a compliment from Jimi, Monika had looked "very displeased." Finally, at around 10:00 p.m., Monika surprised everyone by suddenly getting up to stalk out the door, shouting, "I'm leaving! I'm leaving now!"

Jimi followed her outside, and a loud argument ensued. Worried that the neighbors would complain about the noise, Phillip went outside twice to try to calm things down. He was startled to hear Monika berate Jimi as a "fucking pig," and he became increasingly concerned that she might physically attack Jimi. But when Monika told him to mind his own business, Phillip went back inside.

After half an hour, Jimi also came back inside, where he apologized for Monika's behavior and said he would have to leave. He added how much he'd enjoyed his time at Phillip's and promised to stay in touch. Phillip gave him a business card with his address and watched the two drive away, Monika still screaming at Jimi.

Jimi may have then returned to Monika's flat for a few hours. He was next seen at Pete Cameron's party, arriving alone. Monika came to pick him up after half an hour, and Jimi got Stella Douglas to tell her to leave. Monika kept returning, repeatedly asking to speak to Jimi on the intercom, and when he realized she couldn't be put off, he finally gave up and left the party. It was around 3:00 a.m. on September 18, 1970.

The two returned to the Samarkand, and Monika went to bed after taking one of her sleeping pills, a powerful drug called Vesparax. At some point, Jimi took some of her sleeping pills as well. It was never determined precisely how many

The day after Hendrix passing, the Fillmore East's marquee displays a poignant tribute to him. *Jerry Engel/*New York Post *Archives/ Getty Images*

he took—a toxicologist later said it could have been as few as four or as many as nine. The usual dose was half a tablet, so even if he had taken only four pills, the dose was still eight times higher than recommended—without taking into account that he'd also been drinking alcohol since 5:30 p.m. and had smoked hashish. He'd also taken an amphetamine tablet (a "black bomber") at Pete Cameron's party.

Yet he took these pills with the same recklessness shown when he had swallowed a handful of sleeping pills a few weeks earlier in Denmark. It was later suggested that Jimi may have taken the Vesparax to counteract the effects of the black bomber taken earlier that night, but Vesparax was a much stronger drug. Given that Jimi would be found fully dressed on top of the bed, it suggests he was rapidly overwhelmed by its effect.

In later years, Monika would give many varying accounts of what time she woke up (as well as other events). Tony Brown, who interviewed her extensively over the years, wrote in his book *Hendrix: The Final Days* that "her story would change from one [telephone] call to the next." Whatever the time, at some point she woke up and found Jimi covered in vomit, and she was unable to rouse him.

She next made several phone calls, trying to track down her friend Alvinia Bridges. She was told Alvinia had spent the night with Eric Burdon at the Russell Hotel, and she eventually reached her there, telling her and Eric that she couldn't wake Jimi. Eric told her to slap him a bit and get him some coffee, then hung up. He soon reconsidered, called Monika back, and told her to call an ambulance. Monika was hesitant to do so because of the drugs in the flat, so Alvinia and Eric rushed over to help; in some accounts, Gerry Stickells and another member of Jimi's road crew also came over to help clean up. Eric later told Kathy Etchingham, "I think I saw Jimi on the bed, but I couldn't look because of the mess."

An ambulance was finally called at 11:18 a.m.; it was never determined who made the call. The ambulance, with its two attendants, Reginald Jones and John Saua, arrived at the Samarkand at 11:27 a.m. The door to the flat was wide open and no one was around. Jones and Saua walked in on a scene that Jones later described as "horrific . . . [Jimi] was covered in vomit, tons of it all over the pillow." The vomit was dried, indicating that Jimi had been in that condition for some time, and the attendants couldn't get an aspirator down his throat due to the blockage. "I knew he was dead as soon as I walked in the room," Jones said. "You get a feel for it."

The police were called, and when they arrived to secure the premises, Jimi was taken to St. Mary Abbots Hospital, arriving at 11:45 a.m. He was seen by Dr. John

opposite: Hendrix's casket is carried out following a funeral service at Dunlap Baptist Church in his hometown of Seattle on October 1, 1970. At his family's request, attendance was limited to close friends and relatives. *Michael Ochs Archives/Getty Images*

below: Among the attendees of Jimi's funeral was Miles Davis, pictured here with his wife, Bette Mabry (left) and Devon Wilson. *Bob Peterson/The LIFE Images Collection/ Getty Images*

Bannister and Dr. Martin Seifert, who soon determined that he had been dead for hours. "He was completely cold," said Bannister. "I personally think he probably died a long time before." Professor Robert Donald Teare conducted the autopsy, and the cause of death was determined to be inhalation of vomit due to barbiturate intoxication. Oddly, Teare didn't try to determine the time of death. Later, Dr. Rufus Crompton looked at the original report along with new testimony and estimated that Jimi could have died soon after he'd returned to the Samarkand—between 3:00 and 4:00 a.m.

An unexplained mystery, though, is the fact that although Jimi was found with his hair matted with red wine, his clothes soaked in wine, and with a considerable amount of wine in his stomach and lungs, the autopsy determined there was a very low alcohol content in his body. Monika later said the two drank wine before going to bed, but that wouldn't explain why Jimi's hair and clothing were soaked. Could the wine have been poured over him later in a desperate attempt to wash away the vomit, which by then was too dry? It will never be fully known what role red wine may have played in his death.

Jimi was pronounced dead at 12:45 p.m. Even before an official statement was released, a hospital representative told the media, "We don't know where, how or why he died, but he died of an overdose." BBC Radio One was the first to break the story. Jimi's lawyer, Henry Steingarten, called Al Hendrix in Seattle with the sad news. Leon Hendrix, still serving time in prison, had overheard the other prisoners talking about his brother's death but assumed it was just another rumor. Then, he was called to the chaplain's office, later recalling that he could hear "If 6 Was 9" playing on someone's radio as he walked to the office and felt a sense of growing dread. In the chaplain's office, he was handed the phone and listened, stunned, as his father told him about Jimi's death. "One of the only things keeping me going since I had been locked up was the idea of reuniting with him after I was through with my sentence," he later wrote. "Jimi and I were supposed to go back on the road together and set out on a new journey, but that was never going to happen now."

That evening, some of Jimi's friends gathered at Ronnie Scott's for an impromptu wake. Though distraught over his friend's death, Eric Burdon nonetheless performed that night at the club. While helping clear out Jimi's apartment, he briefly read from a poem (or song lyrics) Jimi had left out, called "The Story of Life." With its references to death, God, and the brevity of existence (something that ends in the "wink of an eye"), Burdon took it for a suicide note. He later stated that he'd "misread" the note. But the mythologizing of Jimi Hendrix had begun.

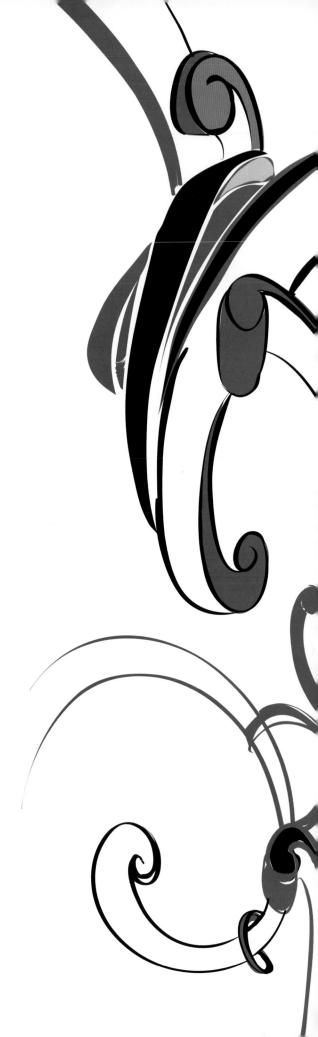

According to Jimi's friends in England, Jimi had wanted to be buried in London, but Al wanted to bring him back to Seattle, and because Jimi hadn't left a will,

his closest blood relative had the final say. The idea of having a large public memorial service was floated but quickly scotched by city authorities. "I think they started getting scared of something like another Woodstock," promoter Tom Hulett, who had worked on all of Jimi's Seattle shows, told *Rolling Stone*. Jimi's body was flown back to Seattle at the end of September, and the funeral was held October 1 at Seattle's Dunlap Baptist Church, at 8445 Rainier Avenue South. Noel Redding, Mitch Mitchell, and Buddy Miles were in attendance, along with others from Jimi's professional life: Michael Jeffrey, Eddie Kramer, Alan Douglas, and Gerry Stickells. Miles Davis, John Hammond Jr., and Devon Wilson also flew in to attend, and even Seattle's mayor, Wes Uhlman, came. Leon was also allowed to attend, under armed guard.

The service was led by Reverend Harold Blackburn. A large floral arrangement made of white and purple flowers in the shape of a guitar stood by the casket. Al didn't speak, but Leon read a poem he'd written, "Star Child of the Universe," putting a copy of it in his brother's casket. Longtime family friend Freddie Mae Gautier read the lyrics of Jimi's song "Angel" as well as a poem written by a Garfield High School student, and Patrinell Wright, later the founder Seattle's Total Experience Gospel Choir, sang "His Eye Is on the Sparrow," "Just a Closer Walk with Thee," and "The Angels Keep Watch over Me." Mitch and Noel were horrified at the open casket, something they'd never experienced at a funeral in England. "Everyone was expected to parade by and look, but I just couldn't," Noel said. The two musicians held hands and broke down in tears.

The pallbearers, chosen by Gautier, were mostly friends from Jimi's youth: James Thomas, the manager of the Rocking Kings; Eddy Rye; Donnie Howell; Billy Burns; and Dave Anderson. The sole exception was Herbert Price, who served as Jimi's chauffeur and valet. Jimi was buried in Greenwood Memorial Cemetery in Renton, just south of Seattle. "When the Saints Go Marching In" was sung at the graveside, and as the coffin was lowered into the grave, people tossed in letters, guitar picks, and, according to Leon, joints.

Following the service, a wake was held at the Seattle Center, site of the 1962 World's Fair, at the Food Circus—the food court of the Center House building (now called the Armory). The event was meant to be a private gathering, but when word got out, fans began turning up. Mitch found the affair "really gauche" but conceded that it was "probably not a bad idea in retrospect." Noel felt it was a "good sendoff" for Jimi: "Buddy Miles, Johnny Winter, Mitch and myself were the nucleus of a jam session that lasted hours. Jimi would have enjoyed it." Jimi's cousin, Eddie Hall, also played what *Rolling Stone* called "a fast and fluid blues guitar."

In his memoir, published in 1999, Al Hendrix wrote that he still found it hard to talk about Jimi's death, but he took some comfort in thinking that Jimi's spirit lived on: "I believe in heaven. . . I like to believe that that's where Jimi is."

CHAPTER 7

THE NEW RISING SON

Al Hendrix inherited Jimi's entire estate. Before the funeral, he'd gone out to New York to meet with Henry Steingarten, Jimi's lawyer, and while there he visited Jimi's apartment and asked for his belongings to be sent to him. Al ended up receiving far fewer items than he'd seen at Jimi's last home—none of his jewelry, and only three of his guitars. Over the following years, Al would see Jimi's personal items turn up for sale at auction houses. Jimi's musical legacy would also be picked over and repackaged in the coming decades, and a series of battles over who would control that legacy ensued.

Jimi at the Winterland Ballroom, San Francisco, February 4, 1968. A skinny kid who taught himself to play a battered, one-string instrument went on to be the kind of guitar hero other musicians dream of becoming. *Baron Wolman/Iconic Images/Getty Images*

It didn't take long for people to take advantage. Soon after Jimi's death, a lawyer friend of Al's introduced him to a group of men who said they wanted to start a nonprofit foundation in Jimi's memory. The plan was to raise money to purchase a plot of land outside Seattle, where a campground for underprivileged youth would be set up, along with a Jimi Hendrix museum. The grounds would also be used for rock concerts, and a scholarship fund was planned. The group wanted the rights to use Al's name in exchange for an upfront cash payment of $1,000, with the promise of more money to come. Al agreed.

The Jimi Hendrix Memorial Foundation sold memberships and peddled memorabilia including buttons and bumper stickers reading "Jimi Hendrix Lives," as well as selling ads for a planned souvenir photo album; the organization also staged four rock concerts in Seattle and Tacoma. But no records were kept detailing how much money was coming in, and the organization began to unravel due to infighting. A former employee reported to the state's Department of Labor that the foundation was breaking minimum-wage laws, and the foundation's charity permit was also revoked. Al went to visit the foundation's Seattle offices one day and found the place empty. No one knew what became of the money. Al had received four further payments of $100 from the group, but then the money stopped coming. A check issued to pay the foundation's city taxes was returned for insufficient funds.

As for Jimi's own earnings, his lawyers told Al there was only $20,000 in his bank account. After working with a local lawyer recommended by a friend, Jimi's former valet, Herbert Price, introduced Al to Leo Branton Jr. Branton had been a lawyer for Nat King Cole and Dorothy Dandridge, and he assured Al that he could handle the estate. "So on a handshake, my dad had a deal," Janie Hendrix told journalist Larry LeBlanc. "If Leo could get anything for my dad—because it seemed like it was a huge mess—then he would be his lawyer for life. It was 'You don't have to pay me anything if I can't get you anything.' It seemed like a great deal for my dad. So he shook his hand."

Branton arranged for Michael Jeffery to buy out Jimi's share of Electric Lady Studios for $240,000 (the studio remains in operation today). Branton then set up an increasingly complicated series of entities to deal with the rights to Hendrix's recordings. In 1974, Branton sold those rights to a Panamanian corporation, Presentaciones Musicales S.A. (PMSA). Depaja, a New York company run by Branton and two other lawyers, represented PMSA in the United States. Bella Godiva Music was established in the United States to handle Jimi's publishing. The rights later passed to other offshore companies: Bureau Voor Muziekrechten Elber B.V. (for recordings in the United States and Canada) and Interlit B.V.I. (for recordings in all other countries). Auteursrechtenmaatschappij B.V. acquired Bella Godiva.

Al was largely unaware of the specifics of how Jimi's estate was being managed, but Branton arranged for Al to receive a regular allowance of $50,000, a substantial sum for a man whose yearly income had been a fraction of that amount, so he was

Historic Performances Recorded at the Monterey Pop Festival, a split LP by Hendrix and Otis Redding, rose to #15 in the US charts following Jimi's death.

happy. Al also received additional money when he needed it for large purchases or cash gifts for his family. Al nonetheless continued working as a gardener, finally retiring in 1979 after heart surgery.

※ ※ ※

The first few years after Jimi's death saw the release of numerous recordings. *Historic Performances Recorded at the Monterey International Pop Festival*, featuring four songs from the Experience's set, had been released at the end of August 1970, and in the wake of Jimi's death, sales pushed it to No. 15 on the charts. A tribute single of "Voodoo Child (Slight Return)" followed, released on October 23, 1970, in the UK only, and topped the charts.

Ed Chalpin wasn't about to be left out, issuing the single "Ballad of Jimi," credited to Curtis Knight and Jimi Hendrix, in the UK in October 1970. A second single, "No Such Animal (Part 1)," was released in the UK in February 1971. Chalpin parlayed his Hendrix recordings into new Curtis Knight albums, as well, including *What'd I Say* (1972) and *In the Beginning* (1973). He wasn't the only person who mined the archives for Hendrix material: Lonnie Youngblood's *Two Great Experiences Together* (1971) and *Rare Hendrix* (1972) and the Isley Brothers' *In the Beginning* (1971) were also released to capitalize on Jimi's death. The recordings were not always what they appeared. Songs would be mixed to push Jimi's guitar part to the forefront (as Ronald Isley admitted they'd done on their release) and were also re-edited and artificially extended. Youngblood's *Two Great Experiences Together* even featured new overdubs by a Hendrix sound-alike.

Of much greater interest was *The Cry of Love*, the first album of new studio recordings released after Jimi's death. Michael Jeffery had arranged for Mitch Mitchell

Among the first posthumous Hendrix releases were two singles issued by Ed Chalpin, "Ballad of Jimi" (credited to Curtis Knight and Jimi Hendrix) and "No Such Animal."

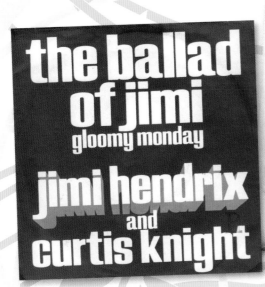

to come over from England and work with Eddie Kramer to sift through the tapes. (Mitchell, Kramer, and Hendrix would all be credited as the album's co-producers.) Jimi had earmarked songs he wanted to consider for his next album, but there was no way of knowing for sure what tracks he would have used. There also weren't enough completed songs for an entire album. Mitch described the process of compiling the album as "a real jigsaw puzzle to put together. You'd find, say, a lead guitar part in one key and then a vocal and rhythm track for the same song in a different key and one had to be speeded up or slowed down to match the other." Mitch himself played a few drum overdubs when needed.

The Cry of Love was released in March 1971, reaching No. 3 in the United States and No. 2 in the UK—it would go on to sell over a million copies. Two singles were released: "Freedom," released in the United States, reached No. 59; "Angel," released in the UK, failed to chart. A proper album of studio recordings was most welcome. Lenny Kaye, in his review in *Rolling Stone*, called it "a beautiful, poignant testimonial, a fitting coda to the career of a man who was clearly the finest electric guitarist to be produced by the Sixties, bar none."

Elsewhere in his review, Kaye speculated that the vaults might be bare after this release: "If *The Cry of Love* had come out while Hendrix was alive, we probably would have said it was a good album, bought a million copies, and left it at that. But now that he's gone, it has to become that much more precious, something to savor slowly because there'll be no others." It was a common perception—Eddie Kramer had previously stated that he felt there was only about two albums worth of material that would be worthy of release. That proved to be a substantial understatement; as of 2016, twelve posthumous studio albums and compilations have been released—a figure that doesn't include box sets or live recordings.

Live releases were especially prolific. There were four live albums with Jimi's performances released in 1971 alone. *Woodstock Two*, released in April, featured

left: A number of LPs of recordings featuring Hendrix soon followed, including the two pictured here: the Isley Brothers' *In the Beginning* and Lonnie Youngblood's *Two Great Experiences Together.*

right: *The Cry of Love* (March 1971) was the first official album of previously unheard material to be released after Hendrix's death.

Though it is billed as the "original motion picture soundtrack," the *Rainbow Bridge* album (1971) does not contain any music from the film. Nonetheless, it was well received, and reached #15 in the US charts.

three more songs from Jimi's set and reached No. 8 in the United States; *Experience*, released in the UK only, had four songs from Jimi's February 24, 1969, appearance at Royal Albert Hall and reached No. 9. *The First Great Rock Festivals of the Seventies: Isle of Wight/Atlanta Pop Festival* had three songs from Hendrix's Isle of Wight appearance and reached No. 47 in the United States; *Isle of Wight*, released in the UK only, had six songs and reached No. 17. The following year, *Hendrix in the West* drew on songs from the Royal Albert Hall, San Diego, Berkeley, and Isle of Wight concerts, reaching No. 47 in the United States, and *More Experience*, released in the UK, presented more songs from the Royal Albert Hall shows.

The *Rainbow Bridge* album was also released in October 1971 in the United States, November in the UK. Despite the album cover copy saying it was an "Original Motion Picture Soundtrack," the album did not actually feature any music from the movie. Instead, it continued the premise of *The Cry of Love*, drawing on tracks in the archives, with Mitch providing a few overdubs. Among the eight tracks was a song called "Look Over Yonder," which Jimi had performed in his Greenwich Village days (when the song was called "Mr. Bad Luck"). There was also a solo studio version of "The Star-Spangled Banner," and a live version of "Hear My Train a Comin'" from his May 30, 1970, performance in Berkeley, taken from the first show.

In his *Rolling Stone* review, Tony Glover noted his puzzlement at the album's presentation as a soundtrack but gave it a thumbs up nonetheless: "In many ways this is one of Hendrix's best albums—it's diverse, but not a goulash." The album fared respectably, reaching No. 15 in the United States and No. 16 in the UK and selling over half a million copies. "Dolly Dagger" was released as a single in the United States, reaching No. 74—it was the last Hendrix single to chart in the United States. In the UK, Jimi's last Top 40 single was a live version of "Johnny B. Goode," released in 1972 to accompany the release of *Hendrix in the West*; it reached No. 35. The last single to chart in the UK was a reissue of "All Along the Watchtower," released in 1990; it reached No. 52.

The *Rainbow Bridge* album fared better than the film. Chuck Wein evinced confidence in his work, telling *Rolling Stone*, "The movie will surprise a lot of people; it shows a side of Jimi that few really knew at all." Michael Jeffery proclaimed, "I think the film says more than *Easy Rider*, really. It's honest." At the time of its premiere, it had a running time of just over two hours, but in response to the negative reviews, it was quickly re-edited. Still, the meandering plotline didn't win over many viewers. Merrell Fankhauser, who later directed the 2013 documentary *Rainbow Bridge Revisited*, admitted that the film's message "kind of got lost a little bit." In *Hendrix: Setting the Record Straight*, John McDermott wrote that the film was "of interest only to the morbidly curious."

The documentary *A Film About Jimi Hendrix* (sometimes simply titled *Jimi Hendrix*), released in December 1973, was received more favorably. "The Hendrix film is not

by any means a biography of the man," Joe Boyd, one of the film's producers, told journalist Judith Sims. "It's an impressionistic film. Our first chore was to show his music, and if we could also get a feeling of what the period and Hendrix were like, that was a bonus; but basically it's a musical film."

The musical sequences are the highlight of the movie. In the days before the Internet, when all manner of live footage became available online, it was exciting to see clips from Jimi's live appearances, since full-length releases of his sets at the Monterey International Pop Festival and Woodstock were still some years off. Two performances in particular stood out. One was a fresh-faced Experience playing "Purple Haze" in 1967 for the TV show *Beat-Club*. Another was more poignant: Jimi, sitting alone on a high chair, playing a solo rendition of "Hear My Train a Comin'."

Along with archive interviews of Jimi, interviewees included Jimi's father and most of his bandmates (Noel Redding declined to participate due to a lawsuit with Hendrix's estate), fellow admirers such as Eric Clapton and Mick Jagger, and such friends as Fayne Pridgon, Albert and Arthur Allen, and others. It's still something of a surface look at the subject, avoiding potential areas of controversy. Jimi's relationship with women and his drug use was discussed, but only briefly. Monika Dannemann says a few words about his death, but most details of Jimi's passing are covered in a short statement before the film's end, emphasizing that doctors determined he did not have a heroin habit.

A Film About Jimi (1973) was described by producer Joe Boyd as "an impressionistic film" rather than a traditional biography.

Boyd, who conducted most of the interviews, admitted that in talking to Hendrix's associates, he quickly realized how contentious Jimi's relationship with Michael Jeffery had been. But he decided not to address the issue in the film as he felt the average viewer wouldn't be interested. Jeffery had agreed to be interviewed but never set a time to do so; Boyd's feeling was that Jeffery felt the film would compete with his own movie, *Rainbow Bridge*.

"We left out a lot of areas, we know that," Boyd admitted. "We never set out to make a complete documentation of his life. There's no way we could include every detail like a written biography. I think I always viewed the film as a means of getting great footage of a great musician out to people who would want to see it." There apparently were a number of people who did want to see it—when the film opened in Los Angeles, one theater pulled in $46,000 in two weeks. The accompanying soundtrack was released prior to the film—June in the UK, where it reached No. 37, and July in the United States, where it reached No. 89.

Studio releases continued. *War Heroes* was released in October 1972 in the UK, reaching No. 23, and in December in the United States, reaching No. 48. (In *Hendrix: Setting the Record Straight*, McDermott suggested the album should've been paired with *Rainbow Bridge* to give a more comprehensive look at Hendrix's unfinished work.) It was also the last Hendrix release Eddie Kramer would work on for some time. Reprise declined to release the next album, *Loose Ends*, described by McDermott as a "patchwork collection of decidedly inferior Hendrix material"; it was issued in the UK in 1974 and failed to chart. The producer, John Jenson, even used a pseudonym as he didn't want his own name on the album.

A new producer was then brought in to oversee Hendrix releases. Branton formed a new company, Are You Experienced? Inc., and hired Alan Douglas to produce Jimi's albums. The first release was *Crash Landing*, which Douglas co-produced with Tony Bongiovi. The album revealed a new approach to working with Jimi's unfinished recordings. Douglas isolated Jimi's performances and brought in session musicians to record new backing tracks. In later years, demos and unreleased tracks would not be reworked in such a fashion—instead, the original takes would be used fill out CD reissues and illustrate the development of a particular song. But at the time of *Crash Landing*'s release, Douglas argued he was improving the material.

He also argued that he was making the material more commercially viable, and in that he was successful. Though short—the album runs just under half an hour—*Crash Landing* generated the most sales since *Rainbow Bridge*, certified gold in the United States. The album was released in March 1975 in the United States, reaching No. 5, and came out in August in the UK, reaching No. 35. The same approach of adding newly recorded overdubs was utilized on *Midnight Lightning*, released in November 1975, which fared less well in the charts (No. 43 in the United States and No. 46 in the UK). But *Nine to the Universe* (1980), which was solely produced by Douglas,

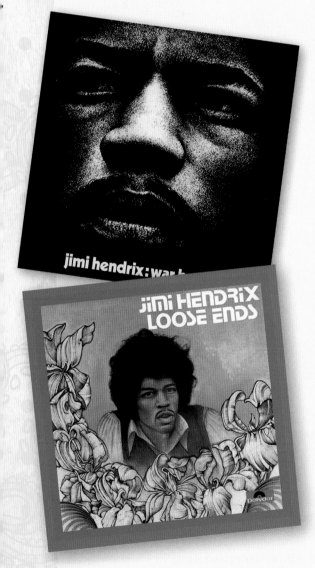

The mid-seventies LPs *War Heroes* and *Loose Ends* continued the steady trail of posthumous releases, but with increasingly diminishing returns.

had no such overdubs. The album peaked at No. 127 in the United States and failed to chart in the UK.

MUCH

There were other personal developments among Jimi's associates in the decade following his death. Just five months after Jimi died, Devon Wilson's life came to a sudden, shocking end when she fell out of a window at New York's Chelsea Hotel; it was never determined if she jumped, fell by accident, or was pushed. Michael Jeffery died on March 5, 1973, in a plane crash. Flying to Great Britain from Spain, his plane collided with another over Nantes, France. The other plane was able to land, but the plane Jeffery was in crashed, killing everyone on board. The crash was blamed on a strike by air traffic controllers in France and faulty radar.

Ed Chalpin's suit against Track and Polydor, which had been pending at the time of Jimi death, finally came to court in 1973. Chalpin ended up losing his case and had to pay attorney's fees. He also had to turn over all extant tapes in his possession, though he was allowed to continue reissuing material he'd already released. He would keep churning out releases for years and even managed to dig up live recordings of Jimi playing with Curtis Knight and the Squires, releasing three such albums in 1973 alone (*What'd I Say*, *Birth of Success*, and *In the Beginning*).

In court, Jimi's sidemen didn't fare nearly as well. Both Noel Redding and Mitch Mitchell pursued legal action for money they felt they were owed and ended up settling. Noel signed away his rights to future royalties for $100,000, while Mitch received $265,000. Diane Carpenter lost her paternity suit against Hendrix's estate in 1972; Tamika Laurice James would not be recognized as Jimi's daughter. But in 1975, a Swedish court ruled in favor of Eva Sundquist's claim that

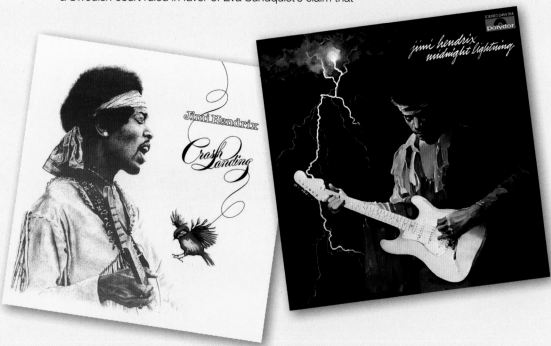

Overseen by producer Alan Douglas, *Crash Landing* and *Midnight Lightning* (both 1975) added new backing tracks to unfinished Hendrix recordings, and proved more commercially successful than other recent LPs.

Jimi was the father of her child, James Henrik Daniel Sundquist. In later years, they would try to establish paternity in the United States as well, and Al would eventually settle with Sundquist for a one-time payment of $1 million.

In the 1980s, the advent of CDs revived interest in Jimi's back catalog, which was reissued. There were also new releases that pleased the fans. *Live at Winterland* (1987) featured songs from the Experience's 1968 shows in San Francisco and sold over two hundred thousand copies. *Radio One* (1988) was drawn from the Experience's appearances on BBC Radio, performances especially exciting for American fans, who'd previously only been exposed to the material on bootleg. Sales were booming; in 1988, *Forbes* magazine estimated income from Hendrix's records and publishing to be $4 million a year, with merchandising adding another $1 million.

Despite this, Jimi was not receiving much recognition in his hometown. In 1980, Seattle radio station KZOK sponsored a fundraising drive to erect a memorial for him, but the city authorities were resistant, pointing to Jimi's drug use, which, in their eyes, made him a poor role model. "It was hell dealing with the city," Janet Wainwright, then the station's promotion director, told the *Seattle Times* in 2011. "We tried everything. Naming a street, one of those little pocket parks you see at the end of some streets. Nobody was interested. I was met with the most vehement objections, including from Walter Hundley, head of the Parks Department, who sat me in his office and basically said they were not going to memorialize a drug addict." Wainwright also recalled getting hate mail, "death threats, people saying Jimi Hendrix was Satan."

Finally, David Hancocks, then director of the Woodland Park Zoo, offered the zoo grounds as a location for a memorial. A mosaic walkway was designed in the zoo's African Savannah section, leading to a "Jimi Hendrix Overlook," which overlooks a rock with a commemorative plaque. The memorial was unveiled in 1983, with Al Hendrix in attendance. Some thought it was racially insensitive to place the plaque in the African Savannah part of the zoo, but Al didn't mind, simply telling reporters, "Jimi liked animals." But the memorial wasn't well maintained. The rock was at one time heated—making it a "hot rock," in reference to Jimi's music—but the heating element eventually failed. Not that anyone observing the rock would know this: visitors weren't allowed to touch it.

In 1984, a bust of Jimi by local sculptor Jeff Day (who lived on Whidbey Island, 30 miles north of Seattle), was donated to Garfield High School, where it's still on display in the library. Day recalled that the school was initially hesitant to take the bust, again due to Jimi's reputation for drug use. Day was surprised to be questioned about the issue during the dedication and responded that he felt the sculpture would be inspirational because of how Jimi overcame his impoverished upbringing. Fred Dente, who had helped to raise funds to cover Day's expenses, wrote a bitter account of the event in a letter to the *Rocket*, Seattle's music paper, complaining that the school's principal refused to let students take part in the ceremony. "KING TV was there, and reported that some in the administration felt that Jimi was a bad role model for the students, along with the usual references to Jimi's substance use and abuse. I'll never forget that day, and the embarrassment I felt for the Hendrix family."

Outside of Seattle, the attitude was more welcoming. In 1991, Warner Bros. paid for a star honoring Jimi to be placed on the Hollywood Walk of Fame in the 6600 block of Hollywood Boulevard. (The total cost was $4,800.) "It's been a long time coming," said Al, who attended the unveiling on November 21 with Leon. "But better late than never." An estimated six hundred people turned up for the ceremony, with one fan, Chris Williams, entertaining the crowd by playing Jimi's songs on guitar. "This is sacred!" he told the *Los Angeles Times*. "A celebration of his music, his existence, his memory. Jimi Hendrix took it all the way, man, as far as you can take it, musically."

Another honor came less than two months later, when Jimi's was inducted into the Rock & Roll Hall of Fame on January 15, 1992. His former bandmates the Isley Brothers were inducted at the same time. Neil Young inducted Jimi, saying at one point, "When you play guitar, you can play, or you can transcend . . . there's no boundaries, how far you can go in your own body and how far your mind can expand when you're playing. Jimi showed me that; I learned that from Jimi. And he was at one with his instrument." The all-star jam that followed the event naturally featured "Purple Haze."

November 27, 1992, would have been Jimi's fiftieth birthday. In a sign that times were changing, Seattle mayor Norm Rice issued a proclamation citing the date as "Jimi Hendrix Day," the first official recognition Jimi received from Seattle's city authorities. Sammy Drain, a friend of Jimi's, had approached the mayor about issuing the proclamation, and he readily agreed. As a mayoral aide stated, "The mayor felt that someone who had contributed to the music industry as Jimi Hendrix had, there was no question he deserved honor and recognition in his hometown."

⁂

These celebrations of Jimi's life came at time when there were new revelations about his death, the result of Kathy Etchingham's investigative efforts. Kathy had divorced her first husband, remarried, had two sons, and worked as a realtor. After an unhappy experience with a reporter following Jimi's death, she stopped giving interviews about her years with him, but she would speak out on occasion. Curtis Knight's 1974 book *Jimi: An Intimate Biography of Jimi Hendrix* included material said to be from an interview with Kathy, though she denied ever speaking to Knight and took legal action in response to the quote.

In 1981, Kathy was similarly upset by her portrayal in David Henderson's 1978 book *'Scuse Me While I Kiss the Sky*, which was about to be published in Great Britain. She contacted Monika Dannemann, by then living in Great Britain, about the possibility of pursuing legal action together. Monika agreed to meet, and Kathy

invited her to her home, asking Mitch and Noel to join them. In the course of their conversation, Monika told them about the day Jimi died, claiming that he had been alive when the ambulance men had arrived and that she had accompanied them to the hospital, where she was assured that Jimi would be fine. She suggested that Jimi's death had come about because he hadn't received proper medical treatment.

Kathy and her husband later visited Monika's home, which Kathy described as a "shrine" to Jimi, filled with Monika's paintings of the man she described as her fiancé and soulmate. Kathy was further put off by Monika's eccentricities, such as when she asked Kathy not to telephone her when the moon was full: "On the full moon Jimi and I are in communication. We go together travelling on the astral plane." Kathy decided to file her complaint about Henderson's book by herself, and the offending material was removed from the UK edition of the book.

But she continued thinking about Monika's story of Jimi's death. If the medical staff had been negligent, someone should have been held responsible. In the early nineties, with the help of a friend, she tracked down the ambulance attendants, Reginald Jones and John Saua, who had not been interviewed during the inquest. They were firm in their recollections of Jimi being dead when they arrived at the hotel room, which they also said was empty—no one had met them, and no one accompanied them to the hospital. Kathy prepared a file with the new information, which she submitted to Great Britain's attorney general, Sir Nicholas Lyell. The file was passed on to Scotland Yard and an investigation ensued in 1993. In the end, the case was not reopened, but the investigations confirmed the accounts of the ambulance attendants and medical staff: Jimi Hendrix was beyond help when Jones and Saua had arrived at the scene. Stories of these new developments ran in *Straight Ahead* magazine in 1992 and *Musician* in 1996. An excellent summation can also be found in Tony Brown's *Hendrix: The Final Days* (1997).

Monika was preparing a book of her own. Kathy was given a copy of the unpublished manuscript, which she found "full of fantasies and mystical ramblings." She took legal action against Monika, who eventually agreed to pay £1,000 in damages and refrain from making false statements about Kathy in the future. Monika violated this agreement with the publication of *The Inner World of Jimi Hendrix* in 1995, but there were some items of interest in the book. Jimi's handwritten lyrics were reproduced, and there were also the photos Monika had taken on September 17, 1970, at her hotel, the last known pictures of Jimi.

Much of the book was devoted to her paintings, most of which depicted Jimi in "otherworldly" situations; in one, he plays guitar while crouched on top of the White House, as a flying saucer soars overhead. She also worked to enhance her credentials as Jimi's fiancé, and the book featured endorsements from Al, June, and Janie. (Al wrote, "I would like to state that my son Jimi Hendrix was engaged to Monika Dannemann and that they planned to get married.") Kathy felt the book contained defamatory statements, and she again took legal action. On April 3, 1996, Monika lost the case and was found guilty of contempt of court. Two days later, on April 5, she was found dead at age forty-nine, having asphyxiated herself in her car. It was another bizarre twist in the story of Jimi's posthumous career.

At the same time, Jimi's family was ramping up their fight to control his music and image. "I don't know what was tougher—going through World War II or battling for Jimi's legacy," Al later wrote in his memoir about the legal battle that commenced in 1992.

In the fall of that year, Leo Branton sent letters to Leon and Janie on behalf of Al, asking them to waive their contingent reversionary rights to Jimi's music in exchange for a cash payment. Leon signed. "My drug addiction was more important to me than anything else, and scrutinizing business deals was of little interest," he said in his memoir. But Janie, believing Jimi's legacy was worth more, did not and hired legal representation. To her surprise, she learned that Branton had been negotiating a deal with MCA to buy the rights to Jimi's music, which were then owned by the various offshore companies Branton had set up. "Jimi had control of his masters," Janie explained to *Celebrity Access*. "So all of the masters ended up being signed over as a sale to these off shore companies. However, my dad was told it was a licensing agreement. . . . In 1993, we discovered that these offshore companies had ownership."

On April 16, 1993, Al sued Branton for "breach of fiduciary duty, fraud, negligent misrepresentation, legal malpractice, restitution based upon rescission of contract, securities law violations, infringement of copyrights, infringement of rights of publicity and declaratory judgments." Branton responded by filing a countersuit for defamation of character. Al's complaint was later amended, with Alan Douglas and Branton's son, Leo Branton III, added to the list of defendants.

The legal wrangling went on for two years. Seattle billionaire Paul Allen, cofounder of Microsoft and a huge Hendrix fan, loaned the family $5.8 million for legal expenses. Allen was making plans to open a Hendrix-themed museum in Seattle that would feature many of the collectables in Allen's own collection. But there was a falling out—temporary, as it turned out—between Allen and the Hendrix family when Allen also wanted rights to Jimi's likeness and music. "They wanted too much, too hard, too fast," said Janie.

In the middle of the legal battles, two more releases produced or co-produced by Alan Douglas came out. *Blues* (1994), co-produced by Bruce Gary of new wave pop act the Knack, focused on Jimi's blues material and included his solo version of "Hear My Train a Comin'" from *A Film About Jimi Hendrix*. The album reached No. 45 in the United States and No. 10 in the UK, selling over half a million copies. The next release, *Voodoo Soup* (1995), attracted controversy. The album was Douglas's concept of what Jimi's fourth album might have been (*The Cry of Love*

In 1995, Jimi's father, Al Hendrix, finally won back control over his son's music.
Robert Knight Archive/Redferns/Getty Images

had not been released on CD at that point), and it drew the fans' ire by again using new drum overdubs on two tracks, "Room Full of Mirrors" and "Stepping Stone," provided by Bruce Gary. The album was released only in the United States and reached No. 66.

The lawsuits were ultimately settled in 1995, with Al winning back the rights to Jimi's music and image. It wasn't without cost. It was agreed that $9 million would be paid to the defendants. The family soon set up Experience Hendrix, the company that would oversee Jimi's legacy from that point on; Al was chairman of the board, Janie was president, and Bob Hendrix, Jimi's cousin, was senior vice president. A licensing deal with MCA was struck, and Experience Hendrix set up its own labels as well: Hendrix Records (jointly run with MCA), which released material by new artists, and Dagger Records, which released Jimi's live shows via mail order.

By a happy circumstance, a Jimi Hendrix tribute concert was planned for that year's Bumbershoot festival, Seattle's yearly arts festival held over Labor Day weekend at the Seattle Center. As early as 1992, Norm Langill, then the president and founder of One Reel, the company then producing Bumbershoot, had thought of having the festival host a Jimi Hendrix electric guitar competition. Langill took the idea to the Hendrix family, who were interested but more concerned with their ongoing litigation at the time.

The year 1995 was not only the twenty-fifth anniversary of Jimi's death, but also Bumbershoot's twenty-fifth anniversary. When the Hendrix family wanted to stage a commemorative festival, they met resistance from city officials. Then Langill stepped up. "I listened to Jimi a lot in the '60s," Langill told the author in 1997. "I remembered

being in Seattle when he died, and they wanted to do a concert for him then. Which would have been very natural at the time, but it never happened. So I said, 'Why don't we do the concert for Jimi now, at the twenty-fifth anniversary?'"

The Hendrix family agreed. The guitar competition was also a part of the event, and there was also a Hendrix "Red House" exhibit, displaying memorabilia and personal artifacts such as the drawings Jimi had done as a child.

The main event was the Jimi Hendrix Tribute Concert, held on September 4 at the Seattle Center's open-air Memorial Stadium. There were opening sets by Abraxas and George Clinton and the P-Funk All Stars, followed by an all-star guitar finale. Noel Redding, Mitch Mitchell, and Buddy Miles were among the musicians—the last time all these men would share the same stage. Other performers included Eric Burdon, Heart's Ann Wilson, Living Color's Vernon Reid, and Pearl Jam's Mike McCready, among others. Hendrix tribute artist Randy Hansen was featured, as was Jay Roberts, the twenty-nine-year-old winner of the guitar competition.

Al Hendrix was honored, coming out on stage to a loud ovation. To his surprise, he was given a gold crown and red robe to wear, and after lighting a specially designed torch that featured a guitar on top, he was led to a throne at the side of the stage (he later jokingly noted that the sound wasn't very good from that position). Four paratroopers from the 101st Airborne Division also dropped into the stadium in acknowledgment of Jimi's own days as a Screaming Eagle.

The show ran late and was further hampered by a thunderstorm. "I remember at one point Buddy went on a tear for about forty-five minutes—almost twenty-five minutes more than he was scheduled to play," Langill said. "And this big thundercloud passed, and Narada [Walden, the show's musical director] turned to me and said, 'That's Jimi telling Buddy to get off the stage!' And it did sort of feel like Jimi was up in the thunderstorm, that there was this hovering electric magnetic presence. That

sounds a little goofy, but you couldn't help but feel that way. 'Cause it's so odd to have a lightning thunderstorm in Seattle." There was another eerie moment at the show's beginning, when a large flock of Canadian geese flew in a *V* formation straight up the stadium and over the top of the stage. "Everybody looked at them and thought, 'Wow, that was weird!'" Langill recalled. "There were a lot of natural forces in play that night. But heck, you remember that until the day you die, that it had those kind of forces of nature."

The next morning, the *Seattle Post-Intelligencer* ran a photo of a teary-eyed Al on the front page. "This festival was yes, to honor Jimi," Janie told *Goldmine*, "but more so to show my dad the love that the fans have for Jimi, and to let him see how big Jimi was. 'Cause I don't even think up until that point he really realized that Jimi was as big of an artist, still, as he was. So he was really touched. And I remember after the concert someone came up to him and said, 'Well, Mr. Hendrix, was it everything that you wanted it to be?' And he said, 'No. It was more.' And that really touched my heart 'cause we did it for him."

❦

In 1997, Experience Hendrix put out its first releases, reissuing the Experience's three albums (the first time the original master tapes were used for CD reissues) and *First Rays of the New Rising Sun*, another variation on what might have been Jimi's fourth album. Eddie Kramer oversaw the remastering and has worked on all subsequent Experience Hendrix releases.

The company also began releasing merchandise. Some fans would become critical over what they regarded as demeaning items, like golf balls emblazoned with Jimi's picture, boxer shorts, or Jimi Hendrix "Road Rage" vanilla-scented car air fresheners. Asked by the *New York Times* about the release of such products, Janie

Hendrix responded, "We definitely don't do it to offend anybody. It's kind of sad. It's like on one hand everybody feels like they own a piece of Jimi. But at the end of the day, who pays the bills? Who takes care of him? Who takes care of his grave? It's really easy to sit back and play Monday morning quarterback, but you don't walk in our shoes."

Promoting Jimi's music remained Experience Hendrix's overwhelming focus. The company's first box set, *The Jimi Hendrix Experience*, was released in 2000, followed by a steady stream of albums and box sets featuring alternate versions of songs and outtakes. In some cases, the releases featured songs that previously appeared on the album Alan Douglas produced, minus the overdubs he'd put on. There were also live releases, both commercially available CDs and DVDs, and the mail order releases on Dagger Records—the label's first release was *Live at the Oakland Coliseum* (1998), from an April 27, 1969, show. As of 2017, live concerts and radio broadcasts are streamed on Experience Hendrix's official website, www.jimihendrix.com.

If the city of Seattle was still largely resistant to having a public memorial for its most famous musician, private individuals were increasingly stepping up to make their own contributions. In 1993, a beautiful mural of Jimi was painted on the wall above Myers Music at 1206 First Avenue, the shop where Al had bought Jimi his first electric guitar. The mural was painted by Dan and Mae Hitchcock, who had previously painted murals and sets for clients ranging from Phil Collins to Southwest Airlines. The mural was unveiled on November 27, Jimi's fifty-first birthday. As luck would have it, there was an APEC conference in town at the time, meaning there were numerous journalists on hand. "It was a Sunday, and the journalists didn't

opposite: The memorial statue on Broadway and East Pine in Seattle has been on display since 1997—the same year that a "Blue Plaque" was placed outside the London flat Hendrix shared with Kathy Etchingham.
Gillian G. Gaar

have anything to do," Dan Hitchcock later recalled. "The story went all the way to China; we got clippings from everywhere from that mural." A commemorative plaque was also installed. Sadly, when the building was sold, the mural was painted over.

In 1997, another memorial appeared on the corner of Broadway and East Pine Streets in Seattle's Capitol Hill neighborhood, outside what was then the headquarters of AEI Music (a company that produces background music tapes for various businesses). The company's president, Mike Malone, oversaw what he called the company's "alternative corporate art collection," which included guitars owned by Bill Haley, Elvis Presley, Chuck Berry, John Lennon, and Jimi Hendrix (a 1970 Fender Stratocaster Sunburst). He also commissioned statues of each artist, made by Seattle sculptor Daryl Smith at Seattle's Fremont Foundry. Smith chose to have Jimi on his knees, leaning back as he plays, wearing an outfit patterned after the clothes he wore during the Monterey International Pop Festival.

The other statues were placed around AEI's offices, but Malone wanted to have Jimi's statue outside and worked with the neighborhood's Chamber of Commerce and other community organizations, with AEI paying for the complete installation. The statue was unveiled on January 21, 1997, with Al, Leon, Janie, and Robert Hendrix in attendance. It was the first time they'd seen the statue, and Smith was nervous. "If they had been disappointed or hadn't liked it, I would've been crushed," he told the author in 1997. "But they liked it real well. Al got tears in his eyes when he saw it; he kind of got misty, so I could tell it had an effect on him."

Despite the rain, more than one hundred people turned out for the event. Malone held up Jimi's guitar for the crowd to see, and Randy Hansen played a short set through clouds of purple smoke. The statue remains a popular photo-op destination due to the high foot traffic in the area. Smith was happy the Hendrix statue was placed outside: "I'm glad it turned out to be Jimi Hendrix. It's really appropriate. Having grown up down by Leschi Park, I'm sure he spent a lot of time on Broadway. And I suppose that often he walked right over that sidewalk. I think that's cool, that he's back on Broadway!"

Jimi's historical presence was being recognized in the UK too. On September 14, 1997, an English Heritage "Blue Plaque" was unveiled on the outside wall of

above: Jimi's brother, Leon, in 1997. *SGranitz/ WireImage/Getty Images*

opposite: On September 14, 1997, an English Heritage "Blue Plaque" was unveiled at 23 Brook Street, London, where Jimi had lived with Kathy Etchingham. Hendrix's bedroom has been recreated at the site. *Anthony Devline/PA Photos/Alamy Stock Image*

23 Brook Street, where Jimi had lived with Kathy Etchingham. Kathy had been petitioning English Heritage for the commemoration since 1992. Pete Townshend unveiled the plaque, and Noel Redding was also in attendance. The event was somewhat marred over tensions regarding Al and Janie's appearance. Kathy had sent Al and Leon invitations, but not Janie: "I didn't want the event to be turned into a promotional exercise for her company," Kathy wrote in her memoir, which was published the following year. Leon did not come to the ceremony, but Janie did; it was a sign of a growing schism in the family. The Brook Street flat would later be opened to the public as a tourist attraction.

Al had separated from his wife June in the early 1980s. She died in 1999, the same year Al published his memoir, *My Son Jimi*. Al died on April 17, 2002, of heart failure at the age of eighty-two. His death triggered another legal battle when it was learned that Leon had been cut out of Al's will. Leon filed suit, seeking to have the will overturned, and later suits followed by other relatives alleging mismanagement of the trusts of which they were beneficiaries. The battle lines were drawn, with Janie and Leon representing different factions of the Hendrix family. That November, Jimi's sixtieth birthday was celebrated with parties held in two different cities, one in Seattle,

Hayley Atwell (as Kathy Etchingham) and André 3000 (as Hendrix) in the 2014 biopic *All Is by My Side; Pictorial Press Ltd./Alamy Stock Photo*

hosted by Experience Hendrix, and one in Los Angeles, hosted by Leon. Leon's paternity was also an issue. In *My Son Jimi*, Al said he didn't believe Leon was his son.

The trial began on June 28, 2004, and ran until September 24 of that year, when Judge Jeffrey Ramsdell read aloud his decision to a packed courtroom. In the end, it was a split decision. Janie and Bob Hendrix were removed as head trustees, but Al's will was upheld—Leon would receive nothing from Al's estate except for a single gold record.

Leon filed an appeal, but the decision stood. It was not the last legal skirmish between Leon and Experience Hendrix. In 2009, Leon and a business partner were sued for trademark infringement. (The case was settled in 2015.) Leon published his own memoir, *Jimi Hendrix: A Brother's Story*, in 2012.

At the time that Judge Ramsdell's decision was announced, Bob Hendrix stated that with the end of legal proceedings, Experience Hendrix was anxious to get back to "keeping the legacy of Jimi Hendrix alive." Since then, two rarities compilations, eleven live albums (including releases on Dagger Records), and four live DVDs have been released. The box set *West Coast Seattle Boy: The Jimi Hendrix Anthology* featured a CD's worth of Jimi's pre-Experience recordings, including his tracks with the Isley Brothers, Don Covay, and Rosa Lee Brooks. Four documentaries have also been released, including *Hear My Train a Comin'*, which debuted on PBS's *American Masters* series in 2013.

Experience Hendrix wasn't involved in every Hendrix-related project. *Jimi: All Is by My Side* (2014) was a feature film that told the story of Jimi's discovery in New York and his rise to fame in London (with André Benjamin cast as Jimi), but the filmmakers weren't given permission to use Jimi's music. There was also some controversy about a scene in which Jimi was seen beating Kathy with a telephone receiver. Kathy said the story came from Curtis Knight's book, *Jimi: An Intimate Biography of Jimi Hendrix*, in which he contended that she told him about the beating. Kathy insisted that not only had she not spoken to Knight, but that the beating itself had never happened.

And a settlement was finally reached with a longtime adversary: Ed Chalpin. Remarkably, Chalpin had managed to put together a six-volume set called *The Authentic PPX Studio Recordings*, released in 1996. After Experience Hendrix was founded, there was further litigation with Chalpin. Eventually, Experience Hendrix prevailed and acquired eighty-eight recordings from Chalpin, including a live performance recorded on December 26, 1965. The company's first release of the material, *You Can't Use My Name: The RSVP/ PPX Sessions*, was released in 2015 and consisted of studio material, including

"How Does It Feel," "Hornet's Nest," and the "practice sessions" from the summer of 1967. Further releases of the material are planned.

"We created a plan a long time ago of what we needed to do," McDermott told *Examiner.com* in 2014:

> "We kind of mapped it out—*First Ray of the New Rising Sun* will be this, with the Purple box [*The Jimi Hendrix Experience*] we're going to create this linear chronological overview of unreleased material, we want to present the Winterland concerts in a specific way, we wanted to do Monterey with a documentary. So we really look at all of the various projects and then figure out whether there's a significant anniversary, and also consult with the label as to what their feelings are. So it is a process. But in many ways it's really about figuring out when is the best time to be able to produce these things and then bring them to the marketplace."

At the time of writing in 2016, the latest Experience Hendrix release was *Machine Gun*, the complete first Band of Gypsys show from December 31, 1969.

⚜ ⚘ ⚜

Greenwood Memorial Park, in Renton, is 17 miles south of the Seattle neighborhoods where Jimi grew up. His initial gravesite at Greenwood had a simple headstone that ironically featured a right-handed guitar. The gravesite attracted visitors from all over the world and is even featured in the 1992 film *Singles*, with Matt Damon's character, the rock musician Cliff Poncier, seen lying beside it in homage to his idol.

In 2003, Jimi, along with other departed Hendrix relatives, was moved to a new site in the cemetery. The memorial now looks like something you might find in ancient Greece. The stately dome is supported by three flat pillars, decorated with etchings of Jimi and his handwritten lyrics. One panel has a large picture of Jimi, with smaller pictures of him as a baby and with his father in the top corners, and some of the lyrics of the last song he ever wrote, "The Story of Life." In the center of the memorial is a large stone square, with a replica of the original headstone and a shimmering purple glass ball on top. The memorial is also decorated with the handwritten lyrics of other Hendrix songs, such as "Angel" and "Voodoo Child (Slight Return)." Other family members, including Jimi's father, Al, and his grandmother Nora, are also buried at the site. Fans come to the memorial every day, some leaving behind coins, notes, or other tokens. "Thank you Jimi," reads one, "for providing me with peace in times of turmoil. . . . The imagination to dream of things beyond today."

Most visitors don't realize it, but the grave of Jimi's mother, Lucille, is not far away, a bit east of the memorial. Neither Jimi or Leon ever knew where their mother was buried, as the grave site was unmarked. It was rediscovered through the efforts of biographer Charles Cross, author of the book *Room Full of Mirrors: A Biography of Jimi Hendrix*. There's now a simple headstone with a picture of Lucille, with a small, shy smile, her hair curling over her forehead, and a flower above her left ear. Underneath her name are the words "Forever in Our Hearts"—the same words as on Jimi's headstone.

Back in Seattle, there are no Blue Plaques marking where Jimi lived. It would be hard to pick one place for such a commemoration as Al moved his family so frequently, but you can find something of Jimi at the Museum of Pop Culture (MoPOP), located at the Seattle Center, the same grounds where all of Jimi's concerts were held once he became a star. MoPOP, originally called the Experience Music Project (the museum's name changed in 2017), is the museum dreamed up by Paul Allen, who had once wanted it dedicated solely to Jimi. By the time the museum opened on June 23, 2000, its scope had broadened to encompass other genres of music, and, eventually, other aspects of pop culture. Exhibits in recent years have focused on the history of *Star Trek*, the costumes of *Star Wars*, and the global phenomenon of Hello Kitty.

There's always a Hendrix exhibit at MoPOP, with Allen and the Hendrix family often working in cooperation; both Al and Janie attended the museum's opening. At the time of this writing in 2017, the museum was hosting an exhibit called "Wild Blue Angel: Hendrix Abroad, 1966–1970," looking at Jimi's touring years. There's a replica of his passport you can look through—Jimi only ever had one—filled with stamps, including the first one he received when he arrived in England on September 24, 1966, full of hope and never imagining what lay ahead. There's a yellow and black poster for his last concert in Seattle on July 26, 1970, at Sick's Stadium: tickets $5 in advance, $6 at the door. There's an invitation to the opening party for Electric Lady Studios on August 26, 1970, as well as the mixing board used in Studio A. ("I spilled beer on that thing," Patti Smith joked when she visited the museum during its opening weekend.) There's also a note Jimi wrote on the Londonderry Hotel's stationery for Kirsten Nefer and Karen Davis, with instructions on meeting up with him at the Isle of Wight concert on August 30, 1970—if he's not at the Sea Grove Hotel,

Hendrix's grave in Greenwood Memorial Park, Renton. *Gillian G. Gaar*

he writes, they're to take a cab to the main stage gate: "Passes will be waiting."

And at last, Seattle now has other plans to honor its famous native son. When a new west–east light rail line opens in 2023, portraits of Jimi will adorn the exteriors of the elevator shafts at Judkins Park Station. It's an appropriate location, as the station will be within walking distance of Jimi Hendrix Park. The park is adjacent to the grounds of the Northwest African American Museum and opened to the public in October 2016, though final development of the area was still being completed in 2017. Jimi's signature is etched into a stairway leading into the park, and the walkway has a timeline of key events in his life. By the time of the grand opening in 2017, a central shelter will have been added, providing a stage area for live shows. "This beautiful park will provide a welcoming and inspiring community gathering space, as well as a place for fans of Jimi's music to celebrate his indelible contributions to the music world," Janie Hendrix states on the park's website.

Perhaps because he had started life with so little, Jimi Hendrix was always a dreamer. As a child, he'd lie in the backyard and gaze up at the stars, dreaming of what life was like in outer space. As a teenager, he'd dreamed of being a rock star. As a successful musician, he told journalists he dreamed of where he might take his music in the future. Fifty years after Hendrix's historic performance at the Monterey International Pop Festival, other young, aspiring musicians strolling through Jimi Hendrix Park might find the inspiration to fuel their own musical dreams as they look at the lyrics to "Little Wing" etched in a purple "ribbon" bordering the walkway, thinking of how a skinny boy who taught himself to play on a battered, one-string instrument went on to be the kind of guitar hero other musicians dream of becoming.

SELECTED LIVE APPEARANCES 1966-1970

1966

September 24	Scotch of St. James, London, England (jam)
September 27	Scotch of St. James, London, England (jam)
September 29	Blaises, London, England (jam)
October 1	Regent Street Polytechnic, London, England (jam)
October 5	Les Cousins, London, England (jam)
October 13	Novelty, Évreux, France
October 14	Unknown venue, Nancy, France
October 15	Salle Des Fêtes, Villerupt, France
October 18	"Musicorama," L'Olympia, Paris, France
October 25	Scotch of St. James, London, England
November 8	Big Apple Club, Munich, Germany (two shows)
November 9	Big Apple Club, Munich, Germany (two shows)
November 10	Big Apple Club, Munich, Germany (two shows)
November 11	Big Apple Club, Munich, Germany (two shows)
November 25	Bag O'Nails, London, England
November 26	Ricky Tick, Hounslow, England
December 10	The Ram Jam Club, London, England
December 16	Chislehurst Caves, Bromley, England
December 21	Blaises, London, England
December 22	Guildhall, Southampton, England
December 26	The Upper Cut, London, England
December 31	Hillside Social Club, Folkestone, England

1967

January 4	Bromel Club, Bromley Court Hotel, Bromley, England
January 7	New Century Hall, Manchester, England
January 8	Tollbar, Mojo A Go-Go, Sheffield, England
January 11	Bag O'Nails, London, England
January 12	The 7½ Club, London, England
January 13	The 7½ Club, London, England
January 14	Beachcomber Club, Nottingham, England
January 15	The Country Club, Kirklevington, England
January 16	The 7½ Club, London, England
January 17	The 7½ Club, London, England
January 18	The 7½ Club, London, England
January 19	Speakeasy, London, England
January 20	Haverstock Hill Country Club, London, England
January 21	Refectory, London, England
January 22	Astoria, Oldham, England
January 24	Marquee Club, London, England
January 25	The Orford Cellar, Norwich, England
January 27	Chislehurst Caves, Bromley, England
January 28	The Upper Cut, London, England
January 29	Saville Theatre, London, England (two shows)
February 1	New Cellar Club, South Shields, England
February 2	Imperial Hotel, Darlington, England
February 3	Ricky Tick, Hounslow, England
February 4	The Ram Jam Club, London, England
February 4	Flamingo Club, London, England
February 6	The Star Hotel, Croydon, England
February 8	Bromel Club, Bromley Court Hotel, Bromley, England
February 9	Locarno, Bristol, England
February 10	Plaza Ballroom, Newbury, England
February 11	Blue Moon, Cheltenham, England
February 12	Sinking Ship Clubland, Stockport, England
February 14	Grays Civic Hall, Essex, England
February 14	Speakeasy, London, England (jam)
February 15	Dorothy Ballroom, Cambridge, England

February 17	Ricky Tick, Thames Hotel, Windsor, England	May 12	"Bluesville '67," Manor House, London, England
February 18	York University, York, England	May 13	Imperial College, London, England
February 19	Blarney Club, London, England	May 14	Belle Vue, New Elizabethan, Manchester, England
February 20	The Pavilion, Bath, England	May 15	Neue Welt, Berlin, Germany (two shows)
February 22	Roundhouse, London, England	May 16	Big Apple Club, Munich, Germany (two shows)
February 23	Worthing Pier Pavilion, Worthing, England	May 18	K52 Club, Frankfurt, Germany (jam)
February 24	Leicester University, Leicester, England	May 19	Konserthallen, Liseberg Nojespark, Gothenburg,
February 25	"Saturday Scene," Corn Exchange, Chelmsford, England		Sweden (two shows)
February 26	"Grand Pop Festival," Cliffs Pavilion,	May 20	Mariebergsskogen, Karlstad, Sweden
	Southend-on-Sea, England	May 21	Falkoner Centret, Copenhagen, Denmark
March 1	Orchid Ballroom, Purley, England	May 22	Kulttuuritalo, Helsinki, Finland
March 4	Le Cadran-Omnibus, Colombes, France	May 23	Klubb Bongo/New Orleans, Malmö, Sweden (two shows)
March 4	Law Society Graduation Ball, Faculté de Droit,	May 24	Stora Scenen & Dans In, Gröna Lund, Tivoli Gardens,
	D'Assas, Paris, France		Stockholm, Sweden
March 5	Twenty Club, Mouscron, Belgium	May 27	Star Palace, Kiel, Germany (two shows)
March 5	Twenty Club, Loison-sous-Lens, France	May 28	Jaguar Club, Scala, Hereford, Germany
March 9	Skyline Ballroom, Hull, England	May 29	"Barbeque 67," Tulip Bulb Auction Hall,
March 10	Club A'Gogo, Newcastle upon Tyne, England (two shows)		Spalding, England
March 11	International Club, Leeds, England	June 4	Saville Theatre, London, England (two shows)
March 12	Gyro Club, Troutbeck Hotel, Ilkley, England	June 18	Monterey International Pop Festival, Monterey, California
March 17	Star-Club, Hamburg, Germany	June 20	Fillmore Auditorium, San Francisco, California
March 18	Star-Club, Hamburg, Germany (two shows)		(two shows)
March 19	Star-Club, Hamburg, Germany (two shows)	June 21	Fillmore Auditorium, San Francisco, California
March 23	Guild Hall, Southampton, England		(two shows)
March 25	Starlight Room, Gliderdrome, Boston, England	June 22	Fillmore Auditorium, San Francisco, California
March 26	Tabernacle Club, Stockport, England		(two shows)
March 28	Assembly Hall, Aylesbury, England	June 23	Fillmore Auditorium, San Francisco, California
March 31	The Astoria, London, England (two shows)		(two shows)
April 1	Gaumont, Ipswich, England (two shows)	June 24	Fillmore Auditorium, San Francisco, California
April 2	Gaumont, Worcester, England (two shows)		(two shows)
April 5	Odeon Cinema, Leeds, England (two shows)	June 25	Golden Gate Park, San Francisco, California
April 6	Odeon Cinema, Glasgow, Scotland (two shows)	June 25	Fillmore Auditorium, San Francisco, California
April 7	ABC Cinema, Carlisle, England (two shows)		(two shows)
April 8	ABC Cinema, Chesterfield, England (two shows)	July 1	Earl Warren Showgrounds, Santa Barbara, California
April 9	The Empire, Liverpool, England (two shows)	July 2	Whisky a Go Go, Los Angeles, California
April 11	The Granada, Bedford, England (two shows)	July 3	Steve Paul's The Scene, New York City, New York
April 12	Gaumont Cinema, Southampton, England (two shows)	July 4	Steve Paul's The Scene, New York City, New York
April 13	Gaumont Cinema, Wolverhampton, England (two shows)	July 5	Rheingold Central Park Music Festival,
April 14	Odeon Cinema, Bolton, England (two shows)		New York City, New York
April 15	Odeon Cinema, Blackpool, England (two shows)	July 8	Coliseum, Jacksonville, Florida
April 16	De Montfort Hall, Leicester, England (two shows)	July 9	Convention Hall, Miami, Florida
April 19	Odeon Cinema, Birmingham, England (two shows)	July 11	Coliseum, Charlotte, North Carolina
April 20	ABC Cinema, Lincoln, England (two shows)	July 12	Coliseum, Greensboro, North Carolina
April 21	City Hall, Newcastle, England (two shows)	July 13	Forest Hills Stadium, New York City, New York
April 22	Odeon Cinema, Manchester, England (two shows)	July 14	Forest Hills Stadium, New York City, New York
April 23	Gaumont Cinema, Hanley, England (two shows)	July 15	Forest Hills Stadium, New York City, New York
April 25	Colston Hall, Bristol, England (two shows)	July 16	Forest Hills Stadium, New York City, New York
April 26	Capitol, Cardiff, Wales (two shows)	July 20	Salvation, New York City, New York
April 27	ABC Cinema, Aldershot, England (two shows)	July 21	Cafe au Go Go, New York City, New York (two shows)
April 28	Adelphi, Slough, England (two shows)	July 22	Cafe au Go Go, New York City, New York (two shows)
April 28	UFO, London, England (jam)	July 23	Cafe au Go Go, New York City, New York (two shows)
April 29	Winter Gardens, Bournemouth, England (two shows)	August 3	Salvation, New York City, New York
April 30	Granada, London, England (two shows)	August 4	Salvation, New York City, New York
May 6	Ballroom of the Stars, The Imperial, Nelson, England	August 5	Salvation, New York City, New York
May 7	Saville Theatre, London, England (two shows)	August 7	Salvation, New York City, New York
May 11	Theatre d'Issy Les Moulineaux, Paris, France	August 8	Salvation, New York City, New York

August 9	Ambassador Theater, Washington, DC
August 10	Ambassador Theater, Washington, DC
August 11	Ambassador Theater, Washington, DC
August 12	Ambassador Theater, Washington, DC
August 13	"Keep the Faith for Washington Youth Fund," Ambassador Theater, Washington, DC
August 15	Fifth Dimension Club, Ann Arbor, Michigan (two shows)
August 18	Hollywood Bowl, Hollywood, California
August 19	Earl Warren Showgrounds, Santa Barbara, California
August 27	Saville Theatre, London, England
August 29	Nottingham Pop and Blues Festival, Sherwood Rooms, Nottingham, England
September 2	ZDF Studio, Berlin, Germany
September 3	Konserthallen, Liseberg Nojespark, Gothenburg, Sweden (two shows)
September 4	Stora Scenen & Dans In, Gröna Lund, Tivoli Gardens, Stockholm, Sweden (two shows)
September 6	Västerås Idrottshall, Västerås, Sweden (two shows)
September 8	Popladan, Hogbo Bruk, Sweden (two shows)
September 9	Mariebergsskogen, Karlstad, Sweden (two shows)
September 10	Stora Salen, Akademiska Föreningen, Lund, Sweden (two shows)
September 11	Stora Scenen & Dans In, Gröna Lund, Tivoli Gardens, Stockholm, Sweden (two shows)
September 12	Stjärnscenen, Liseberg Nojespark, Gothenburg, Sweden (two shows)
September 25	"Guitar In," Royal Festival Hall, London, England
October 6	The Wellington Club, Dereham, England
October 8	Saville Theatre, London, England (two shows)
October 9	"Musicorama," L'Olympia, Paris, France
October 15	Starlight Ballroom, Crawley, England
October 17	Klooks Kleek, Railway Hotel, London, England (jam)
October 22	Hastings Pier, Hastings, England
October 24	Marquee Club, London, England
October 28	California Ballroom, Dunstable, England
November 8	The Union, Manchester, England
November 10	"Hippy Happy Beurs voor Tieners en Twens," Ahoy Hallen, Rotterdam, the Netherlands
November 11	New Refectory, Sussex University, Brighton, England
November 14	Royal Albert Hall, London, England (two shows)
November 15	Winter Gardens, Bournemouth, England (two shows)
November 17	City Hall, Sheffield, England (two shows)
November 18	The Empire, Liverpool, England (two shows)
November 19	The Coventry Theater, Coventry, England (two shows)
November 22	Guild Hall, Portsmouth, England (two shows)
November 23	Sophia Gardens Pavilion, Cardiff, Wales (two shows)
November 24	Colston Hall, Bristol, England (two shows)
November 24	Blackpool Opera House, Blackpool, England (two shows)
November 26	Palace Theatre, Manchester, England (two shows)
November 27	"Festival of Arts," Whitla Hall, Queen's College, Belfast, Northern Ireland (two shows)
December 1	Central Hall, Chatham, England (two shows)
December 2	The Dome, Brighton, England (two shows)
December 3	Theatre Royal, Nottingham, England (two shows)
December 4	City Hall, Newcastle, England (two shows)
December 5	Green's Playhouse, Glasgow, Scotland (two shows)
December 14	Speakeasy, London, England (jam)
December 22	"Christmas on Earth Continued," Grand and National Halls, London, England
December 31	Speakeasy, London, England (jam)

1968

January 4	Lorensberg Cirkus, Gothenburg, Sweden (two shows)
January 5	Jernvallen Sports Hall, Sandviken, Sweden
January 7	Tivolis Koncertsal, Copenhagen, Denmark (two shows)
January 8	Stora Salen, Konserthuset, Stockholm, Sweden (two shows)
January 29	"Musicorama," L'Olympia, Paris, France (two shows)
February 1	Fillmore West, San Francisco, California (two shows)
February 2	Winterland Ballroom, San Francisco, California (two shows)
February 3	Winterland Ballroom, San Francisco, California (two shows)
February 4	Winterland Ballroom, San Francisco, California (two shows)
February 5	Sun Devil's Gym, Arizona State University, Tempe, Arizona
February 6	V.I.P. Club, Tucson, Arizona
February 8	Men's Gym, Sacramento State College, Sacramento, California
February 9	Anaheim Convention Center, Anaheim, California
February 10	Shrine Auditorium, Los Angeles, California
February 11	Robertson Gymnasium, University of California– Santa Barbara, Santa Barbara, California
February 12	Seattle Center Arena, Seattle, Washington
February 13	Ackerman Union Grand Ballroom, University of California, Los Angeles, Los Angeles, California
February 14	Regis College Fieldhouse, Denver, Colorado
February 15	Municipal Auditorium, San Antonio, Texas
February 16	State Fair Music Hall, Dallas, Texas
February 17	Will Rogers Auditorium, Fort Worth, Texas
February 18	Music Hall, Houston, Texas
February 21	Electric Factory, Philadelphia, Pennsylvania (two shows)
February 22	Electric Factory, Philadelphia, Pennsylvania (two shows)
February 23	Masonic Temple, Detroit, Michigan
February 24	CNE Coliseum Arena, Toronto, Ontario, Canada
February 25	Civic Opera House, Chicago, Illinois
February 27	The Factory, Madison, Wisconsin (two shows)
February 28	The Scene, Milwaukee, Wisconsin (two shows)
February 29	The Scene, Milwaukee, Wisconsin (two shows)

March 2	Hunter College, New York City, New York	August 1	City Park Stadium, New Orleans, Louisiana
March 3	Veterans Memorial Auditorium, Columbus, Ohio	August 2	Municipal Auditorium, San Antonio, Texas
March 8	Marvel Gymnasium, Brown University, Providence, Rhode Island	August 3	Moody Coliseum, Southern Methodist University, Dallas, Texas
March 9	State University of New York at Stony Brook, Long Island, New York	August 4	Sam Houston Coliseum, Houston, Texas
March 10	International Ballroom, Washington Hilton Hotel, Washington, DC (two shows)	August 10	Chicago Auditorium, Chicago, Illinois
		August 11	Colonial Ballroom, Davenport, Iowa
		August 16	Merriweather Post Pavilion, Columbia, Maryland
March 15	Atwood Hall, Clark University, Worcester, Massachusetts (two shows)	August 17	Municipal Auditorium, Atlanta, Georgia (two shows)
March 16	Lewiston Armory, Lewiston, Maine	August 18	Curtis Hixon Hall, Tampa, Florida
March 19	Capitol Theatre, Ottawa, Ontario, Canada (two shows)	August 20	The Mosque, Richmond, Virginia (two shows)
		August 21	Civic Dome, Virginia Beach, Virginia (two shows)
March 21	Community War Memorial, Rochester, New York	August 23	New York Rock Festival, Singer Bowl, Flushing Meadow Park, New York
March 22	Bushnell Memorial Hall, Hartford, Connecticut	August 24	Bushnell Memorial Arena, Hartford, Connecticut
March 23	Buffalo Memorial Auditorium, Buffalo, New York	August 25	Carousel Ballroom, Framingham, Massachusetts
March 24	IMA Auditorium, Flint, Michigan	August 26	Kennedy Stadium, Bridgeport, Connecticut
March 25	Otto's Grotto, Cleveland, Ohio (jam)	August 30	Lagoon Opera House, Salt Lake City, Utah
March 26	Public Music Hall, Cleveland, Ohio (two shows)	September 1	Red Rocks Park, Denver, Colorado
March 27	Teen America Building, Lion's Delaware County Fairgrounds, Muncie, Indiana	September 3	Balboa Stadium, San Diego, California
		September 4	Memorial Coliseum, Phoenix, Arizona
March 28	Xavier University Fieldhouse, Cincinnati, Ohio (two shows)	September 5	Swing Auditorium, San Bernardino, California
		September 6	Seattle Center Coliseum, Seattle, Washington
March 29	Chicago University, Chicago, Illinois	September 7	Pacific Coliseum, Vancouver, British Columbia, Canada
March 30	University of Toledo Fieldhouse, Toledo, Ohio	September 8	Coliseum, Spokane, Washington
March 31	Philadelphia Arena, Philadelphia, Pennsylvania	September 9	Memorial Coliseum, Portland, Oregon
April 2	Paul Sauvée Arena, Montreal, Quebec, Canada	September 13	Oakland Coliseum, Oakland, California
April 3	Civic Dome, Virginia Beach, Virginia (two shows)	September 14	Hollywood Bowl, Hollywood, California
April 5	Symphony Hall, Newark, New Jersey	September 15	Memorial Auditorium, Sacramento, California
April 6	Westchester County Center, White Plains, New York	October 5	Honolulu International Center, Honolulu, Hawaii
		October 10	Winterland Ballroom, San Francisco, California (two shows)
April 19	Troy Armory, Troy, New York		
May 10	Fillmore East, New York City, New York (two shows)	October 11	Winterland Ballroom, San Francisco, California (two shows)
May 18	Miami Pop Festival, Gulfstream Race Track, Hallandale, Florida	October 12	Winterland Ballroom, San Francisco, California (two shows)
May 23	Piper Club, Milan, Italy	October 26	Civic Auditorium, Bakersfield, California
May 24	Teatro Brancaccio, Rome, Italy (two shows)	November 1	Municipal Auditorium, Kansas City, Missouri
May 25	Teatro Brancaccio, Rome, Italy (two shows)	November 2	Minneapolis Auditorium, Minneapolis, Minnesota
May 26	Palasport, Bologna, Italy (two shows)	November 3	Kiel Auditorium, Saint Louis, Missouri
May 30	"Monsterkonzert," Hallenstadion, Zurich, Switzerland	November 15	Cincinnati Gardens, Cincinnati, Ohio
		November 16	Boston Garden, Boston, Massachusetts
May 31	"Monsterkonzert," Hallenstadion, Zurich, Switzerland	November 17	Woolsey Hall, Yale University, New Haven, Connecticut (two shows)
June 8	Fillmore East, New York City, New York (jam)	November 22	Jacksonville Coliseum, Jacksonville, Florida
July 6	Woburn Music Festival, Woburn Abbey, Bedfordshire, England	November 23	Curtis Hixon Hall, Tampa, Florida
		November 24	Miami Beach Convention Hall, Miami Beach, Florida
July 15	Sgt. Pepper's, Palma, Majorca, Spain	November 27	Rhode Island Auditorium, Providence, Rhode Island
July 18	Sgt. Pepper's, Palma, Majorca, Spain	November 28	"An Electronic Thanksgiving," Philharmonic Hall, New York City, New York
July 30	Independence Hall, Lakeshore Auditorium, Baton Rouge, Louisiana		
		November 30	Cobo Hall, Detroit, Michigan
July 31	Municipal Auditorium, Shreveport, Louisiana	December 1	Coliseum, Chicago, Illinois

1969

January 8	Lorensbergs Cirkus, Gothenburg, Sweden (two shows)
January 9	Konserthuset, Stockholm, Sweden (two shows)
January 10	Falkoner Centret, Copenhagen, Denmark (two shows)
January 11	Musikhalle, Hamburg, Germany (two shows)
January 12	Rheinhalle, Düsseldorf, Germany (two shows)
January 13	Sporthalle, Cologne, Germany (two shows)
January 14	Halle Münsterland, Müunster, Germany (two shows)
January 15	Kongressaal, Deutsches Museum, Munich, Germany (two shows)
January 16	Meistersingerhalle, Nuremberg, Germany (two shows)
January 17	Jahrhunderthalle, Frankfurt, Germany (two shows)
January 19	Liederhalle, Stuttgart, Germany (two shows)
January 21	Wackenhalle, Strasbourg, France (two shows)
January 22	Konzerthaus, Vienna, Austria (two shows)
January 23	Sportpalast, Berlin, Germany (two shows)
February 18	Royal Albert Hall, London, England
February 24	Royal Albert Hall, London, England
February 24	Speakeasy, London, England (jam)
April 11	Dorton Arena, Raleigh, North Carolina
April 12	Spectrum, Philadelphia, Pennsylvania
April 18	Ellis Auditorium, Memphis, Tennessee (two shows)
April 19	Sam Houston Coliseum, Houston, Texas
April 20	Memorial Auditorium, Dallas, Texas
April 26	Los Angles Forum, Inglewood, California
April 27	Oakland Coliseum, Oakland, California
May 2	Cobo Arena, Detroit, Michigan
May 3	Maple Leaf Gardens, Toronto, Ontario, Canada
May 4	War Memorial Auditorium, Syracuse, New York
May 8	Memorial Coliseum, Tuscaloosa, Alabama
May 9	Charlotte Coliseum, Charlotte, North Carolina
May 10	Charleston Civic Center, Charleston, West Virginia
May 11	State Fairgrounds Coliseum, Indianapolis, Indiana
May 16	Civic Center, Baltimore, Maryland
May 17	Rhode Island Auditorium, Providence, Rhode Island
May 18	Madison Square Garden, New York City, New York
May 23	Seattle Center Coliseum, Seattle, Washington
May 24	San Diego Sports Arena, San Diego, California
May 25	Northern California Folk-Rock Festival, County Fairgrounds, Santa Clara, California
May 30	Waikiki Shell, Honolulu, Oahu, Hawaii
May 31	Waikiki Shell, Honolulu, Oahu, Hawaii
June 1	Waikiki Shell, Honolulu, Oahu, Hawaii
June 20	Newport Pop Festival, Northridge, California
June 22	Newport Pop Festival, Northridge, California
June 29	Denver Pop Festival, Mile High Stadium, Denver, Colorado
August 18	Woodstock Music and Art Fair, Bethel, New York
September 5	United Block Association Benefit, Lenox Avenue and 139th Street, New York City, New York
September 10	Salvation, New York City, New York
December 31	Fillmore East, New York City, New York (two shows)

1970

January 1	Fillmore East, New York City, New York (two shows)
January 28	Winter Festival for Peace, Madison Square Garden, New York City, New York
April 25	Los Angeles Forum, Inglewood, California
April 26	Cal Expo, Sacramento, California
May 1	Milwaukee Auditorium, Milwaukee, Wisconsin
May 2	Dane County Memorial Coliseum, Madison, Wisconsin
May 3	Saint Paul Civic Center, Saint Paul, Minnesota
May 4	"Holding Together" benefit, Village Gate, New York City, New York
May 8	University of Oklahoma Field House, Norman, Oklahoma (two shows)
May 9	Will Rogers Coliseum, Fort Worth, Texas
May 10	San Antonio HemisFair Arena, San Antonio, Texas
May 16	Temple University Stadium, Philadelphia, Pennsylvania
May 30	Berkeley Community Theatre, Berkeley, California (two shows)
June 5	Memorial Auditorium, Dallas, Texas
June 6	Sam Houston Coliseum, Houston, Texas
June 7	Assembly Center Arena, Tulsa, Oklahoma
June 9	Mid-South Coliseum, Memphis, Tennessee
June 10	Roberts Municipal Stadium, Evansville, Indiana
June 13	Baltimore Civic Center, Baltimore, Maryland
June 19	Civic Auditorium, Albuquerque, New Mexico
June 20	Swing Auditorium, San Bernardino, California
June 21	Ventura County Fairgrounds, Ventura, California
June 27	Boston Garden, Boston, Massachusetts
July 4	Atlanta International Pop Festival, Byron, Georgia
July 5	Miami Jai Alai Fronton, Miami, Florida
July 17	New York Pop Festival, Downing Stadium, Randall's Island, New York City, New York
July 25	San Diego Sports Arena, San Diego, California
July 26	Sick's Stadium, Seattle, Washington
July 30	Haleakalā Crater, Maui, Hawaii (two shows)
August 1	Honolulu International Center, Honolulu, Oahu, Hawaii
August 30	Isle of Wight Festival, East Afton Downs, Isle of Wight, England
August 31	Stora Scenen & Dans In, Gröna Lund, Tivoli Gardens, Stockholm, Sweden
September 1	Storen Scenen, Liseberg Nojespark, Gothenburg, Sweden
September 2	Vejlby Risskov Hallen, Aarhus, Denmark
September 3	K. B. Hallen, Copenhagen, Denmark
September 4	"Berlin Super Concert '70," Deutschlandhalle, Berlin, Germany
September 6	Open Air Love & Peace Festival, Mecklenburg Bay, Isle of Fehmarn, Germany
September 16	Ronnie Scott's Jazz Club, London, England (jam)

SELECTED DISCOGRAPHY

Albums

1967   *Are You Experienced* (US: Reprise, UK: Track)
1967   *Axis: Bold as Love* (UK: Track)
1968   *Axis: Bold as Love* (US: Reprise)
1968   *Electric Ladyland* (US: Reprise, UK: Track)
1971   *The Cry of Love* (US: Reprise, UK: Track)
1971   *Rainbow Bridge* (US and UK: Reprise)
1972   *War Heroes* (US: Reprise, UK: Polydor)
1974   *Loose Ends* (UK: Polydor)
1975   *Crash Landing* (US: Reprise, UK: Polydor)
1975   *Midnight Lightning* (US: Reprise, UK: Polydor)
1980   *Nine to the Universe* (US: Reprise, UK: Polydor)
1994   *Blues* (US: MCA, UK: Polydor)

1995   *Voodoo Soup* (US: MCA)
1997   *First Rays of the New Rising Sun* (US and UK: MCA Experience Hendrix)
1997   *South Saturn Delta* (US and UK: MCA/Experience Hendrix)
2000   *Morning Symphony Ideas* (US: Dagger Records)
2004   *Hear My Music* (US: Dagger Records)
2006   *Burning Desire* (US: Dagger Records)
2010   *Valleys of Neptune* (US: Legacy/Experience Hendrix, UK: Sony/Experience Hendrix)
2013   *People, Hell and Angels* (US: Legacy/Experience Hendrix, UK: Sony/Experience Hendrix)

Live Albums

1970   *Band of Gypsys* (US: Capitol, UK: Track)
1970   *Woodstock: MU.S.ic from the Original Soundtrack and More* (US: Cotillion, UK: Atlantic)
1970   *Historic Performances Recorded at the Monterey International Pop Festival* (US: Reprise)
1971   *Woodstock Two* (US: Cotillion, UK: Atlantic)
1971   *The First Great Rock Festivals of the Seventies: Isle of Wight/Atlanta Pop Festival* (US: Columbia, UK: CBS)
1971   *Isle of Wight* (UK: Polydor)
1972   *Hendrix in the West* (US: Reprise, UK: Polydor)
1972   *More Experience* (UK: Ember)
1973   *Soundtrack Recordings from the film Jimi Hendrix* (US and UK: Reprise)
1982   *The Jimi Hendrix Concerts* (US: Reprise, UK: CBS)
1986   *Jimi Plays Monterey* (US: Reprise)
1986   *Johnny B. Goode* (US: Capitol, UK: EMI)
1986   *Band of Gypsys 2* (US: Capitol)
1987   *Live at Winterland* (US: Rykodisc)
1988   *Radio One* (US: Rykodisc, UK: Castle)
1991   *Stages* (US: Reprise, UK: Polydor)
1991   *Live Isle of Wight '70* (UK: Polydor)
1998   *BBC Sessions* (US and UK: MCA/Experience Hendrix)

1998   *Live at the Oakland Coliseum* (US: Dagger Records)
1999   *Live at Clark University* (US: Dagger Records)
1999   *Live at the Fillmore East* (US and UK: MCA/ Experience Hendrix)
1999   *Live at Woodstock* (US and UK: MCA/Experience Hendrix)
2000   *Live in Ottawa* (US: Dagger Records)
2002   *Blue Wild Angel: Live at the Isle of Wight* (US and UK: MCA/Experience Hendrix)
2002   *The Baggy's Rehearsal Sessions* (US: Dagger Records)
2003   *Paris 1967/San Francisco 1968* (US: Dagger Records)
2003   *Live at Berkeley* (US and UK: MCA/Experience Hendrix)
2005   *Live at the Isle of Fehmarn* (US: Dagger Records)
2007   *Live at Monterey* (US and UK: MCA/Experience Hendrix)
2008   *Live in Paris & Ottawa 1968* (US: Dagger Records)
2009   *Live at Woburn* (US: Dagger Records)
2012   *Live in Cologne* (US: Dagger Records)
2013   *Miami Pop Festival* (US: Legacy/Experience Hendrix, UK: Sony/Experience Hendrix)
2015   *Freedom: Atlanta Pop Festival* (US: Legacy/Experience Hendrix, UK: Sony/Experience Hendrix)
2016   *Machine Gun: The Fillmore East First Show* (US: Legacy/Experience Hendrix, UK: Sony/Experience Hendrix)

Box Sets

2000   *The Jimi Hendrix Experience* (US and UK: MCA/ Experience Hendrix)
2010   *West Coast Seattle Boy: The Jimi Hendrix Anthology* (US: Legacy/ Experience Hendrix, UK: Sony/Experience Hendrix)
2011   *Winterland* (US: Legacy/Experience Hendrix, UK: Sony Experience Hendrix)

Best of Collections

1968   *Smash Hits* (UK: Track)
1969   *Smash Hits* (US: Reprise)
1978   *The Essential Jimi Hendrix* (US: Reprise, UK: Polydor)
1979   *The Essential Jimi Hendrix Volume Two* (US: Reprise, UK: Polydor)
1992   *The Ultimate Experience* (US: MCA, UK: Polydor)
1997   *Experience Hendrix: The Best of Jimi Hendrix* (US and UK: MCA/Experience Hendrix)
2001   *Voodoo Child: The Jimi Hendrix Collection* (US and UK: MCA/Experience Hendrix)
2010   *Fire: The Jimi Hendrix Collection* (US: Legacy/Experience Hendrix, UK: Sony/Experience Hendrix)

Singles

1966   "Hey Joe"/ "Stone Free" (UK: Polydor)
1967   "Purple Haze"/"51st Anniversary" (UK: Track)
1967   "Hey Joe"/"51st Anniversary" (US: Reprise)
1967   "The Wind Cries Mary"/"Highway Chile" (UK: Track)
1967   "Purple Haze"/"The Wind Cries Mary" (US: Reprise)
1967   "Burning of the Midnight Lamp"/"The Stars That Play with Laughing Sam's Dice" (UK: Track)
1967   "Foxy Lady"/"Hey Joe" (US: Reprise)
1968   "Up from the Skies"/"One Rainy Wish" (US: Reprise)
1968   "All Along the Watchtower"/"Burning of the Midnight Lamp" (US: Reprise)
1968   "All Along the Watchtower"/"Long Hot Summer Night" (UK: Track)
1968   "Crosstown Traffic"/"Gypsy Eyes" (UK: Track)
1969   "Stone Free"/"If 6 Was 9" (US: Reprise)
1969   "Let Me Light Your Fire"/"Burning of the Midnight Lamp" (UK: Track")
1970   "Stepping Stone"/"Izabella" (US: Reprise)
1970   "Voodoo Child (Slight Return)"/"Hey Joe"/"All Along the Watchtower" (UK: Track)
1971   "Freedom"/"Angel" (US: Reprise)
1971   "Angel"/"Night Bird Flying" (UK: Track)
1971   "Dolly Dagger"/"The Star-Spangled Banner" (US: Reprise)
1971   "Gypsy Eyes"/"Remember"/"Purple Haze"/"Stone Free" (UK: Track)
1972   "Johnny B. Goode"/"Lover Man" (US: Reprise)
1972   "Johnny B. Goode"/"Little Wing" (UK: Polydor)
1972   "The Wind Cries Mary"/"Little Wing" (US: Reprise)
1973   "Hear My Train a Comin'"/"Rock Me Baby" (UK: Reprise)
1982   "Fire"/"Little Wing" (US: Reprise)
1982   "Fire"/"Are You Experienced?" (UK: CBS)
1997   "Dolly Dagger"/"Night Bird Flying" (US and UK: MCA Experience Hendrix)
1999   "The Star-Spangled Banner"/"Purple Haze" (US: MCA Experience Hendrix)
2010   "Valleys of Neptune"/"Cat Talking to Me" (US: Legacy Experience Hendrix)
2010   "Bleeding Heart"/"Jam 292" (US: Legacy/ Experience Hendrix)
2010   "Love or Confusion"/"12 Bar with Horns" (US: Legacy/ Experience Hendrix)
2011   "Fire"/"Touch You" (US: Legacy/Experience Hendrix)
2011   "Johnny B. Goode"/"Purple Haze" (US: Legacy/Experience Hendrix)
2011   "Like a Rolling Stone"/"Spanish Castle Magic" (US: Legacy/Experience Hendrix)
2012   "Can You Please Crawl Out Your Window?"/"Burning of the Midnight Lamp" (US: Sundazed/Experience Hendrix)
2012   "Come On (Let the Good Times Roll)"/"Calling All the Devil's Children" (US: Sundazed/Experience Hendrix)
2013   "Somewhere"/"Foxey Lady" (US: Legacy/Experience Hendrix)
2013   "Fire"/"Foxey Lady" (US: Legacy/Experience Hendrix)
2013   "Dolly Dagger"/"The Star-Spangled Banner" (US: Legacy Experience Hendrix)
2015   "Purple Haze"/"Freedom" (US: Legacy/Experience Hendrix)

GUEST APPEARANCES

Albums

1965	Don Covay & the Goodtimers, *Mercy!* (US: Atlantic)
1967	Curtis Knight, *Get That Feeling* (US: Capitol, UK: London)
1968	McGough & McGear, *McGough & McGear* (UK: Parlophone)
1968	Curtis Knight, *Flashing* (US: Capitol)
1968	Curtis Knight, *The Great Jimi Hendrix in New York* (UK: London)
1969	Eire Apparent, *Sunrise* (US and UK: Buddah)
1969	Curtis Knight, *Instant Groove* (UK: Atco)
1969	Fat Mattress, *Fat Mattress* (US: Polydor, UK: Atco)
1970	Timothy Leary, *You Can Be Anyone This Time Around* (US: Douglas)

1970	Stephen Stills, *Stephen Stills* (US and UK: Atlantic)
1970	Love, *False Start* (US: Blue Thumb, UK: Harvest)
1971	Lonnie Youngblood, *Two Great Experiences Together* (US: Maple)
1971	The Isley Brothers, *In the Beginning* (US: T-Neck)
1972	Curtis Knight, *What'd I Say* (UK: Music for Pleasure)
1972	Lonnie Youngblood, *Rare Hendrix* (US: Trip)
1973	Curtis Knight, *In the Beginning* (US: Ember)
2015	Curtis Knight & the Squires, *You Can't Use My Name: The RSVP/PPX Sessions* (US: Legacy/Experience Hendrix)

Singles

1964	The Isley Brothers, "Testify Part 1"/"Testify Part 2" (US: T-Neck)
1964	Don Covay & the Goodtimers, "Mercy, Mercy"/"Can't Stay Away" (US: Rosemart)
1965	Frank Howard & the Commanders, "I'm So Glad" (US: Barry)
1965	Rosa Lee Brooks, "My Diary"/"Utee" (US: Revis)
1965	The Isley Brothers, "Move Over and Let Me Dance"/ "Have You Ever Been Disappointed" (US: Atlantic)
1965	Little Richard, "I Don't Know What You've Got but It's Got Me Part 1"/"I Don't Know What You've Got but It's Got Me Part 2" (US: Vee-Jay)
1965	Little Richard, "Dancing All around the World"/ "What You've Got" (US: Vee-Jay)
1966	Ray Sharpe with the King Curtis Orchestra, "Help Me (Get the Feeling) Part 1"/"Help Me (Get the Feeling) Part 2" (US: Atco)
1966	Curtis Knight, "How Would You Feel"/"Welcome Home" (US: RSVP)
1966	The Icemen, "(My Girl) She's a Fox"/"(I Wonder) What It Takes" (US: Samar)
1966	Jimmy Norman, "You're Only Hurting Yourself"/"That

	Little Old Groovemaker" (US: Samar)
1966	Curtis Knight & the Squires, "Hornet's Nest"/"Knock Yourself Out" (US: RSVP)
1967	Curtis Knight, "You Don't Want Me"/"How Would You Feel" (UK: London)
1967	Curtis Knight, "Hush Now"/"Flashing" (UK: London)
1968	Billy Lamont, "Sweet Thang"/"Please Don't Leave" (US: 20th Century Fox Records)
1969	Eire Apparent, "Rock 'n' Roll Band"/"Yes I Need Someone" (US and UK: Buddah)
1969	King Curtis, "Instant Groove" (US: Atco)
1970	Love, "The Everlasting First" (US: Blue Thumb, UK: Harvest)
1970	Curtis Knight & the Squires "Ballad of Jimi"/"Gloomy Monday" (UK: London)
1971	The Squires, "No Such Animal Part 1"/"No Such Animal Part 2" (UK: RCA)
1984	Lightnin' Rod, "Doriella Du Fontaine"/"Doriella Du Fontaine (instrumental)" (US: Celluloid)

BIBLIOGRAPHY

Books

Brown, Tony. *Jimi Hendrix: A Visual Documentary*. London: Omnibus Press, 1992.

———. *Hendrix: The Final Days*. London: Omnibus Press, 1997.

Burdon, Eric. *I Used to Be an Animal, But I'm All Right Now*. London: Faber & Faber, 1986.

Cross, Charles R. *Room Full of Mirrors: A Biography of Jimi Hendrix*. New York: Hyperion, 2005.

De Barros, Paul. *Jackson Stret after Hours: The Roots of Jazz in Seattle*. Seattle: Sasquatch Books, 1993.

Etchingham, Kathy. *Through Gypsy Eyes: My Life, the 60s, and Jimi Hendrix*. London: Orion, 1998.

Hendrix, James A., and Jas Obrecht. *My Son Jimi*. Seattle: Aljas Enterprises, 1999.

Hendrix, Janie L., and John McDermott. *Jimi Hendrix: An Illustrated Experience*. New York: Atria Books, 2007.

Hendrix, Leon, and Adam Mitchell. *Jimi Hendrix: A Brother's Story*. New York: Thomas Dunne Books, 2012.

Hopkins, Jerry. *The Jimi Hendrix Experience*. New York: Arcade Publishing, 2014.

Hoskyns, Barney. *Small Town Talk: Bob Dylan, The Band, Van Morrison, Janis Joplin, Jimi Hendrix & Friends in the Wild Years of Woodstock*. Boston: Da Capo Press, 2015.

Jucha, Gary J. *Jimi Hendrix FAQ: All That's Left to Know About the Voodoo Child*. New York: Backbeat Books, 2012.

Kubernik, Harvey, and Kenneth Kubernik. *A Perfect Haze: The Illustrated History of the Monterey International Pop Festival*. Salona Beach, CA: Santa Monica Press, 2011.

McDermott, John, and Eddie Kramer. *Hendrix: Setting the Record Straight*. New York: Warner Books Inc., 1992.

McDermott, John, Eddie Kramer, and Billy Cox. *Ultimate Hendrix: An Illustrated Encyclopedia of Live Concerts and Sessions*. New York: Backbeat Books, 2009.

Mitchell, Mitch. *Jimi Hendrix: Inside the Experience*. New York: Harmony Books, 1990.

Neal, Peter, ed. *Jimi Hendrix: Starting at Zero*. New York: Bloomsbury, 2014.

Potash, Chris, ed. *The Jimi Hendrix Companion: Three Decades of Commentary*. New York: Schirmer Books, 1996.

Redding, Noel, and Carol Appleby. *Are You Experienced?: The Inside Story of the Jimi Hendrix Experience*. Boston: Da Capo Press, 1996.

Roberts, Jon, and Evan Wright. *American Desperado*. New York: Crown Publishers, 2011.

Roby, Steven. *Black Gold: The Lost Archives of Jimi Hendrix*. New York: Billboard Books, 2002.

Roby, Steven, ed. *Hendrix on Hendrix: Interviews and Encounters with Jimi Hendrix*. Chicago: Chicago Review Press, 2012.

Roby, Steven, and Brad Schreiber. *Becoming Jimi Hendrix: From Southern Crossroads to Psychedelic London, the Untold Story of a Musical Genius*. Boston: Da Capo Press, 2010.

Shadwick, Keith. *Jimi Hendrix: Musician*. New York: Backbeat Books, 2012.

Shapiro, Harry, and Caesar Glebbeek. *Jimi Hendrix: Electric Gypsy*. New York: St. Martin's Griffin, 1995.

Smith, Patti. *Just Kids*. New York: Ecco, 2010.

Sounes, Howard. *27: A History of the 27 Clubs through the Lives of Brian Jones, Jimi Hendrix, Janis Joplin, Jim Morrison, Kurt Cobain, and Amy Winehouse*. Boston: Da Capo Press, 2013.

Unterberger, Richie. *The Rough Guide to Jimi Hendrix*. New York: Rough Guides, 2009.

Whitburn, Joel. *Top Pop Albums*, 7th ed. Menomonee Falls, WI: Record Research Inc., 2010.

———. *Top Pop Singles 1955–2015*. Menomonee Falls, WI: Record Research Inc., 2016.

Willix, Mary. *Jimi Hendrix: Voices from Home*. San Diego: Creative Forces Publishing, 1995.

Articles

Albertson, Chris. "Caught in the Act." *DownBeat*, March 5, 1970.

"Andy Summers on Jimi Hendrix." *UniVibes*, May 1996.

Aronowitz, Alfred. "Spaceship Jimi Is Landing." *New York Post*, January 2, 1970.

Barker, Andrew. "Film Review: 'Jimi: All Is by My Side.'" *Variety*, September 23, 2014.

Beers, Carole. "'June' Hendrix, Jimi's Stepmom." *Seattle Times*, August 25, 1999.

Buls, Bruce. "Jimi's Wa-Wa Guitar Brings It on Home." *Seattle Post-Intelligencer*, May 24, 1969.

Burke, Julia. "Kathy Etchingham, Former Partner of Jimi Hendrix, Speaks Out against New Biopic." Skepchick.org, July 25, 2014. www.skepchick.org/2014/07/kathy-etchingham-former-partner-of-jimi-hendrix-speaks-out-against-new-biopic.

Campion, Chris. "Lithofayne Pridgon: Jimi Hendrix's Original 'Foxy Lady.'" *Guardian*, March 22, 2015.

Cianci, Bob. "A Moment in Time with Jimi Hendrix." *Rickresource*, June 27, 2009. www.rickresource.com/forum/viewtopic.php?f=47&t=389689.

De Barros, Paul. "Latest Jimi Hendrix Family Feud Resolved in Settlement," *Seattle Times*, August 13, 2015.

Ferris, Karl. "Jimi Hendrix Experience's 'Are You Experienced?'" RockPoP Gallery, February 22, 2008. www.rockpopgallery.typepad.com/rockpop_gallery_news/2008/02/cover-story---j.html.

Fisher, Annie. Live review of the Jimi Hendrix Experience at the Singer Bowl, August 23, 1968. *Village Voice*, August 29, 1968.

Fricke, David. "100 Greatest Guitarists: David Fricke's Picks." *Rolling Stone*, December 2, 2010. www.rollingstone.com/music/lists/100-greatest-guitarists-of-all-time-19691231.

Gaar, Gillian G. "Experience Music Project's evolution," *Goldmine*, September 8, 2000.

———. "Hendrix's Seattle," *Goldmine*, September 8, 2000.

———. "In from the Storm: Jimi Hendrix: His Legacy and the City of Seattle." *Goldmine*, June 30, 1997.

———. "John McDermott on What's Next from the Jimi Hendrix Archives." originally published on *Examiner.com*, March 3, 2014.

———."The Long-Awaited Experience Music Project Museum Opens in Seattle." *Goldmine*, September 8, 2000.

Glover, Tony. Review of Rainbow Bridge. *Rolling Stone*, December 9, 1971.

Gressel, Janine. "Wet Crowd Watches Hendrix in Ballpark." *Seattle Times*, July 27, 1970.

Gold, Noë. "Jimi Hendrix and Leonard Nimoy with Chuck Dunaway." Doctor Noe's Gadget, May 29, 2012. www.doctornoemedia.blogspot.com/2012/05/jimi-hendrix-and-leonard-nimoy-with.html.

Helmore, Edward. "How I Helped to Make Jimi Hendrix a Rock 'n' Roll Star." *Guardian*, September 14, 2013.

"Hendrix Estate Claim Denied to Illegitimate Daughter." *Rolling Stone*, February 3, 1972.

Hodenfield, Chris. "Experience Break-Up: Noel Splits and Jimi Moves Uptown." *Circus*, November 1969.

Hopkins, Jerry. "A Piece of Jimi Hendrix's Rainbow." *Rolling Stone*, December 2, 1976.

Jimi Hendrix. Special edition, *Guitar Player*, September 1975.

"Jimi's Private Parts." The Smoking Gun. www.thesmokinggun.com/documents/crime/jimis-private-parts.

Johnson, Pete. "Jimi Hendrix in Concert at Bowl." *Los Angeles Times*, September 16, 1968.

Jones, Peter. "Jimi Hendrix: Mr. Phenomenon!" *Record Mirror*, December 10, 1966.

Kaye, Lenny. Review of *The Cry of Love*. Rolling Stone, April 1, 1971.

Kershaw, Sarah. "Rock Idol's Legacy Devolves into Family Feud." *New York Times*, July 23, 2003.

Kreps, Daniel. "Jimi Hendrix's Estate Settles Licensing Legal Battle." *Rolling Stone*, August 15, 2015.

Lacitis, Erik. "Seattle Area's Many Jimi Hendrix Memorials." *Seattle Times*, August 14, 2011.

———. "Vision for Hendrix Park as Vibrant as Namesake." *Seattle Times*, August 14, 2011.

Lambert, Ken. "Jimi Hendrix Brother Gets None of the $80 Million Estate." *Seattle Times*, September 25, 2004.

LeBlanc, Larry. "In the Hot Seat with Larry LeBlanc." *Encore CA*, February 4, 2010. encore.celebrityaccess.com/?encoreId=232&articleId=33881.

Lewis, Mike. "Judge Splits Decision on Hendrix Estate." *Seattle Post-Intelligencer*, September 25, 2004.

"Lithofayne Pridgon Interview." *Gallery*, September 1982.

Lydon, Michael. "A Shoddy Jimi Hendrix Record?" *Rolling Stone*, January 20, 1968.

MacDonald, Patrick. "Jimi Remembered: 20 Years after His Death, The Legendary Guitarist Is More Popular Than Ever." *Seattle Times*, September 18, 1990.

Mayer, Steven. "Hendrix Concert in Bakersfield the Stuff of Legend." *Bakersfield.com*, September 18, 2015.

———. "When Jimi Hendrix Came to Bakersfield: Part II." *Bakersfield.com*, September 25, 2015.

Meyer, Josh. "Jimi Hendrix Gets Star on Walk of Fame." *Los Angeles Times*, November 22, 1991.

Niesel, Jeff. "Bassist Billy Cox Aspires to Keep Jimi Hendrix' Legacy Alive with Experience Hendrix." *Cleveland Scene*, March 9, 2016.

O'Brien, Christine. "An Interview with Cynthia Plaster Caster." originally published on www.doors.com.

Papazian, Rita. "Almost Famous: Former Trendsetter Recalls Jimi Hendrix and the 60s." *Shoreline Times*, April 1, 2010.

"Rainbow Bridge: Hendrix In Hawaii." *Rolling Stone*, August 5, 1971.

Reid, Graham. "Jimi Hendrix and Alan Douglas: The Fireball and the Keeper of the Flame." Elsewhere, March 8, 2010. www.elsewhere.co.nz/absoluteelsewhere/2164/jimi-hendrix-and-alan-douglas-the-fireball-and-the-keeper-of-the-flame.

Live review of the Jimi Hendrix Experience at the Honolulu International Center, October 5, 1968. *Honolulu Advertiser*, October 7, 1968.

Roby, Steven. "Interview with Stella Douglas." SteveRoby.wordpress.com, October 2007.

Schwartz, Susan. "On With Hendrix." *Seattle Times*, September 7, 1968.

Scott, Jane. "Jimi Hendrix Experience Is the Wildest Thing Here." *Cleveland Plain Dealer*, March 27, 1968.

Shelton, Robert. Live review of the Jimi Hendrix Experience at the Singer Bowl, August 23, 1968. *New York Times*, August 25, 1968.

Sims, Judith. "Behind the Making of *A Film about Jimi Hendrix*." *Rolling Stone*, November 8, 1973.

Sisario, Ben. "A Hendrix Castle Where Musicians Still Kiss the Sky." *New York Times*, April 25, 2010.

Stout, Gene. "A Lick in Time." *Seattle Post-Intelligencer*, September 5, 1995.

Street, Andrew P. "Jimi & Me: Why Hendrix's Ex-Lover Is Taking on Hollywood." *Evening Standard*, August 7, 2014.

"Tribute and Tribulation." Seattle Post-Intelligencer, August 30, 1995.

Vulliamy, Ed. "Jimi Hendrix: You Never Told Me He Was That Good." *Guardian*, August 7, 2010.

Wasserman, John L. "Jimi Hendrix at Berkeley." *San Francisco Chronicle*, June 1, 1970.

Weber, Bruce. "Alan Douglas, Who Mined Hendrix Archive, Dies at 82." *New York Times*, June 14, 2014.

Yagi, Anuhea. "Remembering Rainbow Bridge." *MauiTime*. August 26, 2010. www.mauitime.com/culture/remembering-rainbow-bridge.

Websites

www.authentichendrix.com

www.crosstowntorrents.org

www.earlyhendrix.com

www.electricladystudios.com

www.findagrave.com

www.handelhendrix.org

hendrix.guide.pagesperso-orange.fr

www.jimihendrix.com

www.jimihendrix-lifelines.net

www.jimihendrixmemorial.com

www.jimihendrixparkfoundation.org

www.montereyinternationalpopfestival.com

www.rockprophecy.com

www.tcm.com

www.wikipedia.org

INDEX

Gillian G. Gaar has written for numerous publications, including *Mojo*, *Rolling Stone*, and *Goldmine*. Her previous books include *She's A Rebel: The History of Women in Rock & Roll*, *Entertain Us: The Rise of Nirvana*, *Return of the King: Elvis Presley's Great Comeback*, *The Doors: The Illustrated History*, and *Boss: Bruce Springsteen and the E Street Band — The Illustrated History*. She lives in Seattle.

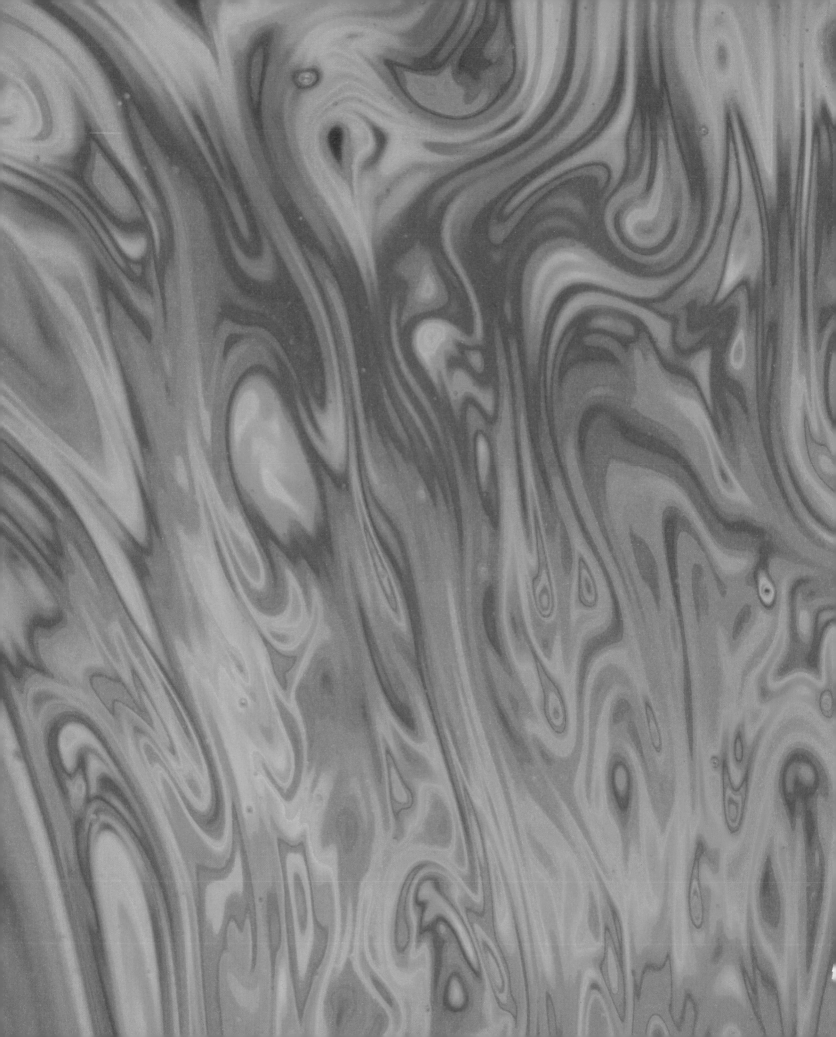